WORKBOOK / TAPE MANUAL

ELLIN S. FELD   ELLEN VON NARDROFF

Columbia University

Upsala College

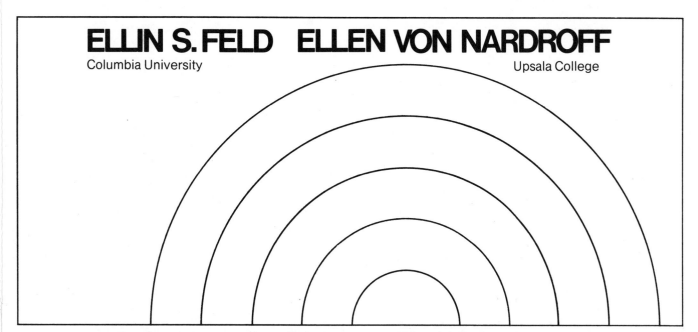

ZIELSPRACHE: DEUTSCH

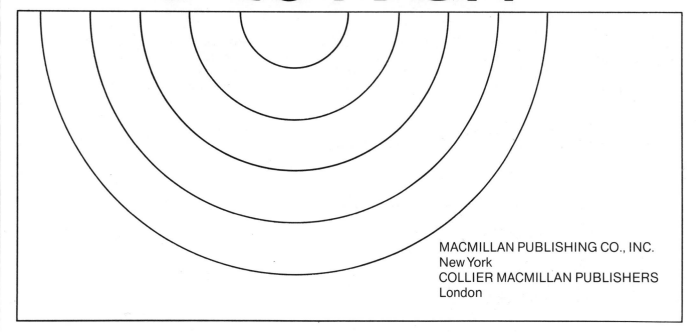

MACMILLAN PUBLISHING CO., INC.
New York
COLLIER MACMILLAN PUBLISHERS
London

Macmillan Publishing Co., Inc.
866 Third Avenue, New York, New York 10022

Collier Macmillan Canada, Ltd.

Printed in the United States of America

ISBN 0-02-336830-6

9 8 7

ISBN   0-02-336830-6

TO THE STUDENT

We have made every effort in this *Workbook/Tape Manual* to provide you with a useful and enjoyable supplement to the basic textbook *ZIELSPRACHE: DEUTSCH*.

The *Workbook*, for home or class use, has a variety of exercises intended to help you review and reinforce the vocabulary and structures of each textbook lesson, and to give you additional practice in composition.

The *Tape Manual* (pages distinguishable by the gray edges) contains the material you will need for the eighteen language laboratory lessons that correspond to the lessons in the textbook. Each tape lesson has two parts.

Part I contains approximately 15 minutes of exercises that concentrate on pronunciation. It begins with a reading and repetition of the introductory conversation contained in the textbook lesson, proceeds to the practice of several individual sounds, and concludes often with tongue twisters, limericks or dictations. This part of the tape should be used soon after the instructor has introduced the new lesson in class. Whenever possible you should record and play back the exercises to give yourself the chance to evaluate your own pronunciation as you hear it juxtaposed to that of the native speaker.

Part II of each tape also contains approximately 15 minutes of taped material, with the emphasis on communication. The material is designed to provide additional practice in using and understanding the spoken language. Even exercises that practice structure are, whenever possible, set in conversational patterns. In addition, there are several exercises on each tape that are intended to focus your attention on understanding and responding to stories, descriptions, fairy tales, and private conversations (a man and his psychiatrist; a thief and his lawyer, etc.). In early lessons these stories, descriptions and conversations are repeated so you have a second chance to listen to them. In later lessons they are not repeated, but if you have difficulty, you should simply rewind your tape and listen again. Try to relax when you listen. You will find that you understand much more when you are not tense. You should not be concerned if you miss a word here or there--you will probably understand the main ideas anyway. Part II of each tape should be used when the class is close to the end of the textbook lesson, and not before the reading text (*Lesestück*) has been studied. In other words it should be used as a review and reinforcement of what you have already learned.

CONTENTS

PART ONE
WORKBOOK

PART TWO
TAPE MANUAL

ZIELSPRACHE: DEUTSCH

Part One

Workbook

LEKTION EINS

I. Gegenteile und Kontraste (Opposites and Contrasts)

In the blank write the letter of the word from the right-hand column that is the opposite or clear contrast.

1. neu __H__		a. interessant
2. dort __E__ (*THERE*)		b. spielen
3. dick __F__		c. die Stadt
4. gehen __i__		d. ja
5. der Mann __j__		e. hier
6. arbeiten __b__		f. schlank
7. nein __d__		g. der Student
8. langweilig __a__		h. alt
9. das Dorf __c__		i. kommen
10. der Professor __g__		j. die Frau

II. Was gehört zusammen? (What goes together?)

In the blank write the letter of the word from the right-hand column that is in some way related to the word in the left column.

1. der Film __g__		a. wohnen
2. die Diskothek __h__		b. arbeiten
3. das Büro __b__		c. trinken
4. das Bier __c__		d. die Vorlesung
5. der Hörsaal __d__		e. Ingrid
6. Tennis __i__		f. auf Wiedersehen
7. der Name __E__		g. das Kino
8. tschüß __f__		h. tanzen
9. das Zimmer __a__		i. spielen

III. Give the German equivalents of the following words and phrases.

1. I hope   *hoffentlich*
2. by the way   *übrigens*
3. Excuse me!   *Verzeihung!*
4. unfortunately   *leider*
5. So long!   *tschüß!*
6. Thanks a lot!   *vielen Dank!*
7. really   *wirklich*
8. only   *nur*
9. That doesn't matter.   *das macht nichts*
10. maybe   *vielleicht*
11. probably   *wahrscheinlich*
12. very   *sehr*
13. or   *oder*
14. nothing   *nichts*
15. afterward   *nachher*
16. always   *immer*
17. exactly   *genau*
18. gladly   *gern*

IV. Give the correct form of the definite and indefinite article.

1. *die* *eine* Professorin   2. *das* *ein* Bier
3. *das* *ein* Büro   4. *der* *ein* Assistent
5. *die* *eine* Diskothek   6. *das* *ein* Dorf
7. *der* *ein* Film   8. *die* *eine* Freundin
9. *der* *ein* Hörsaal   10. *die* *eine* Karikatur
11. *das* *ein* Kino   12. *die* *eine* Lektion
13. *das* *ein* Mädchen   14. *der* *ein* Name

15. *das* *ein* Seminar   16. *die* *eine* Stadt

17. *die* *eine* Universität   18. *die* *eine* Vorlesung

19. *das* *ein* Zimmer   20. *die* *eine* Amerikanerin

V. Give the pronoun for each underlined noun.

1. Hoffentlich ist <u>Sabine</u> nicht pleite. *sie*

2. Wo ist <u>ein Kino</u>? *es*

3. <u>Mein Freund</u> ist nicht hier. *er*

4. Dort ist <u>ein Büro</u>. *es*

5. <u>Ein Mann</u> sitzt dort. *er*

6. <u>Die Vorlesung</u> ist interessant. *sie*

7. <u>Eine Assistentin</u> liest dort. *sie*

8. <u>Ein Seminar</u> ist nicht immer interessant. *es*

9. <u>Meine Freundin</u> ist schlank. *sie*

10. <u>Der Film</u> ist alt. *er*

VI. Insert the proper form of the verb.

1. Ein Student *spricht* mit Elisabeth. (sprechen)

2. Wer *liest* in Zimmer vier? (lesen)

3. *Arbeitest* du immer? (arbeiten)

4. Wann *öffnet* das Kino? (öffnen)

5. *Fährst* du nachher in die Stadt? (fahren)

6. Ich *finde* Professor Bauer langweilig. (finden)

7. Sie (they) *fragen* Professor Schneider. (fragen)

8. *Sind* Sie aus München? (sein)

9. Was *tut* wir nachher? (tun)

10. *Habt* ihr Geld? Ich *bin* pleite. (haben; sein)

VII. Supply the correct form of the appropriate verb.

1. Hier _____ man Tennis.

2. Hier _____ man Bier.

3. Hier _____ man Tango.

4. Hier _____ man Comics.

5. Hier _____ man „Auld Lang Syne".

6. Hier _____ man deutsch.

VIII. Translate.

1. Then he is coming. _____

2. Does she find Professor Bauer interesting? _____

_____

3. Is she going to come along? _____

4. They are landing in Frankfurt. _____

5. Yes, we do have money. _____

IX. Describe a friend using the following cues.

his (her) name is ... _____

he (she) is a student and also _____

an assistant for (für) Professor X _____

lives in (name of city) _____

finds the city interesting _____

has a room there _____

is always broke _____

is very friendly and likes to talk _____

is not fat but (rather) slender _____

probably doesn't work much _____

reads comics _____

likes to drink, but only Coca Cola _____

plays the guitar (die Gitarre) and sings _____

by the way, the guitar is new _____

he (she) is really O.K. _____

LEKTION ZWEI

I. Gegenteile und Kontraste

Write the letter of the word from the right-hand column that is the opposite or clear contrast.

1. bleiben _____   a. schon

2. da _____   b. hören

3. einfach _____   c. gehen

4. manchmal _____   d. Auf Wiedersehen!

5. nicht genug _____   e. schwer

6. noch nicht _____   f. hier

7. ohne _____   g. immer

8. sehen _____   h. zu viel

9. die Frau _____   i. mit

10. Guten Tag! _____   j. der Herr

II. Was gehört zusammen?

Write the letter of the word from the right-hand column that is in some way related.

1. das Handwerk _____   a. das Problem

2. der Studienbewerber _____   b. momentan

3. die Psychologie _____   c. warum

4. sagen _____   d. der Studienplatz

5. das Geld _____   e. komisch

6. die Karikatur _____   f. das Seelenleben

7. fragen _____   g. jodeln

8. gerade _____   h. verdienen

9. es schwer haben _____   i. sprechen

10. singen _____   j. der Klempner

III. Give the German equivalents.

1. Hello! _____

2. on vacation _____

3. still _____

4. How are you? _____

5. nice _____

6. as a plumber _____

7. of course _____

8. not yet _____

9. at the moment _____

10. maybe _____

11. It's not possible. _____
    (It won't work.)

12. What a shame! _____

13. I hope _____

14. the lesson _____

15. from where _____

16. afterward _____

17. That doesn't matter. _____

18. Excuse me! _____

19. by the way _____

20. gladly _____

IV. Complete each sentence according to the information in Lektion Zwei by selecting the appropriate noun from the group below. Use the noun with its definite article, indefinite article, kein, or no article, whichever is appropriate.

Handwerk	Geschäft	Glück	Computer
Medizin	Ecke	Taxifahrer	Sohn
Jugend	Studienplatz	Klempner	

1. Frau Schmidt geht durch _____ .

2. Frau Schmidt kommt um _____ .

3. Martin Meyer hat noch _____ .

4. Ulrike Schmidt studiert _____ .

5. _____ hat es heute schwer.

6. _____ verdient genug Geld.

7. Für _____ ist Martin zu ungeschickt.

8. Hoffentlich hat Martin Meyer bald mehr _____ .

9. Martin arbeitet als _____ .

10. In Deutschland bestimmt _____ , wer studiert.

11. Das ist Herr Meyer; er hat _____ , Martin.

V. Insert the proper form(s) of the verb(s).

1. Warum _____ du nicht Präsident? Das _____ ein ordentlicher Beruf.
   (werden; sein)

2. Er _____ sie sehr oft in Frankfurt; sie _____ dort als
   Taxifahrerin. (treffen; arbeiten)

3. Wann _____ du ihn? _____ er nicht in Stuttgart? (sehen; wohnen)

4. _____ ihr ihn langweilig? (finden)

5. Sie _____ noch keinen Studienplatz; vielleicht _____ sie
   Klempnerin. (haben; werden)

6. Man _____ das Büro bald. (öffnen)

VI. Make sentences using the following elements; then rewrite, changing all nouns
to pronouns.

1. Für / der Klempner / sein (to be) / die Wasserleitung / interessant.

   _____

   _____

2. Ohne / die Freundin / kommen / Peter / nicht.

   _____

   _____

3. Der Student / haben / nichts / gegen / der Professor.

   _____

   _____

4. Ulrike / kennen / der Herr / nicht.

   _____

   _____

5. Die Studentin / finden / die Vorlesung / langweilig.

   _____

   _____

VII. Negate the following sentences.

1. Kennt er hier eine Diskothek? _____

2. Spielt der Film hier? _____

3. Hast du Geld? _____

4. Ist der Professor langweilig? _____

5. Hat er einen Studienplatz? _____

6. Liest er in Zimmer vier? _____

7. Ist er Student? _____

8. Spielt er gut? _____

9. Hast du ein Problem? _____

10. Kennt sie den Amerikaner? _____

VIII. Interview. Der Psychologe (psychologist) fragt; der Patient sagt nicht viel. Translate this dialog into German.

Der Psychologe	*Der Patient*
1. Where do you come from?	From Ottweiler.
_____	_____
2. Where do you live?	In Neunkirchen.
_____	_____
3. Occupation?	I have no occupation.
_____	_____
4. Do you like to work?	Sometimes.
_____	_____
5. Interesting! Do you like to go on vacation?	Yes.
_____	_____
6. What interests you?	Nothing.
_____	_____
7. Do you find (the) life difficult?	Yes, of course.
_____	_____

8. Interesting! Do you sometimes drink too much?   Yes, I'm having a tough time.

   _____   _____

   _____   _____

9. Why are you having a tough time?   I have no luck.

   _____   _____

10. Really?   Yes.

   _____   _____

11. Do you have a problem?   Yes.

   _____   _____

12. What is it?   I have no emotional life
                                          (emotions).

   _____   _____

13. Excuse me?   No emotional life.

   _____   _____

14. Very interesting! Yes, you do have a problem ...

   _____

LEKTION DREI

I. Gegenteile und Kontraste

Give the letter of the opposite or clear contrast.

1. alt _____	a. böse
2. geben _____	b. jung
3. einfach _____	c. die Dame
4. auf Urlaub gehen _____	d. arbeiten
5. die Tochter _____	e. bleiben
6. der Herr _____	f. fahren
7. halten _____	g. der Sohn
8. nie _____	h. immer
9. gehen _____	i. schwer
10. nett _____	j. nehmen

II. Was gehört zusammen?

Give the letter of the word that is in some way related.

1. der Polizist _____	a. fahren
2. der Sauertopf _____	b. der Strafzettel
3. das Buch _____	c. der Bahnhof
4. der Zug _____	d. die Geschichte
5. die Haltestelle _____	e. entschuldigen
6. die Ausrede _____	f. der Bus
7. der Porsche _____	g. böse

III. Schreiben Sie auf deutsch.

Give the definite article with each noun.

1. otherwise _____ 2. again _____

3. in front of _____ 4. to earn _____

5. sometimes _____   6. already _____

7. correct _____   8. on time _____

9. too bad! _____   10. heavy _____

11. alarm clock _____   12. perhaps _____

13. but _____   14. but rather _____

15. history _____   16. sick _____

17. exactly _____   18. not yet _____

19. never _____   20. bed _____

IV. Rewrite, adding the modal; translate each new sentence.

1. Er spricht mit Tina. (müssen)

_____

2. Ich beschreibe das Problem. (wollen)

_____

3. Sie liest nie das „Wallstreet Journal". (wollen)

_____

4. Ich bleibe nicht hier. (mögen)

_____

5. Man trifft dort viele Leute. (können)

_____

6. Er liest in Zimmer vier. (sollen)

_____

7. Ich verdiene nicht genug. (können)

_____

8. Du fährst nicht schnell. (dürfen)

_____

9. Seht ihr das nicht? (können)

_____

10. Der Wecker ist kaputt. (müssen)

_____

11. Die Leute warten dort.   (können)

_____

12. Parkt ihr hier?   (dürfen)

_____

13. Wir sind pünktlich.   (sollen)

_____

14. Sie werden nicht alt.   (wollen)

_____

15. Warum tut ihr das?   (müssen)

_____

V. Rewrite as polite commands or requests.

   Example: Der Professor sagt, ich soll die Lektion lesen.
   Der Professor sagt: „Lesen Sie die Lektion."

1. Frau Schmidt sagt, ich soll ein Bier nehmen.

_____

2. Der Polizist sagt, ich soll auf das Schild schauen.

_____

3. Der Assistent sagt, ich soll den Professor fragen.

_____

4. Der Polizist sagt, ich soll nicht an der Bushaltestelle parken.

_____

5. Die Frau sagt, ich soll nachher ins Büro kommen.

_____

6. Der Klempner sagt, ich soll nicht so ungeschickt sein.

_____

7. Der Professor sagt, ich soll Klempner werden.

_____

VI. Rewrite as familiar singular commands or requests.

Example: Udo sagt, ich soll den Professor fragen.
Udo sagt: „Frag den Professor."

1. Die Tante sagt, ich soll nicht so schnell fahren.

_____

2. Sabine sagt, ich soll das lesen.

_____

3. Die Großmutter sagt, ich soll den Koffer nehmen.

_____

4. Ingrid sagt, ich soll pünktlich sein.

_____

5. Peter sagt, ich soll nicht lachen.

_____

6. Udo sagt, ich soll hier bleiben.

_____

7. Tante Ella sagt, ich soll mehr arbeiten.

_____

VII. Rewrite as statements. Start with the underlined word or words and add the modal.

1. Gehen wir bald. (müssen) _____

2. Tun wir es nachher. (können) _____

3. Fahren wir dort um die Ecke. (sollen) _____

4. Fragen wir den Polizisten dort. (wollen) _____

5. Parken wir nicht hier. (dürfen) _____

6. Treffen wir ihn in Chicago. (können) _____

VIII. Translate:

My Aunt Tulla (Meine Tante Tulla)

My aunt Tulla always drives fast, but she never gets a ticket. She always finds an excuse. Here is one (eine): She says, "Sorry, officer, please don't be angry. I've been driving for 20 years. I drive well, and I never drive too fast. But today... I have a daughter, her name is Angela... She is very sick. She has to lie in bed, she can't talk, she can't sit or stand, she doesn't want to play, nothing interests her. She is so sick..."

And what does the policeman say? Does he give Aunt Tulla a ticket? No! He says kindly: "Yes, of course, Mrs. Müller. I understand (verstehen). I have a child, too, a son... But please, Mrs. Müller, you (man) are not allowed to drive 80 miles (Meilen). You are not allowed to drive faster than (mehr als) 55. I hope Angela gets well (gesund) soon. Good bye, Mrs. Müller. And please, don't drive faster than 55."

My aunt can find an excuse for every situation.

_____

_____

_____

_____

_____

_____

_____

_____

_____

_____

_____

_____

_____

_____

_____

_____

_____

_____

_____

LEKTION VIER

I. Gegenteile und Kontraste

Write the letter of the opposite or clear contrast.

1. der Dialekt _____   a. nichts

2. das Restaurant _____   b. morgen

3. heute _____   c. Mutters Essen

4. rechts _____   d. woher

5. die Schwester _____   e. das Hochdeutsch

6. etwas _____   f. links

7. wohin _____   g. der Bruder

II. Was gehört zusammen?

Give the letter of the word that is in some way related.

1. der Verkäufer _____   a. der Winter

2. das Geld _____   b. die Medizin

3. das Essen _____   c. der Geburtstag

4. die Gesundheit _____   d. die Jeans

5. lernen _____   e. das Wort

6. das Raumschiff _____   f. die Bank

7. schenken _____   g. das Restaurant

8. tragen _____   h. das Kaufhaus

9. kalt _____   i. die Schule

10. sprechen _____   j. der Astronaut

III. Fill in the appropriate forms of the words given.

essen	tragen	verwandt	ein Restaurant
haben	verstehen	der Fahrstuhl	ein Sonderangebot
schenken	etwas	der Geburtstag	

1. Kassettenspieler gibt es in Stock 10. Ich fahre mit _____.

2. Wir _____ Hunger. Dort links ist _____. Dort können

wir _____.

3. Morgen hat mein Freund _____. _____ wir ihm _____.

4. Sie ist meine Schwester. Wir sind _____.

5. Er spricht Dialekt. Ich kann ihn nicht _____, ich spreche nur Hochdeutsch.

6. Ein Teenager _____ gern Jeans und T-Shirts.

7. Das Kaufhaus hat heute _____ für Taschenrechner: nur 50 Mark.

IV. Give the German equivalents.

1. Great! _____

2. there are _____

3. Bless you! _____

4. Anything else? _____

5. I hope _____

6. on vacation _____

7. I'm hungry. _____

8. after lunch _____

9. tomorrow _____

10. That's no problem. _____

11. We don't like excuses. _____

12. It's her birthday. _____

13. Excuse me, please. _____

14. on time _____

15. Stop! Enough! _____

16. at home _____

17. certainly _____

18. He's having a tough time. _____

19. Thanks a lot. _____

20. So long! _____

V. Supply the definite article for each case indicated.

Nom.		Acc.	Dat.
_____	1. T-Shirt	_____	_____
_____	2. Schule	_____	_____
_____	3. Raumschiff	_____	_____
_____	4. Kalender	_____	_____
_____	5. Fernsehen	_____	_____
_____	6. Essen	_____	_____
_____	7. Arbeit	_____	_____
_____	8. Bett	_____	_____
_____	9. Ding	_____	_____
_____	10. Leben	_____	_____
_____	11. Wecker	_____	_____
_____	12. Bank	_____	_____

VI. Assume that you have not heard the underlined noun. Using <u>wer</u>, <u>wen</u> or <u>wem</u>, ask a question to elicit the noun.

> Example: Er sagt das <u>dem Polizisten</u>.
> *Wem sagt er das?*

1. Man soll <u>den Verkäufer</u> fragen. _____

2. Sie schenkt es <u>der Schwester</u>. _____

3. Sie wollen <u>Ingrid und Peter</u> nicht helfen. _____

4. Mit <u>einem Teenager</u> kann man einfach nicht sprechen. _____

_____

5. <u>Der Polizist</u> dankt ihnen. _____

6. <u>Der Assistent</u> sitzt im Büro. _____

7. Sie kann <u>den Klempner</u> nicht finden. _____

8. Sie muß <u>ihre Tante</u> abholen. _____

9. Für <u>meinen Vater</u> habe ich nichts. _____

10. Er geht nachher zu dem Professor. _____

11. Er spielt gegen seinen Freund. _____

12. Die Taxifahrerin war nicht sehr freundlich. _____

VII. Rearrange the sentences in the appropriate sequence by placing a number before each sentence (i.e., put (1) before the first sentence, (2) before the second, etc).

_____ Christine fotografiert die Klasse und Herrn Frieling, und jedes (every) Kind bekommt eine Fotografie.

_____ In der Schule zeigt sie der Klasse die Kamera.

_____ Sie bekommt eine Kamera von Renate.

_____ „Das ist schön," sagt Herr Frieling, „jetzt kannst du die Klasse fotografieren."

_____ Christine hat heute Geburtstag.

_____ Christine kommt mit der neuen Kamera in die Schule.

VIII. Rewrite the sentences, replacing each underlined noun with a pronoun.

1. Renate ist mit der Tante im Kaufhaus.

_____

2. Ohne seine Frau geht der Mann nie ins Kino.

_____

3. Außer der Schwester kommt auch der Sohn.

_____

4. Für meinen Vater will ich das Tonbandgerät kaufen.

_____

5. Fragen Sie den Polizisten. Vielleicht ist das Geschäft nicht weit von hier.

_____

6. Was wollen Uta und Jürgen dem Vater schenken?

_____

7. Ich habe nichts gegen die Leute.

_____

8. Er bekommt eine Kamera von seiner Freundin.

_____

IX. Composition

The following is a conversation between you and a friend. Supply your parts of the conversation according to the cues. Do not attempt to translate the cues literally.

Ein Freund von Ihnen hat morgen Geburtstag, und sie wollen ihm etwas schenken.

Sie: (Explain to your girl friend why you want to get something for him and ask her for help because you don't know what to get.)

_____

_____

_____

Freundin: Ja, ich weiß, er möchte einen Kassettenspieler haben. Sein alter Kassettenspieler ist kaputt. Er hat so viele Kassetten, und er kann sie nicht spielen.

Sie: (Express very positive reaction to the suggestion and also your gratitude. You mention that there is a store not far from here, around the corner from the railroad station where they have players. Express the hope that they still have one; they are having a special on cassette players.)

_____

_____

_____

_____

_____

Freundin: Gut, ich komme mit. Vielleicht finde ich auch etwas für das Geburtstagskind.

Sie gehen mit der Freundin ins Geschäft, und da treffen Sie ihren Freund, das Geburtstagskind.

Geburtstagskind: Tag, was macht ihr denn hier? Ich will einen Spieler kaufen. Ihr auch?

Sie: (Say something that will dissuade him from buying one.)

_____

_____

_____

_____

LEKTION FÜNF

I. Gegenteile und Kontraste

1. klein _____   a. der Onkel

2. kaufen _____   b. der Export

3. alt _____   c. etwas

4. rechts _____   d. verkaufen

5. der Import _____   e. neu

6. die Tante _____   f. groß

7. nichts _____   g. reparieren

8. woher _____   h. gewagt

9. geben _____   i. wohin

10. der Dialekt (deutsch) _____   j. links

11. vorsichtig _____   k. bekommen

12. kaputt machen _____   l. das Hochdeutsch

II. Select the word that best fits the context. Change each definite article to the appropriate form of the indefinite article.

die Beleidigung	der Mechaniker	die Rolltreppe
das Familienmitglied	das Museum	das Taxi
der Fahrstuhl	das Museumsstück	Stammkundin
der Führerschein	das Ritual	

1. Sie kauft ihr Benzin immer bei einer bestimmten Tankstelle; sie ist dort

_____.

2. Wenn man 6 Leute und 7 Koffer zum Bahnhof bringen will, braucht man

_____.

3. Der Deutsche behandelt sein Auto fast wie _____.

4. Wenn der Anlasser nicht richtig funktioniert, bringt man den Wagen zu

_____.

5. Wenn ein Wagen schon sehr alt ist, spricht man von _____.

6. Wenn ein Kaufhaus sehr groß ist, hat es _____ und

_____ .

7. Wenn man ein Ford T-Model sehen will, besucht man _____ .

8. Man darf nie ohne _____ fahren.

9. Wenn man zu einem Polizisten sagt: „Sie Sauertopf!", dann ist das _____

_____ .

10. Das Autowaschen ist in Deutschland manchmal _____ .

III. Was ist das?

Wenn ein Rechner sehr klein ist, heißt er *Taschenrechner*.

Wenn eine Uhr sehr klein ist, heißt sie _____ .

Wenn ein Buch sehr klein ist, heißt es _____ .

Wenn ein Kalender sehr klein ist, heißt er _____ .

IV. Wußten Sie.........? (Did you know?)

Rewrite as questions, beginning each with: „Wußten Sie, daß..."

1. Das Verb „dieseln" ist mit einem Ingenieur verwandt.

_____

2. Ein Porsche hat seinen Namen von einem Ingenieur, Ferdinand Porsche.

_____

3. Man darf in Deutschland nicht mit dem Fahrrad auf die Autobahn.

_____

4. „Ladybug" heißt auf deutsch „Marienkäfer", und „Junebug" heißt auf deutsch „Maikäfer".

_____

_____

5. Man trinkt in Deutschland das Bier nie eiskalt.

_____

6. Man kann in Deutschland bei McDonald's Bier kaufen.

_____

V. Rewrite, replacing names with appropriate possessive adjectives; then use the phrase with the prepositions indicated.

    Example: Peters Auto; mit; für
               sein Auto; mit seinem Auto; für sein Auto

1. Brigittes Geburtstag; seit; für

_____

2. Alfreds Geburtstag; seit; für

_____

3. Tante Irmas Kamera; von; ohne

_____

4. Onkel Ernsts Party; zu; für

_____

5. Herrn und Frau Müllers Haus; aus; um

_____

6. Herrn und Frau Kappels Tochter; von; für

_____

7. Christines Auto; mit; für

_____

VI. Rewrite as indirect questions, starting with Können Sie mir sagen, ...

1. Wohin fährt der Bus?

_____

2. Wer kann meinen VW reparieren?

_____

3. Wann fährt der nächste Zug?

_____

4. Woher kommt ein Datsun?

_____

5. Wo kann ich einen Wagen leihen?

_____

6. Warum ist das Benzin hier so teuer?

_____

7. Muß man hier lange warten?

_____

8. Was ist das?

_____

9. Wie schnell darf man hier fahren?

_____

10. Wem soll ich das geben?

_____

VII. Translate.

Das Statussymbol

My uncle Bruno is still young. So he says. He's 65. He loves his bicycle. It has a diesel-engine with 5 HP. He always says: "Quality is a matter of prestige for me!"

When my uncle has to fix his bike, it's almost a ritual. And I'm supposed to help him. After one minute, he always says that I'm too clumsy, that I can never be(come) a mechanic. Then he shows me how I'm supposed to do it; but I can never do it.

When I want to borrow his bike, he gets nervous and says: "Drive carefully and slowly. Don't play the racedriver. You're too young, you don't have any life experience!" Then I say to him: "Uncle Bruno, it's a bike, not a space ship! Of course, I can drive a bike!"

Yes, my uncle loves his bike, his status symbol. But otherwise, he's very nice.

_____

_____

_____

_____

_____

_____

_____

_____

_____

_____

_____

_____

LEKTION SECHS

I. Gegenteile und Kontraste

1. die Beleidigung _____		a. pleite
2. gewagt _____		b. bekommen
3. alles _____		c. schnell
4. bewundern _____		d. der Schauspieler
5. der Bruder _____		e. das Kompliment
6. damals _____		f. gestern
7. schicken _____		g. vorsichtig
8. morgen _____		h. verreisen
9. zu Hause bleiben _____		i. kritisieren
10. der Zuschauer _____		j. die Schwester
11. reich _____		k. nichts
12. langsam _____		l. jetzt

II. Was gehört zusammen?

1. der Sauertopf _____		a. der Bruder
2. das Benzin _____		b. der Regisseur
3. die Werkstatt _____		c. der Anruf
4. der Verkehr _____		d. der Volkswagen
5. das Transportmittel _____		e. meckern
6. das Familienmitglied _____		f. die Tankstelle
7. der Film _____		g. der Polizist
8. das Telefon _____		h. reparieren

III. Are the following nouns singular or plural? What case or cases are they? Give all possibilities.

Example: unsere Hamburger
         pl. nom. and pl. acc.

1. Ihren Examen _____

2. die Semester   _____

3. seine Töchter   _____

4. seinen Koffer   _____

5. deine Kamera   _____

6. den Autos   _____

7. ihrem Wecker   _____

8. unseren Wagen   _____

9. eurer Mutter   _____

10. seinen Schlüssel   _____

11. Ihr Onkel   _____

12. den Mechanikern   _____

IV. Put the following telephone conversation in the proper sequence by placing a number in the blank before each remark or response. Begin by putting (1) in front of the opening greeting, (2) in front of the other speaker's response, etc.

Speaker A	*Speaker B*
_____ An der Bushaltestelle, Ecke Schillerstraße, wo du letztesmal gewartet hast.	_____ Nein, er ist momentan verreist, und meine Mutter meckert, wenn ich ihren Wagen will.
_____ Ich habe eine Einladung zu Peters Party. Gehst du auch hin?	_____ Tag Helge, was gibt's Neues?
_____ Dann können wir mit dem Bus fahren. Kann ich dich vielleicht treffen?	_____ Ich kann nicht. Mein Wagen ist in der Werkstatt.
_____ Hallo, Michael, hier Helge.	_____ Gut. Also abgemacht. Bis Freitag.
_____ Kannst du vielleicht den Wagen von deinem Vater leihen?	_____ Schmidt hier.
_____ Willst du mich abholen?	_____ Ja, natürlich, dann können wir zusammen hingehen.
_____ Tschüß!	_____ Ja, gern, wo denn?

V. <u>Kreuzworträtsel</u> (Crossword Puzzle)

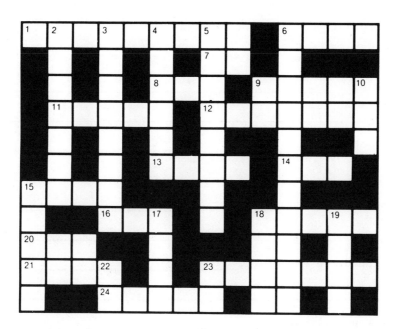

Waagerecht (⟶)

1. anderes Wort für „selbstverständlich"
6. „Bitte nehmen Sie die Kamera." „Vielen ...!"
7. Ich weiß nicht, ... er mich kennt.
8. Das ist mein Bruder, ich helfe ...
9. Wenn man blind ist, kann man nicht ...
11. Sie sind ..., denn sie haben viel Geld.
12. So heißt ein Wagen (teuer und schnell).
13. Der Polizist ist ..., er gibt mir keinen Strafzettel.
14. Was ist mit deinem Auto ...?
15. Mein Vater hat viel für ... Auto bezahlt.
16. ... heißt Anna.
18. ... das Autowaschen ist in Deutschland ein Ritual.
20. ... nach Hause!
21. gehen Sie dort um die ...
23. Ich muß zum Bahnhof, ich muß meine Schwester ...
24. Du ... auf meinem Platz!

Senkrecht (↓)

2. Wenn man seine Hausaufgabe nicht gemacht hat, muß man eine gute ... haben.
3. ..., wissen Sie, wie er heißt?
4. Kannst du mir Geld ...?
5. Sie arbeitet wie ein ..., sehr schnell und genau.
6. Ein deutscher Ingenieur hat ihn gebaut.
10. nicht alt
15. Können Sie mir ..., wie alt er ist?

17. Mein Bruder ist ... ein Jahr alt.
18. ... ihr das Schild dort?
19. Ich möchte zur Party kommen, ... ich kann nicht.
22. Das ist mein Tonbandgerät, ... ist neu.

VI. Use the appropriate past tense to ask the question; then respond to the question as in the example.

Example: Sie konkurriert mit den anderen.
Hat sie immer mit den anderen konkurriert?
Ich weiß nicht, ob sie immer mit den anderen konkurriert hat.

1. Sie hat viel Geld. _____

_____

2. Er plant alles sehr genau. _____

_____

3. Sie produzieren gute Autos. _____

_____

4. Die Lufthansa landet in Frankfurt. _____

_____

5. Er schickt alles pünktlich. _____

_____

6. Sie verkaufen nur Kameras. _____

_____

7. Sie verreist nur im Winter. _____

_____

8. Sie sind so langweilig. _____

_____

VII. Composition

Supply your part of the telephone conversation according to the English cues.

Telefongespräch

Ihr Gesprächspartner, Horst Naumann, ist mit Ihnen in einem Seminar, aber Sie finden ihn langweilig. Ihr Telefon läutet.

Sie: (answer the telephone)

_____

Horst: Hallo, hier Horst Naumann. Du weißt, ich bin im Seminar bei Professor Halpert.

Sie: (Give indication of recognition and the usual general inquiry about his state of health.)

_____

Horst: Gut, danke. Sag mal, ich bin neu hier. Ich war letztes Jahr in Hamburg. Dort ist das Leben interessant. Gibt es hier abends (in the evening) etwas zu tun?

Sie: (Respond affirmatively and with enthusiasm since you want to defend your small town and its offerings; name several things one can do: movies, how many there are and what is playing in a couple of them right now; no disco yet, but soon; sometimes a lecture or a concert (das Konzert).)

_____

_____

_____

_____

Horst: Na, also keine große Auswahl (selection), aber für so eine Stadt.... Sag mal, was machst du am Freitag? Vielleicht köonnen wir zusammen etwas tun.

Sie: (You want to get out of this; so you quickly bring up your unfortunate lack of money because father or mother hasn't sent your check, and you still have to eat before you get it.)

_____

_____

_____

Horst: Das macht nichts. Ich bezahle alles. Ich hatte gestern Glück in der Lotterie.

Sie: (Express your thanks; you really can't accept (annehmen); maybe another time (ein andermal).)

_____

_____

Horst: Dann leihe ich dir das Geld. Du Kannst es mir dann zurückgeben, wenn der Scheck kommt.

Sie: (Refuse with thanks because you don't like to borrow money; just for insurance against this persistent person you mention something about possibly going on a trip on Friday.)

_____

_____

_____

Horst: Wie kannst du das machen? Ohne Geld?

Sie: (Invent something about a friend with a car going somewhere or other interesting where you have never been.)

_____

_____

_____

Horst: Also dann, vielleicht ein andermal. Bis morgen im Seminar. Tschüß.

Sie: (Express thanks for the call and say goodbye.)

_____

LEKTION SIEBEN

I. Was gehört zusammen?

1. der Film _____	a. die Eltern
2. die Note _____	b. der Lehrling
3. das Interview _____	c. die Woche
4. das Gymnasium _____	d. der Regisseur
5. der Rucksack _____	e. die Prüfung
6. das Telefon _____	f. gewaltig
7. sehr groß _____	g. der Reporter
8. der Tag _____	h. das Abitur
9. das Kind _____	i. der Anruf
10. die Berufsschule _____	j. trampen

II. From the list select the verb that fits the context and use it in the appropriate tense.

abholen	aufhören	kennenlernen
anfangen	aufpassen	mitkommen
ansehen	herumreisen	zurückkehren

1. Am Montag (Monday) fängt die Woche an, am Sonntag _____ sie _____.

2. Gestern ist er verreist; übermorgen _____ er _____.

3. Weil er von den Ferien träumt, _____ er in der Klasse nicht _____.

4. Jan war in Amerika und _____ dort _____.

5. Wir trampen nach Alaska; willst du _____?

6. Dein Freund ist sehr nett; wo _____ du ihn _____?

7. Können wir mit dem Essen _____, oder sollen wir warten?

8. Wer _____ morgen die Tante am Bus _____?

9. Wenn mich der Professor _____, werde ich nervös.

III. Rewrite using the past tense of the modal indicated.

1. Er hat im Ausland studiert. (wollen)

_____

2. Sie sind im Oktober verreist. (müssen)

_____

3. Sie hat das Kind am Kindergarten abgeholt. (sollen)

_____

4. Wir sind mit Rucksack und Schlafsack getrampt. (wollen)

_____

5. Sie sind dort nicht gelandet. (dürfen)

_____

6. Ich habe ihn nicht überholt. (können)

_____

7. Du hast doch die Universität besucht. (wollen)

_____

8. Man hat den Computer vorsichtig behandelt. (müssen)

_____

IV. Fill in the correct definite article. Then rewrite the sentence, using the plural of the noun. Change the verb form when necessary.

1. Er dankt _____ Schauspieler.

_____

2. Sie hilft _____ Bruder.

_____

3. Er spricht oft über _____ Examen.

_____

4. Wohin gehst du mit _____ Koffer?

_____

5. Kannst du _____ Koffer bringen?

_____

6. Sie kommen mit _____ Auto.

_____

7. Kennen Sie _____ Studenten?

_____

8. Wann hat _____ Klasse angefangen?

_____

9. _____ Schwester ist sehr intelligent.

_____

10. Ist das _____ Amerikanerin?

_____

11. _____ Leistung war durchschnittlich.

_____

12. Wann bekommen wir _____ Note für _____ Prüfung?

_____

V. Ask a new friend questions about his/her recent trip. Use the cues given in the appropriate tense.

    Example: wo / sein
              Wo warst du?

1. wo / sein _____

2. in Amerika / sein _____

3. dort / studieren _____

4. wo / landen _____

5. wer / dich / abholen _____

6. wo / wohnen _____

7. viel Englisch / lernen _____

8. wann / Semester / aufhören _____

9. was / dann / machen _____

10. viel / herumreisen _____

11. auch nach Kalifornien / trampen _____

12. Florida / besuchen wollen _____

13. was / dich / interessieren _____

14. viele Leute / kennenlernen _____

15. Reporter / dich / interviewen _____

16. warum / zurückkommen wollen _____

VI. Answer, using the plural form of the noun.

    Example: Was tut ein Assistent?
              Er arbeitet für die Professoren.

1. Was tut ein Klempner? _____

2. Was tut ein Regisseur? _____

3. Was tut ein Zeitungsverkäufer? _____

4. Was tut ein Taxifahrer? _____

5. Was tut ein Polizist? _____

6. Was tut ein Mechaniker? _____

7. Was tut ein Professor? _____

8. Was tut ein Student? _____

9. Was tut ein Reporter? _____

10. Was tut ein Uhrenverkäufer? _____

VII. Translate

I Was an Exchange Student in Germany

I must say, Germany is O.K. I returned from Heidelberg yesterday. I was in
Germany from the beginning of November until the end of June. I studied in Heidelberg.
I got to know a lot of people. They were very nice and always willing to (wanted to)
help me. I already knew (some) German, but I learned a lot more. I lived with a
family; they were great! They have two daughters and three sons. I hitchhiked with
them to Austria. There I visited the house where Freud had lived. That was very
interesting for me because I'm studying psychology. In January I worked for (bei)
a filling station. It was not hard because they had self-service (Selbstbedienung).
I earned enough money so that I could go on a trip. I would really like to go to
Germany again. I must say, Germany is O.K. I would also like to see Switzerland.
Perhaps I can study in Basel where Carl Gustaf Jung was a student, and I would like
to· visit Zürich because Jung worked there... Yes, I have to earn more money....

NAME _____ INSTRUCTOR _____ CLASS _____

_____

_____

_____

_____

_____

_____

_____

_____

_____

_____

_____

_____

_____

_____

_____

_____

_____

_____

_____

LEKTION ACHT

I. Gegenteile und Kontraste

1. ein bißchen _____   a. normal

2. suchen _____   b. arbeiten

3. führen _____   c. sitzen

4. immer noch _____   d. folgen

5. stehen _____   e. viel

6. pikiert _____   f. finden

7. Ferien haben _____   g. nicht mehr

8. verrückt _____   h. freundlich

9. fliehen _____   i. zurückkehren

II. Was gehört zusammen?

1. die Datenverarbeitung _____   a. die Zeitung

2. der Lehrer _____   b. das Glück

3. die Schreibmaschine _____   c. das Laboratorium

4. der Stuhl _____   d. der Computer

5. die Anzeige _____   e. die Kinder

6. die Daumen drücken _____   f. der Sekretär

7. Freud _____   g. entdecken

8. experimentieren _____   h. das Geld

9. Columbus _____   i. das Über-Ich

10. die Bezahlung _____   j. sitzen

III. Identify the following nouns as to case and number. Give all possibilities.

1. ihrem Problem _____   2. unsere Kamera _____

3. der Tochter _____   4. den Museen _____

5. meinen Brüdern _____   6. einer Diskothek _____

7. keinen Wecker _____   8. die Jahre _____

9. unsere Geräte _____   10. den Resultaten _____

IV. Change to the present tense.

1. Da ist er vom Stuhl gefallen. _____

2. Sie haben die Anzeigen gelesen. _____

3. Er hat sie pikiert angesehen. _____

4. Hat sie die Stellung bekommen? _____

5. Natürlich hat er zu viel gegessen. _____

6. Die Kinder sind um zwei nach Hause gegangen. _____

7. Warum hat sie immer schlechte Noten bekommen? Weil sie nicht aufgepaßt hat.

_____

8. Ist sie auch mitgekommen? _____

9. Warum ist er nicht in den USA geblieben? _____

10. Hast du es wirklich aufgegeben? _____

V. Manchmal findet man etwas schwer, manchmal findet man etwas leicht. Was finden Sie schwer oder leicht?

Give five things you find easy or hard.

Example: *Es ist schwer, im Zoo zu arbeiten, wenn man nicht tierliebend ist.*

1. _____
2. _____
3. _____
4. _____
5. _____

VI. <u>Composition</u>

A. Sie sehen eine Anzeige für eine Stellung. Sie schreiben einen Brief.

Write a letter of application stating how you fulfill the requirements for the following job.

Anzeige

Verkäufer(in), Buchhandlung (bookstore). Dynamisch, freundlich. Erfahrung mit Büchern. Abitur oder Äquivalent. Muß Englisch und/oder Französisch lesen. Bezahlung offen. Sehr angenehme Arbeitsbedingungen. Schriftliche Bewerbung an Herrn Otto Flisker, Bahnhofstraße 18.

Herrn
Otto Flisker
Bahnhofstraße 18

Sehr geehrter Herr Flisker,

_____

_____

_____

_____

_____

_____

_____

_____

_____

_____

Hochachtungsvoll

_____

B. Sie bekommen die Stellung und arbeiten 3 Monate in dem Geschäft. Aber die Stellung ist sehr langweilig und die Arbeitsbedingungen sind gar nicht angenehm. Sie geben die Stellung auf. Hier sind die Arbeitsbedingungen.

1. Verkäufer und Verkäuferinnen müssen um 8 Uhr im Geschäft sein. Dann fängt die Arbeit an.

2. Um 8:30 öffnet das Geschäft.

3. Verkäufer dürfen nicht im Geschäft lesen. Die Bücher sind nur für die Kunden da.

4. Um 12 Uhr essen die Frauen zu Mittag; die Männer essen um eins.

5. Im Katalog stehen die Titel von allen Büchern im Geschäft. Wenn ein Kunde nach einem Buch fragt, müssen Sie schnell herausfinden, ob wir das Buch haben.

6. Um 4 Uhr trinken die Frauen ihren Tee oder Kaffee; die Männer warten bis 4:20.

7. Am Freitag bekommen Sie Ihren Scheck.

Tell your parents in a letter that you have given up the job and tell them (by way of explanation) about each of these regulations in the appropriate past tense.

Liebe Eltern!

_____

_____

_____

_____

_____

_____

_____

_____

_____

_____

_____

_____

_____

_____

LEKTION NEUN

I. By adding the prefix <u>un-</u> to a German adjective you get the opposite. Add <u>un-</u> and translate the new word.

1. interessant _____

2. wahrscheinlich _____

3. natürlich _____

4. ordentlich _____

5. schön _____

6. pünktlich _____

7. amerikanisch _____

8. beliebt _____

9. vorsichtig _____

10. wichtig _____

11. glücklich _____

12. akzeptabel _____

13. angenehm _____

14. bekannt _____

15. möglich _____

16. gesund _____

II. <u>Was ist das?</u>

Identify each object by selecting the appropriate word from the list; supply the definite article.

Anzeige	Flugzeug	Sonnenschirm
Autoschlange	Mittelmeer	Sand
Blockhütte	Olivenbaum	Zelt
Bohrer		

1. Ich stehe im Bergwald; Herr Fischer hat mich gebaut. _____

2. Wenn man nicht gern in der Sonne sitzt, sitzt man unter mir. _____

3. Man findet mich im Süden; ein Produkt von mir ist im Martini.

_____

4. Wenn auf den Autobahnen viel Verkehr ist, findet man mich da.

_____

5. Der Zahnarzt muß mich haben, wenn er die Zähne repariert.

_____

6. Man findet mich bei Pan Am, Lufthansa, Swiss Air, usw. _____

7. Man findet mich zwischen Afrika und Europa. _____

8. Man findet mich am Strand und in der Sahara. _____

9. Wenn man nicht im Hotel schlafen will, nimmt man mich mit. _____

10. Wenn man eine Stelle finden will, sucht man mich in der Zeitung.

_____

III. Answer with a phrase, using the preposition and noun given.

1. Wo warst du gestern? (auf, Party) _____

2. Wohin gehst du jetzt? (in, Stadt) _____

3. Wo sitzt die Katze? (auf, Dach) _____

4. Wo wartet er? (hinter, Reisebüro) _____

5. Wohin soll ich das legen? (auf, Stuhl) _____

6. Wo hast du das gehört? (in, Vorlesung) _____

7. Wo hast du das gesehen? (in, Geschäft) _____

8. Wo ist mein Schlüssel? (unter, Zeitung) _____

9. Wohin fahrt ihr nächstes Jahr? (in, Schweiz) _____

10. Wohin soll ich den Koffer stellen? (in, Ecke) _____

IV. Answer the questions, using the past tense of _können_.

Example: Warum bist du nicht mitgekommen?
          Ich konnte nicht mitkommen.

1. Warum hast du das nicht gelesen? _____

2. Hat er das nicht herausgefunden? _____

3. Hast du ihm nicht ausgeholfen? _____

4. Hast du nicht mit ihm gesprochen? _____

5. Warum ist er nicht dort geblieben? _____

6. Ist der Plan nicht gelungen? _____

7. Haben sie es nicht getan? _____

8. Habt ihr ihn nicht verstanden? _____

9. Hat er keinen Vortrag gehalten? _____

10. Hat er keine Jeans getragen? _____

V. Answer the questions, adding the items in parentheses; begin each sentence with the subject.

1. Wann ist er in die Stadt gegangen? (um acht)

_____

2. Mit wem ist er gestern ins Kino gegangen? (seine Schwester)

_____

3. Wo hat sie damals mit ihm gesessen? (unter, Sonnenschirm)

_____

4. Wohin hat sie am Sonntag mit ihnen eine Reise gemacht?. (in die Vereinigten Staaten)

_____

_____

5. Wie ist er heute an den Strand gefahren? (mit, Bus)

_____

VI. <u>Was ist das?</u>

Translate.

1. die Mathematiklehrerin _____

2. die Großeltern _____

3. die Wildkatze _____

4. die Tageszeitung _____

5. die Herrentoilette _____

6. die Damentoilette _____

7. der Reisescheck _____

8. der Zeltplatz _____

9. das Charterflugzeug _____

10. der Nervenarzt _____

11. die Busreise _____

12. die Lebensgefahr _____

13. der Busfahrer _____

14. die Fahrprüfung _____

15. der Kaufpreis _____

16. der Untertitel _____

17. das Wirtschaftswunder _____

18. das Bergdorf _____

19. die Liebesgeschichte _____

20. der Sonnenhut _____

VIII. Translate.

I was on Vacation with my Parents

In July, my parents said: "You can come with us, or stay with (bei) your aunt Abigail and work in the house, play with the cat, sell newspapers, or do whatever (was) you want." I didn't want to stay with my aunt Abigail; she is a grouch. I didn't want to work in the house or sell newspapers, and I don't like cats. What did I do? I went to Oregon with my parents.

My parents don't like sleeping (to sleep) in a tent; they sleep in a hotel. They don't eat hamburgers at (bei) McDonald's; they eat in a restaurant. They don't like to swim, they don't climb (on) mountains, they don't sail.... Why did I go with them? Well, because I don't like Aunt Abby, and I'm only 12 years old. I had to go with them. And what did I do? I slept in hotels, I ate in restaurants. I didn't swim, I didn't climb mountains, I didn't sail .... My vacation was boring as hell!

_____

_____

_____

_____

NAME _____ INSTRUCTOR _____ CLASS _____

_____

_____

_____

_____

_____

_____

_____

_____

_____

_____

_____

_____

_____

_____

LEKTION ZEHN

I. <u>Was gehört zusammen?</u>

1. Schwyzer Dütsch _____   a. Italien

2. der Klempner _____   b. der Dieb

3. die Brieftasche _____   c. das Konto

4. die Bank _____   d. die Wohnung

5. der Lesesaal _____   e. das Gebirge

6. das Penthaus _____   f. das Essen

7. der Käse _____   g. die Sprache

8. der Römer _____   h. das Geld

9. der Einbrecher _____   i. der Schraubenschlüssel

10. die Alpen _____   j. die Bücher

II. Change to the simple past tense.

1. Er hat es nicht behauptet.

_____

2. Die Polizei hat die Bank zu spät erreicht.

_____

3. Die Leute in der Bank haben nichts bemerkt.

_____

4. Wir haben gar nichts berührt.

_____

5. Die Millionärin hat zwei Nummernkonten gehabt.

_____

6. Wir haben unser Geld bei dieser Bank deponiert.

_____

7. Wie hat man das erklärt?

_____

8. Sie sind in der Nacht aus dem Fenster geklettert.

_____

9. Wann hat sie sie abgeholt?

_____

10. Tante Irene hat das gewußt.

_____

III. Fill in the correct form of the <u>der-</u> or <u>ein-</u>word.

1. Sie kann _____ Kreuzworträtsel lösen. (all-)

2. Das steht in _____ Zeitung. (dies-)

3. _____ Zahnarzt heißt Dr. Schmerzlos. (sein)

4. Er will nichts mehr von _____ Schwierigkeiten hören. (mein)

5. _____ Kind schläft in diesem Zimmer. (ihr)

6. _____ Schiffsreise ist teuer. (jed-)

7. Sie sitzt sehr oft an _____ Fenster. (dies-)

8. Hat er _____ Artikel über Freud schon geschrieben? (sein)

9. _____ Studenten finden ihn langweilig. (manch-)

10. Mit _____ Leuten spricht sie nicht gern. (solch-)

11. Mach _____ Fenster auf. (dein)

12. Er möchte _____ Familie kennenlernen. (mein)

IV. Rewrite, replacing each noun by a pronoun or pronoun substitute.

1. Was hat der Dieb mit dem Schraubenschlüssel getan?

_____

2. Seine Töchter haben meine Familie dort besucht.

_____

3. Der Einbrecher hat auf diesen Moment gewartet.

_____

4. Ihre Schwester hat ihr beim Einmaleins geholfen.

_____

5. Unser Sohn wartet schon lange auf einen Studienplatz.

_____

6. Denkt sie oft an ihre Freunde?

_____

7. Mit den Kindern will mein Mann nicht verreisen.

_____

8. Nach der Party habe ich lange geschlafen.

_____

9. Die Geschichte steht natürlich in der Zeitung.

_____

10. Ich habe etwas über Safaris gelesen.

_____

V. Definieren Sie die folgenden Wörter.

    Example: Rechtsanwalt
                Man braucht einen Rechtsanwalt, wenn man in Schwierigkeiten ist.

              Geschäft
                Man geht in ein Geschäft, wenn man etwas kaufen will.

1. Diskothek _____

2. Parkplatz _____

3. Restaurant _____

4. Führerschein _____

5. Altersheim _____

6. Telefon _____

7. Abitur _____

8. Visum _____

9. Zahnarzt _____

10. Reisebüro _____

11. Laboratorium _____

12. Schreibmaschine _____

13. Stellung _____

14. Nummernkonto _____

15. Deutschlehrer _____

VI. Kreuzworträtsel

(Use ss for ß.)

Waagerecht (⟶)

1. Wagen
3. Whisky und Soda
5. Präposition
6. Ich brauche ... für meine Kamera.
8. Männername
11. Ich, Über-Ich, ...
12. Deutsche Mark
13. ... Sie die Zeitung?
15. Es macht ...!
17. Konjunktion
20. Großvater
21. Männername
23. See in den USA
26. Zielsprache: ...
29. Konjunktion

Senkrecht (↓)

1. Männername
2. großartig
3. Kommst ... mit?
4. Kilometer
5. ...: Deutsch
7. Bundesrepublik Deutschland
9. ..., zwei, drei
10. Frauenname
14. Sie hat ein Kind; ... ist erst zwei.
16. Er ist ... langweilig!
18. ein deutsches Auto
19. ... komme mit.
22. ... nicht so viele Comics, Kinder!
24. Raumschiff von einem anderen Planeten
25. Er fährt an die Ost ... .
27. Weltorganisation
28. Zentimeter

VII. Sie sind Reporter bei einer deutschen Zeitung. Sie sollen einen Artikel über einen Gangster schreiben. Sie haben ihn interviewt, und hier sind Ihre Notizen. Schreiben Sie jetzt den Artikel mit dem Titel: „Wie man Gangster wird."

(Feel free to fill in more details and elaborations than these sparse notes allow; i.e., make it a good story!)

geboren / Hamburg

wohnen / bei Tante / Sauertopf / meckern

Schule / Noten nicht gut / Lehrer nicht nett

nach Schule / keine Stellung / unterqualifiziert

immer Probleme / immer erfolglos

Gangster kennenlernen / Assistent geworden

jetzt / kein Assistent mehr

viel verdienen / einen internationalen Ruf

Nummernkonto / Schweiz

oft Reisen / Safaris usw.

_____

_____

_____

_____

_____

_____

_____

_____

_____

_____

_____

_____

_____

_____

LEKTION ELF

I. Select the correct verb to complete the expression; then write a short sentence in the future tense with each expression. Use each verb only once unless otherwise indicated.

Example: es schwer _____
es schwer *haben*
Er wird es bestimmt schwer haben.

bekommen   essen   halten
besuchen   haben   machen (3 times)
drücken

1. Angst _____

_____

2. zu Abend _____

_____

3. einen Vortrag _____

_____

4. es eilig _____

_____

5. eine Schule _____

_____

6. einen Spaziergang _____

_____

7. die Daumen _____

_____

8. eine Reise _____

_____

9. Geschäfte _____

_____

II. Rewrite in the simple past tense.

1. Sie schlägt mit der Hand auf den Tisch und lacht.

_____

2. Er widerspricht seiner Frau, weil er es nicht glaubt.

_____

3. Sie schreien und meckern.

_____

4. Wir gehen nach Hause und spielen Bridge.

_____

5. Er schläft ein und träumt von einem Ungeziefer.

_____

6. Er wirft den Fisch ins Wasser und kehrt nach Hause zurück.

_____

7. Sie sitzen im Zimmer und hören Radio.

_____

8. Er erwacht und sieht auf die Uhr.

_____

9. Er steht da und sagt nichts.

_____

10. Ich liege im Bett und kann nicht schlafen.

_____

III. <u>Was bin ich?</u>

1. Ich habe einen Roman geschrieben und Preise gewonnen. _____

2. Ich gehe in die Häuser, nachts, und wenn die Leute nicht zu Hause sind. Ich nehme
   mit, was ich finden kann: Fernseher, Kassettenspieler, usw.

   _____

3. Ich frage die Leute. Ich will alles wissen. Dann schreibe ich einen Artikel. Wenn
   die Leute ihn lesen, meckern sie und sagen: „Das stimmt nicht, das habe ich nicht

   gesagt! Dieser Idiot!" _____

4. Export, Import, die Wirtschaft, das Sozialprodukt, die Währung, Inflation, diese Dinge interessieren mich.

_____

5. Ich tippe, ich telefoniere, ich schreibe, ich sage den Leuten, daß Herr X oder Frau X jetzt nicht mit ihnen sprechen kann. Ich frage, ob sie später kommen können. Ich rufe das Restaurant an und reserviere Plätze für X, wenn er oder sie mit einem Partner Geschäfte machen will.

_____

6. Ich liebe die Schweiz, weil es dort Berge gibt. Viele Berge. Berge sind interessant. Manche Leute fallen von den Bergen, aber ich nicht! Bis jetzt bin ich noch nicht gefallen.

_____

7. Die Formel $E = mc^2$ interessiert mich. Die Quantenmechanik, die Thermodynamik, Moleküle, Atome, Positrone, Neutrinos, Quarks... diese Dinge interessieren mich sehr.

_____

8. Indianapolis im Mai, ja, das interessiert mich! _____

IV. Wenn, wann, als?

Fill in the correct word.

1. _____ ich erwachte, war es schon zehn Uhr.

2. Ich möchte wissen, _____ der Zug ankommt.

3. _____ ich etwas gesagt habe, hat er mir immer widersprochen.

4. _____ Sie nicht wissen, ob es richtig oder falsch ist, fragen Sie den Professor.

5. _____ der Fischer den Butt sah, bekam er Angst.

6. Die Polizei konnte nicht feststellen, _____ der Dieb in der Bank war.

7. _____ die Polizei kam, floh der Dieb durchs Fenster.

8. Man kann den Safe nicht öffnen, _____ man die Kombination nicht weiß.

9. Bitte sagen Sie mir, _____ das passiert ist.

V. Give the correct part of the day in both forms, e.g.: am Morgen; morgens.

1. Wenn man von neun bis fünf arbeitet, steht man um diese Zeit auf. Sonntags

vielleicht nicht. _____

2. Wenn man von neun bis fünf arbeitet, hat man um diese Zeit frei, so daß man etwas essen kann. Manche Studenten stehen um diese Zeit auf und gehen zum „Frühstück" in die Mensa.

_____

3. Die Zeit zwischen Mittagessen und Abendessen heißt so.

_____

4. Die Cocktailstunde ist um diese Zeit. Die Diskotheken öffnen. Wenn man gearbeitet hat, ist man um diese Zeit müde (tired). Manche jungen Leute fangen dann zu leben an.

_____

5. Normale Menschen schlafen un diese Zeit. Manche Leute können oder wollen dann nicht schlafen und gehen aus oder sitzen vor dem Fernseher. Eltern warten manchmal um diese Zeit auf ihre Teenager.

_____

VI. Answer negatively as in the example; use the plural of the noun.

Example: Hast du am Montag eine Vorlesung?
Nein, montags habe ich keine Vorlesungen.

1. Fährt der Bus am Sonntag?

_____

2. Hält er am Freitag einen Vortrag?

_____

3. Gibt er am Montag ein Examen?

_____

4. Macht ihr am Dienstag einen Spaziergang?

_____

5. Macht sie am Mittwoch eine Bergtour?

_____

6. Hast du am Samstag die Zeitung gelesen?

_____

7. Haben wir am Donnerstag eine Prüfung?

_____

VII. Translate. Use simple past except where indicated.

Yesterday I read this story by (von) Franz Kafka (pres. perf.). A man woke up one morning and was a vermin. He was not surprised; no, he looked at (auf) his alarm clock and saw that it was already late. He wanted to get up and go to work, but naturally, he couldn't. Soon he heard his mother; she said: "Gregor, it's late!" And his father and his sister asked: "What's the matter, Gregor, are you sick? Why don't you come out of your room?" Gregor said: "No, I'm not sick, I'm fine, thank you. I'll be ready (fertig) soon." Later, when his mother saw him, she screamed. Mothers are proud when they can say, "My son, the doctor!" Or "My son, the lawyer!" Gregor's mother had to say, "My son, the vermin!" Of course, she screamed! Gregor did not go to the office (on) that day. I think he never went to the office again (pres. perf.). I am not yet finished with the story. I was lying in bed when I was reading it, and I got scared (pres. perf.). I'll tell you more about it later when I'm finished with it.

_____

_____

_____

_____

_____

_____

_____

_____

_____

_____

_____

_____

_____

_____

_____

_____

_____

_____

LEKTION ZWÖLF

I. Gegenteile und Kontraste

1. Europäer _____   a. der Freund

2. auswandern _____   b. anfangen

3. auf den Arm nehmen _____   c. Amerikaner

4. der Gegner _____   d. ernst nehmen

5. zuende sein _____   e. zu Hause bleiben

II. Was gehört zusammen?

1. abschaffen _____   a. tragen

2. der Garten _____   b. das Motorrad

3. das Auspuffgas _____   c. die Musik

4. die Einwegflasche _____   d. die Energie

5. Lust haben _____   e. eliminieren

6. der Sturzhelm _____   f. das Wasser

7. die Schallplatte _____   g. pflanzen

8. anhaben _____   h. die Umweltverschmutzung

9. besonders _____   i. die Wegwerfgesellschaft

10. der Europäer _____   j. wollen

11. zuende sein _____   k. vor allem

12. die Atomkraft _____   l. der Schweizer

13. der Fluß _____   m. fertig sein

III. Identify these verb forms as subjunctive (s) or indicative (i) or both (s and i).

1. ich hielte _____   2. er schliefe _____

3. wir blieben _____   4. ihr schriebet _____

5. sie arbeitete _____ 6. sie landeten _____

7. Sie ließen _____   8. ich finge _____

9. du könntest   _____   10. es gefiel   _____

11. er bewunderte   _____   12. wir glaubten   _____

13. sie wüßte   _____   14. sie kamen   _____

15. es gäbe   _____   16. sie hält   _____

IV. Select the appropriate verb and use it in its correct form. Do not use any verb more than once.

telefonieren	geben	schlafen
können	haben	sagen
teilnehmen	gehen	sehen
sein		

1. Wenn er ein Optimist _____, dann glaubte er an die Zukunft.

2. Wenn sie _____, würde sie nach Kanada auswandern.

3. Wenn es nach mir _____, hätten wir hier keine Mülldeponie.

4. Wenn es Schnee _____, fahre ich in die Berge.

5. Wenn du an der Demo _____, können wir nachher eine Spritztour machen.

6. Wenn sie recht _____, dann ist das Problem noch schlimmer.

7. Wenn ich nicht so lange _____, würde ich pünktlich zur Klasse kommen.

8. Wenn wir jetzt _____, könnten wir ihn noch erreichen.

V. Combine the elements to form phrases in the nominative case (d- = definite article).

1. d- / neu / Lederjacke _____

2. manch- / amerikanisch / Studenten _____

3. jed- / deutsch / Auto _____

4. dies- / arm / Familie _____

5. d- / interessant / Roman _____

VI. Combine the elements to form phrases in the appropriate case (d- = definite article).

1. von / dies- / alt / Freund _____

2. bei / all- / klein / Kindern _____

3. für / jed- / deutsch / Familie _____

4. in / dies- / technisch / Artikeln _____

5. mit / d- / teuer / Motorrad _____

6. nach / manch- / groß / Demonstrationen _____

7. ohne / d- / neu / Mülldeponie _____

8. seit / d- / interessant / Vortrag _____

9. gegen / jed- / überzivilisiert / Menschen _____

10. um / d- / neu / Motorrad _____

VII. Composition

Sie sind Reporter für eine Zeitung. Auf dem Weg zur Arbeit sehen Sie eine große Demonstration. Sie möchten herausfinden, warum man demonstriert, aber Sie können niemand interviewen, weil alle Leute brüllen. Sie sehen die folgenden Schilder. Später schreiben Sie einen Artikel.

In brief, fake it! Write a report, basing it on the signs you have seen as if you had interviewed several people. Use lots of adjectives!

Weg mit dem Reaktor!   *Der Reaktor macht uns kaputt!*

Wir wollen keine Radioaktivität!   *Reaktor und Krieg ruinieren die Welt!*

Unsere Kinder müssen gesund bleiben!   *Angst macht uns kaputt!*

Ohne Kinder keine Zukunft!   *Was macht ihr mit eurem Müll??*

_____

_____

_____

_____

_____

_____

_____

_____

_____

_____

LEKTION DREIZEHN

I. <u>Kontraste</u>

Find opposites.

1. verschwinden _____

2. gewinnen _____

3. gut _____

4. erst- _____

5. intelligent _____

6. ankommen _____

7. Schluß machen _____

8. streiten _____

9. erwachen _____

II. Schreiben Sie auf deutsch.

1. I am sorry. _____

2. He was sorry. _____

3. Are you sorry? _____

4. Was she sorry? _____

5. I know that they were sorry. _____

6. Who is sorry? _____

7. They will be sorry. _____

8. Why are you sorry? _____

9. If he were sorry, he wouldn't do that. _____

_____

10. I wish I could say that I'm sorry. _____

_____

III. Combine the sentence pairs.

Example: Sie aß zu Abend. Dann ging sie ins Kino.
Nachdem sie zu Abend gegessen hatte, ging sie ins Kino.

1. Er schoß das dritte Tor. Dann stand das Spiel 1:3.

_____

2. Sie gingen weg. Dann kam er.

_____

3. Ich nahm eine Stunde an der Diskussion teil. Dann hatte ich keine Lust mehr.

_____

4. Sie sah fern. Dann ging sie ins Bett.

_____

5. Er las die Anzeige in der Zeitung. Dann ging er ins Personalbüro der Fabrik.

_____

6. Der Zahnarzt behandelte meinen Zahn. Dann bekam ich Zahnschmerzen.

_____

7. Er sagte die Katastrophe voraus. Dann passierte sie wirklich.

_____

8. Wir reisten in der ganzen Welt herum. Dann wollten wir wieder nach Hause.

_____

9. Sie drückten mir die Daumen. Dann klappte es.

_____

10. Ich schlief trotz des schweren Essens ein. Dann träumte ich von einer Explosion.

_____

IV. Translate.

1. That was the game of the year.

_____

2. Those (das) are the difficulties of the German language.

_____

3. It takes place on the first day of the month.

_____

4. He is the center forward of our team.

_____

5. The Swiss Frank is the currency of Switzerland.

_____

6. She is the pride (der Stolz) of her parents.

_____

7. The films of this German movie director won prizes.

_____

8. The quality of this car is excellent.

_____

9. Would you like to meet the dean of our university?

_____

10. Do you know the title of the article?

_____

11. He will arrive at the end of the week.

_____

12. Uncle Sam is the symbol of the United States.

_____

V. Express wishes according to the example.

  Example: Ich kann nie ein Tor schießen.
            Ich wollte, ich könnte mal ein Tor schießen.

1. Ich darf nie spät nach Hause kommen.

_____

2. Ich habe nie recht.

_____

3. Sie kommen nie pünktlich.

_____

4. Er stimmt nie mit mir überein.

_____

5. Hier passiert nie etwas.

_____

6. Ich kann ihn nie überreden.

_____

7. Wir reisen nie ins Ausland.

_____

8. Sie hören nie auf.

_____

9. Sie kommt nie in die Vorlesung.

_____

10. Er nimmt mich nie auf seinem Motorrad mit.

_____

VI. Write sentences with the following verbs that take the dative case.

1. helfen   _____

2. danken   _____

3. gefallen   _____

4. leid tun   _____

5. widersprechen _____

6. gelingen   _____

7. Spaß machen   _____

8. antworten   _____

VII. Translate.

Trainer: Why didn't you stop that ball?

_____

Torwart: I couldn't. Didn't you see that?

_____

Trainer: Of course, I saw it! You were too slow. When did you go to bed yesterday?

_____

_____

Torwart: At eight!

_____

Trainer: I don't believe that! I'm sure you went out with your girlfriend and danced 'til one.

_____

_____

Torwart: I didn't go out. I never go out before a game.

_____

Trainer: Don't contradict me. I saw you.

_____

Torwart: Where?

_____

Trainer: In the Super-Disco.

_____

Torwart: You're crazy! I don't know that disco.

_____

Trainer: O.K. Maybe it was your brother. I'm sorry.

_____

Torwart: No, you're not sorry! You want to fight (streiten). You don't like my game.

_____

_____

Trainer: You're right. I don't like your game. And the fans don't like it either. Did you hear what they were shouting?

_____

_____

Torwart: Yes! They shouted: "Who is the coach of this miserable team??"

_____

_____

Trainer: You see what I mean? If you played better, they wouldn't say that!

_____

_____

Torwart: You're an idiot. I wish they would fire (feuern) you!

_____

Trainer: You've got to have the last word!

_____

Torwart: No, you!

_____

LEKTION VIERZEHN

I. Gegenteile und Kontraste

1. beenden _____   a. nehmen

2. größer _____   b. gestorben

3. sparsam _____   c. unglücklich

4. geboren _____   d. das Dach

5. der Gegner _____   e. anfangen

6. geben _____   f. langsam gehen

7. verlieren _____   g. der Partner

8. laufen _____   h. kleiner

9. der Keller _____   i. finden

10. zufrieden _____   j. verschwenderisch

II. Was gehört zusammen?

1. ins Exil gehen _____   a. die steigenden Preise

2. die Bude _____   b. Du sollst nicht stehlen.

3. erfahren _____   c. die Flasche

4. der Verwandte _____   d. auswandern

5. die Inflation _____   e. das Zimmer

6. bekannt _____   f. das Projekt

7. das Glas _____   g. der Onkel

8. anrufen _____   h. die Information

9. arbeiten an _____   i. der Ruhm

10. die Bibel _____   j. das Telefon

III. Change to past contrary-to-fact.

1. Wenn er nicht so verschwenderisch wäre, würde er sein Konto nicht so oft
   überziehen.

   _____

   _____

2. Wenn mein Wagen nicht so gut liefe, würde ich ihn verkaufen.

_____

3. Wenn sie zu ihrem Vater ginge, würde er ihr das Geld geben.

_____

4. Wenn es keine Inflation gäbe, würden 50 Mark genügen.

_____

5. Wenn sie einen warmen Mantel hätte, würde sie keinen neuen kaufen.

_____

IV. Translate.

1. Wenn sie eine Reise machten, nahmen sie uns mit.

_____

2. Er sollte nicht so verschwenderisch sein, sonst hat er bald kein Geld mehr.

_____

3. Hätten Sie Zeit, mir einen Gefallen zu tun?

_____

4. Wenn er kein so netter Mensch gewesen wäre, hätte er ihnen etwas anderes gesagt.

_____

5. Bei den steigenden Preisen könnte ich das nicht bezahlen.

_____

6. Konnten sie ihr bei der Arbeit helfen?

_____

7. Wenn er gestern angekommen wäre, könnten wir heute mit dem Projekt anfangen.

_____

8. Ich hatte ihn nicht darum gebeten, aber er wollte es unbedingt tun.

_____

9. Wenn ich bei McDonald's gegessen hätte, wäre ich nicht pleite.

_____

V. Translate.

1. That was an expensive phone call.

_____

2. The new car is not running well.

_____

3. (On) the next day I received his check.

_____

4. My next term paper is due soon.

_____

5. This interesting invention will revolutionize the world.

_____

6. She told me about your good progress (pl.) in (the) school.

_____

7. What's the name of the young man?

_____

8. Some young people don't have an understanding father.

_____

VI. Was hätten Sie anders getan? (What would you have done differently?)

1. would have tried to get better grades

_____

2. wouldn't have griped so much

_____

3. would have helped my brothers and sisters with their (beim) multiplication tables

_____

4. would have written a good term paper for psychology

_____

5. would have come to class on time

VII. <u>Composition</u>

In the following telephone conversation between Otto and his father, you fill in
Otto's part of the conversation as indicated in the English description. Do not
attempt to translate literally; find your own way of expressing the sentiments.

Vater: Was, wieder hundert Mark? Du denkst wohl, ich heiße Rockefeller!

Otto: (inflation; a hundred marks isn't enough these days)

_____

_____

Vater: Ja, die Inflation, die Inflation! Glaubst du, daß die Inflation nur dich
betrifft? Ich weiß auch, was Inflation ist!

Otto: (We have it tough these days; but he wouldn't ask if it weren't so urgent.)

_____

_____

_____

_____

Vater: Ja, eine Lederjacke gehört zu den wichtigen Dingen im Leben! Wie wäre es mit
einer Stellung? Du bist schon lange genug Student!

Otto: (Admits his father is right; he would if he could. Admits 16 semesters is a
bit extreme but he promises to get done in three or four semesters. Then his
father will be proud of his rock star.)

_____

_____

_____

_____

Vater: Rock-Star??? Rock-Star??? Ich denke, du studierst Wirtschaftswissenschaft!

Otto: (Did once, but after he had overdrawn his account three times the bank told
him that economics was not the right profession for him.)

_____

_____

_____

LEKTION FÜNFZEHN

I. Make nouns of the following verbs and translate the nouns.

   Example: erfinden: *die Erfindung = invention*

1. sich erholen: _____

2. sich erkälten: _____

3. empfehlen: _____

4. sich verändern: _____

5. übereinstimmen: _____

6. erscheinen: _____

7. stören: _____

8. lösen: _____

9. erklären: _____

10. einführen: _____

11. behaupten: _____

12. entdecken: _____

13. bewundern: _____

14. bezahlen: _____

15. entschuldigen: _____

II. Make nouns of the following verbs and translate the nouns.

   Example: anrufen: *der Anruf = phone call*

1. tanzen: _____

2. besuchen: _____

3. gewinnen: _____

4. verkaufen: _____

5. anfangen: _____

6. schlafen: _____

7. versuchen: _____

8. schlagen: _____

9. schreien: _____

10. streiten: _____

11. berichten: _____

12. laufen: _____

13. kaufen: _____

14. fallen: _____

15. sitzen: _____

III. Select the correct verb and complete the sentence. Use a negative where appropriate. Use each verb once.

sich trimmen   sich interessieren für   sich erholen
sich erkälten   sich vorstellen   sich zusammennehmen
sich verändern   sich anstrengen

1. Du hast Halsschmerzen, weil du _____ hast.

2. Er sieht gern Horrorfilme, weil er _____.

3. Ich esse zu viel, weil ich _____ kann.

4. Sie fahren auf Urlaub, weil sie _____ müssen.

5. Es ist mir gelungen, weil ich _____ habe.

6. Ich kann es nicht glauben, weil ich _____ kann.

7. Er hat mich nicht erkannt, weil ich _____ habe.

8. Ihr habt abgenommen, weil ihr _____ habt.

IV. Make sentences in the present perfect tense, using the following phrases.

Haus brennen   ihm den Namen nennen
ihn kennen   nach Hause rennen
dir Krokodil aus Florida mitbringen sich das denken
nicht daran denken

1. _____

2. _____

3. _____

4. _____

5. _____

6. _____

7. _____

V. Answer the following questions according to the example. Note that questions 5, 6 and 7 are in the past.

    Example: Warum strengst du dich nicht an? (können)
               Wenn ich könnte, würde ich mich anstrengen.

1. Warum nimmst du nicht zu? (können)

_____

2. Warum stimmst du nicht mit mir überein? (können)

_____

3. Warum nimmt er nicht daran teil? (müssen)

_____

4. Warum rufst du ihn nicht an? (Nummer wissen)

_____

5. Warum hast du sie nicht angerufen? (Nummer wissen)

_____

6. Warum bist du nicht mitgekommen? (sich nicht erkälten)

_____

7. Warum hast du es nicht bemerkt? (achten auf)

_____

VI. <u>Gestern war ein miserabler Tag!</u>

Rewrite the following events as events that almost happened.

1. Ich stehe zu spät auf.

_____

2. Ich vergesse meinen Führerschein.

_____

3. Mein Wagen springt nicht an.

_____

4. Ich fahre gegen einen Baum.

_____

5. Ich bekomme einen Strafzettel.

_____

6. Ich komme zu spät zur Vorlesung.

_____

7. Ich widerspreche meinem Professor.

_____

8. Ich schlafe in der Vorlesung ein.

_____

9. Später gelingt mir mein Experiment nicht,

_____

10. und im Laboratorium findet eine Explosion statt.

_____

VII. Make two sentences for each of the following expressions, one referring to a person and one referring to a thing.

    Example: erzählen von
                Von wem hat er dir erzählt?
                Wovon hat er dir erzählt?

1. träumen von _____

_____

2. meckern über _____

_____

3. denken an _____

_____

4. beginnen mit _____

_____

5. stolz sein auf _____

_____

6. Angst haben vor _____

_____

7. sich wundern über _____

_____

VIII. Schreiben Sie auf deutsch.

Besuch beim Arzt

Yesterday I had to go to the doctor because I had a sore throat. I wish I hadn't gone! He said: "Oh, I almost didn't recognize you! You've gained weight! What's the matter? What do you eat? What? Hamburgers and milk shakes? Eat vegetables and drink mineral water. And cut your intake in half. Have you given up smoking? No? Why not? You must stop. You'll get lung cancer. Self discipline and willpower! You're a young person. Get hold of yourself! Do you take pills? What? Pills against stress?? Yes, that's our young generation! When you're fifty you can start with them. And sleeping pills, too? Unbelievable! Exercise daily! And jogging is good too, if you can't fall asleep at night. No, I can't give you a prescription for pills for (gegen) a sore throat. You don't need anything. It will be better (besser) tomorrow. I recommend that you lead a healthy life, that's the best thing. Lose weight and stop taking pills. And don't eat so much. Good bye!"

I wish I had stayed home in bed. But he was right: my sore throat is better. Hm! Shall (sollen) I try to give up smoking? I have to think it over...

_____

_____

_____

_____

_____

_____

_____

_____

_____

_____

_____

LEKTION SECHZEHN

I. Gegenteile und Kontraste

1. abfahren _____   a. pünktlich

2. sich erinnern _____   b. klein

3. die Fremdsprache _____ c. nächst-

4. früh _____   d. ankommen

5. gleich _____   e. vergessen

6. riesig _____   f. die Muttersprache

7. die Verspätung _____   g. später

8. vorig- _____   h. spät

II. Was gehört zusammen?

1. benutzen _____   a. die Stellung

2. der Wartesaal _____   b. die Zeitung

3. das Flugzeug _____   c. gebrauchen

4. gutaussehend _____   d. tragen

5. der Job _____   e. das Kommunikationsmittel

6. der Kanister _____   f. der Bahnhof

7. der Kiosk _____   g. schön

8. die Sprache _____   h. das Benzin

9. schleppen _____   i. Lufthansa

III. Rewrite each sentence changing the adjectives first to the comparative, then to the superlative form.

1. Die guten Wohnungen sind in den alten Straßen.

_____

_____

2. Er macht viele Fehler, wenn er schreibt.

_____

_____

3. Mein langes Examen war nicht mein schweres Examen.

_____

_____

4. Ich muss heute meinen warmen Mantel tragen.

_____

_____

5. Er war mit seiner jungen Tochter da.

_____

_____

6. Ich kann den grossen Koffer tragen.

_____

_____

IV. Combine all the clauses in each group as relative clauses with the first sentence.

  Example: Das ist der Deutschprofessor. Er gibt allen Studenten gute Noten und
            alle Studenten bewundern ihn.
            *Das ist der Deutschprofessor, der allen Studenten gute Noten gibt,
            und den alle Studenten bewundern.*

1. Das ist der bekannte Mittelstürmer. Er ist sehr arrogant, alle Trainer hassen
   ihn, alle Reporter schreiben über ihn, und sein Spiel ist wirklich sehr gut.

_____

_____

_____

2. Das ist eine beliebte Tennisspielerin. Sie ist sehr arrogant, alle bewundern sie,
   alle sprechen von ihr, und ihr Rückhandschlag ist gefährlich.

_____

_____

_____

3. Wir haben ein sehr gutes Deutschbuch. Wir können es empfehlen, es ist nicht sehr teuer, man kann gut damit arbeiten, sein Titel ist „Zielsprache:Deutsch".

_____

_____

_____

4. Das sind die amerikanischen Deutschstudenten. Sie lernen schon zwei Semester Deutsch, sie finden die Klassen nie langweilig, der Professor gratuliert ihnen jeden Tag, ihr Enthusiasmus ist überwältigend, und man muß sie bewundern.

_____

_____

_____

_____

V. Sie wollen nach München. Sie haben eine Vorlesung bis vier Uhr, aber die Universität ist nur fünf Minuten vom Bahnhof.

Consult the following train schedule and then answer the questions.

Fahrplan

Zeit	Zug-Nr.	Abfahrt Frankfurt (M) Hbf in Richtung	Gleis
16.26 ⚒ außer ⑥, nicht 24., 31. XII.	E 3460	Ffm Süd 16.31—Offenbach 16.36—Hanau 16.45—Fulda 17.57	8
16.26 ⚒ außer ⑥, nicht 24., 31. XII.	5164	Ffm Flughafen 16.36—Mainz-Bischofsheim 16.56—Wiesbaden 17.13 ✈ Hält nicht in Ffm Sportfeld und Wiesbaden Ost und verkehrt nicht über Mainz	21
:16.28 Blauer Enzian → an ⑥ und am 24., 25., 31. XII., 4. bis 6. IV. und 25. V. nur bis Dortmund ←	IC 120	Wiesbaden 16.55—Koblenz 17.56—Bonn 18.29—Köln 18.51—Wuppertal 19.30—Hagen 19.49—Dortmund 20.12—Hamm außer ⑥ 20.38—Bielefeld außer ⑥ 21.07—Hannover außer ⑥ 22.02—Peine außer ⑥ 22.26—Braunschweig außer ⑥ 22.42 ◆ ✕	7
16.31	E 3155	Langen 16.41—Darmstadt 16.51—Heidelberg 17.50—Karlsruhe 18.31—Freiburg 20.20 🚭 5)	11
:16.32 ⑥ und ⑦ vom 2. II. bis 30. III., 7., 12. und 13. IV., auch 30. IX.	D 1424	Wiesbaden 17.00—Koblenz 18.12—Bonn-Beuel 18.55—Köln 19.16—Düsseldorf 19.57—Oberhausen 20.20—Dortmund 21.02 ☕	18
:16.33 Heinrich der Löwe	IC 529	Würzburg 17.53—München 20.22 ◆ ✕	6
16.35 ⚒ außer ⑥, nicht 24., 31. XII.	E 3584	Frankfurt West 16.39—Bad Vilbel 16.52—Stockheim 17.47	16
16.35 ⚒ außer ⑥, nicht 24., 31. XII.	E 3738	Frankfurt-Höchst 16.43—Farbwerke Hoechst 16.46—Niedernhausen 17.04—Limburg 17.47	2
:16.37 Schauinsland ① bis ⑤, nicht 22. XII. bis 1. I., 4. bis 7. IV., 26. V.	IC 577	Mannheim 17.21—Karlsruhe 17.58—Baden-Baden 18.14—Freiburg 19.02—Basel Bad Bf 19.39—SBB 19.46 ✕	9
:16.40	D 815	Darmstadt 16.56—Heidelberg 17.32—Stuttgart 19.06—Ulm 20.20—Augsburg 21.12—München 21.56, 🚌 Friedrichshafen Stadt 22.30 ☕ 🚭	12

E = Eilzug (express train)
D = D-Zug
IC = Intercity-Zug

Fragen

1. Wieviele Züge fahren zwischen vier und fünf nach München?

_____

2. Wann fährt der schnellere Zug nach München ab? Was für ein Zug ist das? Was ist
   die Nummer des Zuges? Wann kommt er in München an? Wie lange dauert die Fahrt?
   Von welchem Gleis (track) fährt er ab?

_____

_____

3. Wann fährt der langsamere Zug ab? Wann kommt er in München an? Was für ein Zug
   ist es? Was ist die Nummer des Zuges? Wie lange fährt er von Frankfurt nach
   München? Von welchem Gleis fährt er ab?

_____

_____

4. Wieviele Züge auf diesem Fahrplan haben Namen? Welche Züge sind es. Wie heissen
   sie?

_____

_____

5. Mit welchem Zug würden Sie fahren, wenn Sie so bald wie möglich ankommen wollten?

_____

6. Welcher Zug nach München hat ein Zugrestaurant?

_____

VI. Schreiben Sie einen Brief an Ihren Freund (Ihre Freundin) München, den (die) Sie
besuchen werden. Geben Sie ihm (ihr) genaue Information über Ihre Reisepläne (das
Datum, den Zug, mit dem Sie fahren, wann er abfährt, wo er hält, wann er in München
ankommt). Fragen Sie, ob er (sie) Sie abholen kann, oder wie Sie zu ihm (ihr) kommen
können (Bus, U-Bahn usw, welche Haltestelle...)

_____

_____

_____

_____

_____

_____

LEKTION SIEBZEHN

I. Here is an easy way to increase your vocabulary. Make adjectives from the following nouns and translate them.

    Example: die Demokratie
              demokratisch = demokratic

              der Terrorist (wk.)
              terroristisch = terrorist (adj.)

1. die Biologie   _____

2. die Astronomie   _____

3. die Geographie   _____

4. der Journalist (wk.) _____

5. die Psychologie   _____

6. der Idiot (wk.)   _____

7. die Soziologie   _____

8. die Anthropologie   _____

9. die Technologie   _____

10. der Optimist (wk.)   _____

11. die Energie   _____

12. der Pessimist (wk.) _____

13. das Mikroskop   _____

14. der Kommunist (wk.) _____

15. der Marxist (wk.)   _____

16. der Protestant (wk.) _____

II. Vocabulary Review

A. Translate the following word pairs. Note the change in meaning when a prefix is added to a verb.

1. fahren – erfahren   _____

2. kaufen – verkaufen   _____

3. lassen - verlassen   _____

4. sagen - voraussagen   _____

5. lesen - vorlesen   _____

6. schreiben - beschreiben   _____

7. kennen - erkennen   _____

8. warten - erwarten   _____

9. nehmen - zunehmen   _____

B. Now do the same with the following groups.

1. sprechen - besprechen - versprechen

_____

2. finden - erfinden - herausfinden

_____

3. kommen - mitkommen - vorkommen

_____

4. drücken - ausdrücken - bedrücken

_____

5. hören - aufhören - zuhören

_____

6. stehen - aufstehen - entstehen - verstehen

_____

7. suchen - besuchen - versuchen - untersuchen

_____

III. Wo ist Willy?

Change from passive to active. Keep the same tense.

1. Vielleicht ist er von einem Krokodil gefressen worden.

_____

2. Vielleicht ist er von der Polizei mitgenommen worden.

_____

3. Vielleicht ist er von einem Geheimagenten besucht worden.

_____

4. Vielleicht ist er von einem Polizeiwagen gestoppt worden.

_____

5. Vielleicht ist er von seinen Freunden überredet worden, zu Hause zu bleiben.

_____

IV. Change to the passive voice in the simple past tense.

1. Man fragte sie darüber. _____

2. Man behauptete das oft. _____

3. Man rief ihn nachts um zwei an. _____

4. Man erkannte die Diebe nicht. _____

5. Man beschrieb den Täter genau. _____

V. Continue the statements, using the modal with the passive infinitive of the verb given.

    Example: Hans arbeitet. (nicht wollen; stören)
              Er will nicht gestört werden.

1. Mein T-Shirt ist schmutzig. (müssen; waschen)

_____

2. Alfred ist der beste Kandidat. (müssen; wählen)

_____

3. Das ist Trinkwasser. (nicht dürfen; verschmutzen)

_____

4. Mein Wagen ist total kaputt. (nicht können; reparieren)

_____

5. Elisabeth hat kein Telefon. (nicht können; anrufen)

_____

6. Mike ging inkognito auf die Party. (nicht wollen; erkennen)

_____

7. Peter ist sehr vorsichtig. (nicht möchten; überraschen)

_____

8. Die Kinder meckerten. (wollen; mitnehmen)

_____

VI. Complete the following statements according to the example.

Example: Du glaubst, dein Bruder fährt schnell. (meine Schwester)
          Aber meine Schwester fährt noch schneller.

1. Du glaubst, deine Mutter ist sparsam. (mein Vater)

_____

2. Er arbeitet viel. (wir)

_____

3. Ihre Prüfung war schwer. (unsere Prüfungen)

_____

4. Dort ist es kalt. (hier)

_____

5. Er kann gut deutsch. (ich)

_____

6. Skifahren ist gefährlich. (Autofahren)

_____

7. Sie ist verrückt. (er)

_____

8. Eure Mannschaft hat schlecht gespielt. (unsere Mannschaft)

_____

9. In Italien ist es warm. (in Afrika)

_____

10. Mein Soziologieprofessor ist nett. (mein Deutschprofessor)

_____

VII. Rewrite, changing each adjective or adverb to the superlative.

1. Am Nordpol ist es kalt. _____

2. So kommen wir schnell hin. _____

3. Sie hatten viel verdient. _____

4. An dieser Stelle ist das Wasser tief. _____

5. Dieser Sport ist gefährlich. _____

6. PCB ist giftig. _____

7. Wasser ist gesund. _____

8. Sie hat mich scharf kritisiert. _____

9. Ich lese gern Detektivromane. _____

VIII. Translate

Telefongespräch

Angie: Hi, Debbie. How are you? I haven't heard (anything) from you since Monday. What are you doing?

_____

_____

Debbie: Hi, Angie. I wanted to call you earlier. But I have an exam next week. And for the last three days I've been writing a term paper.

_____

_____

_____

Angie: On (About) what?

_____

Debbie: "Mass Media and Democracy."

_____

Angie: That sounds interesting. More interesting than your last topic, what was it? "Difficulties of the Aged (older people)"?

_____

_____

Debbie: Yes. (the) Younger people have problems, too, perhaps worse problems. I could write more about that topic!

_____

_____

Angie: I believe you. - I'm looking for another job because I don't like working (to work) in an office. I really would rather work in a zoo or drive a truck. That would be more interesting than the work I have to do now!

_____

_____

_____

_____

_____

Debbie: Has something happened?

_____

Angie: No, I simply don't like my job.

_____

Debbie: But you're earning money. I have to be even (noch) thriftier than last year. Everything has gotten more expensive.

_____

_____

Angie: Yes, I know! By the way, did I tell you that my car was stolen?

_____

_____

Debbie: No! Really?

_____

Angie: Yes! It was found near (bei) a filling station. Now the brakes don't work anymore (nicht mehr).

_____

_____

Debbie: Why don't you sell it?

_____

Angie: It has to be fixed first. Then I'll buy a smaller car. - But that's not all. My cat disappeared. And I quarrelled with my boyfriend, and he disappeared, too.

_____

_____

_____

Debbie: What did you quarrel about?

_____

Angie: About my cat that disappeared.... O.K., Debbie, I have to say good-bye. I have to type this stupid letter, and Mr. Klein is always in a hurry.

_____

_____

_____

Debbie: O.K., Angie, I'll call you later, after (the) dinner. I heard the craziest story about your boyfriend. I've got to tell (it to) you. Bye!

_____

_____

_____

Angie: Now I'm really curious! Don't forget to call! Bye!

_____

_____

LEKTION ACHTZEHN

I. Each of the following nouns has as a component an adjective that you have had. Translate.

1. die Blindheit _____

2. die Ewigkeit _____

3. die Müdigkeit _____

4. die Persönlichkeit _____

5. der Sozialismus _____

6. die Höflichkeit _____

7. die Leichtigkeit _____

8. die Zufriedenheit _____

9. die Sparsamkeit _____

10. die Dummheit _____

II. Each of the following nouns is related to a verb that you have had. Translate.

1. der Vorschlag _____

2. die Unterbrechung _____

3. die Unterhaltung _____

4. das Verbot _____

5. die Verfolgung _____

6. die Erwartung _____

7. die Verständigung _____

8. der Vergleich _____

9. die Abfahrt _____

10. der Gebrauch _____

III. Translate

1. We had miserable weather.

2. We've heard something new.

_____

3. Haven't you anything more interesting to say?

_____

4. I won't buy bad quality.

_____

5. I don't like to swim in cold water.

_____

6. We're in great danger.

_____

7. We would help poor students if we could.

_____

8. German beer is better than American beer.

_____

9. I don't expect much new from him.

_____

10. Are gray cats hard to see at night?

_____

IV. Change the following quotes to indirect discourse.

1. Sie sah mich an und sagte: „Hilf dir selbst, dann hilft dir Gott."

_____

2. Er fragte mich: „Sind alle Katzen nachts grau?"

_____

3. Sie sagten: „Die dümmsten Bauern haben die dicksten Kartoffeln."

_____

4. Sie sagte: „Es gibt hier seit Jahren keine unberührte Natur mehr."

_____

5. Er sagte: „Ich werde mich scheiden lassen."

_____

6. Sie sagten: „Wir können leider nicht."

_____

7. Sie sagte: „Es tut mir leid, aber ich habe eine Verabredung."

_____

8. Er fragte: „Waren Sie wirklich in großer Gefahr?"

_____

9. Sie fragten ihn: „Was haben Sie getan?"

_____

10. Sie sagte: „Leider habe ich das nicht gewußt."

_____

V. Translate.

1. Die Ersten werden die Letzten sein.

_____

2. Die Vorsichtigeren wollten es sich noch einmal überlegen.

_____

3. Hilf der Blinden über die Straße.

_____

4. Nur eine Verrückte kann so etwas sagen.

_____

5. Er hat zugenommen. Jetzt sagen die Schlanken „Dicker" zu ihm.

_____

6. Der Bus war gegen einen Baum gefahren; es gab Tote.

_____

7. „Na, Kleiner, wo warst du denn?" sagte die Mutter zu ihrem Jüngsten.

_____

8. Das konnte nur einem Ungeschickten passieren.

_____

9. Neugierige riefen an und fragten, was geschehen wäre.

_____

10. Die Intelligenten verstanden es, die Dummen nicht.

_____

VI. <u>Composition</u>

Write at least five sentences on each of the following.

1. Stimmt es, daß Gold jede Tür öffnet? Geben Sie ein Beispiel dafür und eins dagegen.

_____

_____

_____

_____

_____

_____

_____

_____

_____

2. „Morgen, morgen, nur nicht heute, sagen alle faulen (lazy) Leute." Was bedeutet
   dieses Sprichwort? Gehören Sie zu den „faulen Leuten"? Wieso oder wieso nicht?

_____

_____

_____

_____

_____

_____

_____

_____

_____

ZIELSPRACHE: DEUTSCH

Part Two

Tape Manual

LEKTION EINS
PART I

EXERCISE I. Listen to the conversations in Lektion Eins.

Professor Schneider ist O.K., / aber Professor Bauer.../

Universität Saarbrücken. / Eine Studentin geht in ein Büro. / Dort arbeitet ein Mann. / Sie fragt: /

Studentin: Verzeihung, / sind Sie Professor Schneider? /
Mann: Nein, leider nicht. / Ich bin nur sein Assistent. /
Studentin: Wo liest Professor Schneider? / Ich bin neu hier. /
Mann: Zimmer vier. / Übrigens, / mein Name ist Arnold Weber. / Heißen Sie nicht Elisabeth Müller? /
Studentin: Nein, das ist meine Freundin. / Also dann, / vielen Dank und auf Wiedersehen. /
Mann: Tschüß! / —Hm, nicht sehr freundlich! /

Peter Hansen, ein Student, sitzt im Hörsaal. / Er spricht mit Sabine Hoffmann. /

Peter: Das Seminar von Professor Bauer ist doch stinklangweilig. / Findest du nicht auch? /
Sabine: Genau. / Woher kommt er denn? /
Peter: Er ist aus München. / Das hört man doch. /
Sabine: Professor Schneider ist aber O.K. / Seine Vorlesung ist wirklich interessant. /
Peter: Was tun wir nachher? /
Sabine: Ingrid und ich fahren in die Stadt. / Vielleicht gehen wir ins Kino. / Der alte King-Kong-Film spielt. / Oder in die neue Diskothek. / Ingrid tanzt doch so gern. / Kommst du mit? /
Peter: Ja, gern. / Hoffentlich habt ihr Geld. / Ich bin nämlich pleite. /
Sabine: Das macht nichts. / Ingrid hat immer viel Geld. /

Now repeat each phrase or sentence after the speaker.

In this lesson you will first practice the pronunciation of simple vowels in German. In a later exercise the ch will be practiced.

EXERCISE II. Listen and repeat each word after the speaker. First the long <u>a</u>:

ja//   Name//   aber//   fragen//   fahren//

Now the short <u>a</u>:

Mann//   Stadt//   hat//   dann//   schlank//

Now indicate whether you hear a long <u>a</u> or a short <u>a</u> by putting a check mark in the appropriate column in your workbook.

	long <u>a</u>	*short <u>a</u>*		*long <u>a</u>*	*short <u>a</u>*		*long <u>a</u>*	*short <u>a</u>*
1.	_____	_____	2.	_____	_____	3.	_____	_____
4.	_____	_____	5.	_____	_____			

EXERCISE III. Now practice the long o. Repeat.

oder//   wo//   wohnen//   Lektion//   woher//

Now the short o:

von//   sondern//   dort//   hoffentlich//   Dorf//

Now indicate by a check mark whether you hear a long o or a short o.

	long o short o			long o short o			long o short o
1.	_____	_____	2.	_____	_____	3.	_____	_____
4.	_____	_____	5.	_____	_____			

EXERCISE IV. Now practice the long u. Listen and repeat.

du//   tun//   tut//   gut//   Fuß//

Now the short u.

und//   Bus//   Kunst//   Mutter//   Butter//

Now indicate by a check mark whether you hear a long u or a short u.

	long u short u			long u short u			long u short u
1.	_____	_____	2.	_____	_____	3.	_____	_____
4.	_____	_____	5.	_____	_____			

EXERCISE V. Now practice the long i.

vier//   Kino//   spielen//   wie//   viel//

And now the short i.

finden//   mit //   nicht//   singen//   Film//

Now indicate in your workbook whether you hear a long i or a short i.

	long i short i			long i short i			long i short i
1.	_____	_____	2.	_____	_____	3.	_____	_____
4.	_____	_____	5.	_____	_____			

EXERCISE VI. Now practice the long e

sehr//   Amerika//   geht//   lesen//   wer//

And now the short e.

sprechen//   gern//   Lektion//   Professor//   Student//

Do you hear a long _e_ or a short _e_? Check the appropriate column.

long e	_short e_		_long e_	_short e_		_long e_	_short e_
1. _____	_____	2. _____	_____	3. _____	_____		
4. _____	_____	5. _____	_____				

EXERCISE VII. In this exercise you will practice the ch in German. Repeat each word after the speaker. First the soft or front ch.

ich//   nicht//   nämlich//   wirklich//   Mädchen//

Now the hard or back ch.

doch//   auch//   machen//   macht//   Buch//

Now repeat each sentence after the speaker.

Ich mache nichts.//

Ich mache es auch.//

Das Mädchen macht es nicht.//

Das macht nichts.//

Das macht doch nichts.//

EXERCISE VIII. In this exercise you will have a dictation. First you will hear each full sentence. Then each sentence will be broken up into units. Write what you hear. Then each sentence will be repeated so that you can check what you have written.

No. 1.: _____

No. 2.: _____

No. 3.: _____

LEKTION EINS
PART II

EXERCISE I. Answer each question affirmatively; then repeat the correct response given by the speaker.

Example: Lesen Sie gern Comics?
Ja, ich lese gern Comics.

EXERCISE II. Listen to the statement; then form questions, as in the example. Repeat the question after it has been given by the speaker.

Example: Ich singe gern Auld Lang Syne.
Singst du auch gern Auld Lang Syne?

EXERCISE III. Answer the questions using the information provided by the speaker and printed in your workbook. Begin your answer with the last element in the question. Repeat the correct form after the speaker.

Example: Was singt ihr nachher? (Jingle Bells)
Nachher singen wir Jingle Bells.

1. (die „Times")   4. (in Stuttgart)
2. (Coca Cola)   5. (Tennis)
3. (nichts)

EXERCISE IV. In this exercise you will hear statements. Pretend you have not heard the last element in the statement, and ask a question concerning that element. You will use one of the following interrogatives: <u>wo</u>, <u>wie</u>, <u>wann</u>, <u>woher</u>. Repeat the correct form of the question after the speaker has given it.

Example: Die Universität ist in Heidelberg.
Wo ist die Universität?

EXERCISE V. Listen to each of the following passages. They will be read twice. After the second reading you will be asked to complete a statement based on the information you have heard.

Passage No.1

Now listen to the passage one again.

Now select the correct phrase to complete the sentence by checking the appropriate letter in your workbook.

Linxweiler ist   a) eine Stadt wie (like) Chicago
                  b) eine Universität
                  c) ein Dorf wie Dullsville
                  d) ein Büro

Passage No.2

Now listen again.

Now complete the statement by checking the correct letter in your workbook.

Veronika ist   a) Professorin
                 b) Filmstar
                 c) Assistent
                 d) Studentin

Passage No.3

Now listen again.

Complete the statement by checking the correct letter in your workbook.

Seppl wohnt in   a) San Francisco
                   b) Amsterdam
                   c) München
                   d) Paris

LEKTION ZWEI
PART I

EXERCISE I. Listen to the entire conversation of <u>Lektion Zwei</u>.

Wasserleitung oder Psychologie? /

Frau Schmidt geht durch ein Geschäft. / Sie kommt um eine Ecke und trifft Herrn Meyer. / Er sieht sie und sagt: /

Herr Meyer: Guten Tag, Frau Schmidt. / Kennen Sie mich noch? /
Frau Schmidt: Ja natürlich, Herr Meyer. / Wie geht's? /
Herr Meyer: Danke, gut. /
Frau Schmidt: Und was macht die Familie? /
Herr Meyer: Mein Sohn Martin ist gerade auf Urlaub zu Hause. /
Frau Schmidt: Das ist aber schön. / Studiert er nicht Psychologie? /
Herr Meyer: Nein, leider noch nicht. / Er hat noch keinen Studienplatz. / Momentan arbeitet er als Taxifahrer in Frankfurt. / Vielleicht nächstes Semester. /
Frau Schmidt: Das Problem kennen wir auch. / Meine Tochter Ulrike studiert nämlich Medizin, / und da geht's ja auch nicht ohne den Numerus clausus. /
Herr Meyer: Ja, die Jugend hat es heute schwer. /
Frau Schmidt: Bestimmt. /
Herr Meyer: Manchmal sage ich: warum wird Martin nicht Klempner? / Das ist ein ordentlicher Beruf. / Und man verdient genug. / Aber für ein Handwerk ist Martin zu ungeschickt. / Und das Seelenleben interessiert ihn einfach mehr als die Wasserleitung. /
Frau Schmidt: (*lacht*) Wie schade! / Na, hoffentlich hat er bald mehr Glück. /

Now repeat each phrase or sentence after the speaker.

In this lesson you will first practice the pronunciation of the German umlauted vowels. Later exercises will help you practice the German r.

EXERCISE II. Listen and repeat each word after the speaker. First the long <u>ä</u>:

nächst-//   Mädchen//   nämlich//   fährt//   Universität//

Now the short <u>ä</u>:

Geschäft//   fällt//   hätte//   Hände//   Männer//

Now indicate by a check mark whether you hear a long <u>ä</u> or a short <u>ä</u>.

long ä	*short ä*	*long ä*	*short ä*	*long ä*	*short ä*
1. _____	_____	2. _____	_____	3. _____	_____
4. _____	_____	5. _____	_____		

EXERCISE III. Now practice the long <u>ö</u>.

hören//   Hörsaal//   schön//   Löhne//   Söhne//

Now the short ö

öffnen//   Köln//   völlig//   Hölle//   können//

Now indicate in your workbook whether you are hearing a long ö or a short ö.

   long ö short ö   *long ö short ö*   *long ö short ö*

1. _____ _____   2. _____ _____   3. _____ _____

4. _____ _____   5. _____ _____

EXERCISE IV. Now you will practice the long ü.

Übung//   Büro//   für//   übrigens//   natürlich//

Try the short ü.

tschüß//   Glück//   zurück//   Hülle//   Fülle//

Do you hear long ü or short ü? Check the appropriate column.

   long ü short ü   *long ü short ü*   *long ü short ü*

1. _____ _____   2. _____ _____   3. _____ _____

4. _____ _____   5. _____ _____

EXERCISE V. In this exercise you will practice the German r. Listen and repeat. First the r in initial position.

Resultat//   Rand//   Riß//   Rom//   Rum//   Regen//   Rübe//   Röcke//

Now the r in medial position:

fahren//   Beruf//   interessieren//   studieren//   Urlaub//   andere//

Now try the r in combination with other consonants:

brennen//   bringen//   Drang//   drin//   fragen//   Freund//   Gras//

groß//   krank//   Kram//   Professor//   Problem//   treffen//   trinken//

Now try the r in final position after a long or accented vowel:

der//   mehr//   schwer//   Professor//   sehr//   vier//   wer//   woher//

And now the final r in an unaccented syllable:

ander//   aber//   Klempner//   Semester//   Tochter//

Fahrer//   Wasser//   Wunder//   Zimmer//

Now repeat these sentences after the speaker:

Der Klempner ist im Zimmer.//

Wer ist er?//

Klempner ist ein ordentlicher Beruf.//

Er hat ein großes Problem.//

Er arbeitet mehr, aber es ist schwer.//

LEKTION ZWEI
PART II

EXERCISE I. Listen to the following statements; then formulate the questions to which these statements are the answers. Use du forms when a "you" question is called for. Repeat the correct question after it has been given by the speaker.

Example: Ja, ich habe einen Studienplatz.
           Hast du einen Studienplatz?

EXERCISE II. After listening to the following statements, indicate in your workbook whether they are true or false.

	True	*False*		*True*	*False*		*True*	*False*
1.	_____	_____	2.	_____	_____	3.	_____	_____
4.	_____	_____	5.	_____	_____			

EXERCISE III. Das stimmt nicht! Each of the following statements is incorrect. Correct each one first by negating the information given; then give the correct information. Repeat the correct sentences after the speaker.

Example: Frankfurt ist ein Dorf.
           Frankfurt ist kein Dorf. Frankfurt ist eine Stadt.

Now begin.

EXERCISE IV. In this exercise you will hear some descriptions. Each description will be given twice. After the second reading you will be asked to answer a question or complete a statement.

Passage No.1

Now listen to the same passage one again.

Now answer the following question by checking the appropriate letter in your workbook.

1. Warum arbeitet Maria in einem Café?

> a) Sie tanzt gern.
> b) Sie hat nicht genug Geld.
> c) Sie ist zu ungeschickt für Mathematik.
> d) Sie hat kein Glück.

Passage No.2

Now listen to the same passage once again.

Now complete the statement by selecting the appropriate letter in your workbook.

2. Fritz Schmidt ist   a) Student
                        b) Taxifahrer
                        c) Professor
                        d) Klempner

Passage No.3

Now listen to the passage once again.

Now complete the statement by selecting the correct letter in your workbook.

3. Ida Groß ist   a) Klempnerin
                   b) Amerikanerin
                   c) Großmutter
                   d) Professorin

LEKTION DREI
PART I

EXERCISE I. First listen to the entire conversation of Lektion Drei.

Tante Irene muß warten.../

Polizist: Junger Mann, / hier dürfen Sie nicht halten oder parken. /
Udo: Warum nicht, Herr Wachtmeister? /
Polizist: Schauen Sie mal auf das Schild da. / Oder können Sie nicht lesen? /
   Bushaltestelle. / Wollen Sie vielleicht einen Strafzettel? /
Udo: Nein, danke. / Ich muß aber meine Tante am Zug abholen. / Und ich möchte doch
   pünktlich sein. / Sonst muß die nette alte Dame warten. /
Polizist: Ja, ja, die Ausrede kenne ich. / Fahren Sie um die Ecke. / Dort ist ein
   Parkplatz. / Dort kann man parken, so lange man will. /

Udo: Tag, Tante Irene, / wartest du schon lange? / Gib mir doch den Koffer. /
Tante: Kannst du nie pünktlich sein, Udo? / Müßt ihr jungen Leute immer zu spät
   kommen? /
Udo: Entschuldige bitte, / sei nicht böse, Tante. / Direkt vor dem Bahnhof will ich
   parken. / Da muß ein Bulle kommen. / Ich soll auf den Parkplatz. / Fast fünf
   Minuten von hier. /
Tante: Ja, ja, mach Schluß, Udo. / Ich mag keine Ausreden. / Komm, nimm bitte den
   Koffer. / Gehen wir. / Und bitte, fahr heute nicht so schnell. /
Udo: Mensch, Tante, / du bist mal wieder ein richtiger Sauertopf! /

Now repeat each phrase or sentence after the speaker.

In this next section you will practice the pronunciation of diphthongs and the l.

EXERCISE II. First the diphthong au. Repeat after the speaker.

Auto//   Ausrede//   schauen//   Sauertopf//

aus//   auch//   Frau//   genau//

Now the eu which is usually spelled e u but sometimes ä u. Repeat.

Leute//   heute//   deutsch//   Freund//

neu//   teuer//   Eule//   läuft//

Now the ei. Repeat.

leider//   langweilig//   heißen//   mein//   sein//

Verzeihung//   beschreiben//   bleiben//   Arbeit//   Polizei//

EXERCISE III. Remember that ei is spelled e i. Do not confuse it with the long i sound which is sometimes spelled i e. In your workbook you will find a set of word pairs. The speaker will say one of the words in each pair. Circle the word you hear.

1. Leid   Lied   2. blieben   bleiben   3. schienen   scheinen

4. briet   breit   5. Beine   Biene   6. schrie   Schrei

EXERCISE IV. Now you will practice the German 1. Remember to place the tip of your tongue behind your upper teeth. First in initial position. Repeat.

lange//   Leute//   liegen//   lachen//   leben//   lesen//

Now the l in medial position. Repeat.

Bulle//   alle//   spielen//   halten//   bald//   Schild//

Geld//   Glück//   bleiben//   Klempner//   Film//   pleite//

schlank//   wollen//   sollen//

Now the l in final position. Repeat.

schnell//   Krokodil//   Spiel//   viel//   Fall//   manchmal//   will//   soll//

Now repeat the following sentences after the speaker.

Hilde will alles lesen.//

Er will bald viel Geld.//

Alle Leute lachen laut.//

Wir wollen lange leben.//

Der Klempner hat viel Glück.//

Helene ist schlank.//

EXERCISE V. Now you will practice a tongue twister, called Zungenbrecher in German. First you will hear the speaker say the entire tongue twister. Just listen.

Wenn Fliegen hinter Fliegen fliegen, dann fliegen Fliegen Fliegen nach.
(When flies fly behind flies, they are following flies in flight.)

Now repeat after the speaker.

Now try saying the entire tongue twister faster and faster.

LEKTION DREI
PART II

EXERCISE I. Answer each question, which will be said twice, using the modal auxiliary printed in your workbook and given by the speaker. Repeat the correct answer after the speaker. Follow the example.

> Example: Warum liest du das? Warum liest du das? (müssen)
> *Ich muß das lesen.*

Now begin.

1. (können)   4. (mögen)   7. (können)

2. (sollen)   5. (dürfen)   8. (wollen)

3. (wollen)   6. (müssen)   9. (dürfen)

EXERCISE II. Respond to the statement with a wir-command, using the words provided in your workbook and given by the speaker. Then repeat the correct form after the speaker. Follow the example.

> Example: Hier ist ein Parkplatz. (parken)
> *Parken wir hier.*

Now begin.

1. (spielen)   3. (fragen)   5. (deutsch sprechen)

2. (halten)   4. (warten)   6. (lesen)

EXERCISE III. Finish the speaker's words with a du-command form as in the example. Then repeat the correct form after the speaker.

> Example: Warum willst du nicht auf Urlaub gehen?
> *Geh auf Urlaub.*

Now begin.

EXERCISE IV. Change the following familiar commands to formal comman~ them after the speaker.

EXERCISE V. Was bin ich von Beruf? (What's my professi~ following three descriptions you will hear the word~ workbook the profession that has been described of course!)

No.1: _____

No.2: _____

No.3: _____

EXCERCISE VI. Ist das richtig oder falsch? True or false? Listen to each of the
following statements, and indicate in your workbook whether it is true or false.

	Richtig (True)	Falsch (False)		Richtig (True)	Falsch (False)
1.	_____	_____	8.	_____	_____
2.	_____	_____	9.	_____	_____
3.	_____	_____	10.	_____	_____
4.	_____	_____	11.	_____	_____
5.	_____	_____	12.	_____	_____
6.	_____	_____	13.	_____	_____
7.	_____	_____	14.	_____	_____

LEKTION VIER
PART I

EXERCISE I. First listen to the entire conversation of Lektion Vier.

Sie will einen Taschenrechner... /

Nach dem Mittagessen. / Renate und Annette kommen aus einem Restaurant. /

Renate: Ich muß nach Stuttgart. / Meine Schwester hat morgen Geburtstag. / Ich
    möchte ihr einen Taschenrechner kaufen. / Kommst du mit? /
Annette: Was will sie denn mit einem Taschenrechner? / Sie ist doch erst sieben. /
Renate: Was weiß ich! / Sie träumt auch von einer Digitaluhr mit Kalender, / einem
    Computer, / einem Elektronenmikroskop, / einer Spiegelreflexkamera... /
Annette: Will sie sonst noch etwas? /
Renate: Vielleicht ein Raumschiff. / -Das Kaufhaus hat ein Sonderangebot für
    Taschenrechner. /
Annette: Gut, gehen wir. /

Im Kaufhaus. / Renate fragt einen Verkäufer: /

Renate: Verzeihung, / wo gibt es Taschenrechner? /
Verkäufer: Stock vier. / Da gibt es Kassettenspieler, / Tonbandgeräte / und auch
    Taschenrechner. / Dort rechts ist die Rolltreppe. / Dort links geht's zum
    Fahrstuhl. /
Renate: Ich danke Ihnen. /
Annette: Was will das Fräulein Einstein nur mit dem Ding? /
Renate: Sie will das Ding haben, / sie hat Geburtstag, / also schenke ich es ihr. /
    Sonst muß ich ihr immer beim Einmaleins helfen. /
Annette: Ah, jetzt verstehe ich. / Klasse! / Kauf dem Wunderkind einen
    Taschenrechner! /

Now repeat each phrase or sentence after the speaker.

In this lesson you will practice the glottal stop and the s-sound.

EXERCISE II. This exercise will help you practice the glottal stop. Remember that
German words are not run together in a sentence. Each word is pronounced as a
separate unit. Before each word that begins with a vowel you should hear a glottal
stop, that is, a slight clicking sound. Listen and repeat after the speaker.

Er lernt das Einmaleins.//	Er arbeitet in Amerika.//
Ich esse alles gern.//	Er ist ungeschickt.//
Aber die Uhr ist alt.//	Das Auto ist alt und kaputt.//
Er ist Amerikaner.//	Die Ausrede kenne ich auch.//
Das ist ein elegantes Auto.//	

EXERCISE III. Now you will practice the German s-sound. Remember that before a vowel or between two vowels the single s is voiced, s as in sehen. Repeat after the speaker. First before a vowel:

Seminar//   sagen//   Sauertopf//   sitzen//

sondern//   Sohn//   sieben//   sind//

Now between two vowels:

Gesundheit//   Vorlesung//   Resultat//   lesen//

Now you will practice the unvoiced s. It is used in final position or before a consonant, s as in liest. Repeat after the speaker.

Bus//   ist//   hast//   nichts//   erst//   etwas//   links//

The double ss or ß is always unvoiced. Repeat after the speaker.

heißen//   wissen//   tschüß//   Schluß//   Wasser//   groß//   Assistent//

Now the speaker will say one of the two words printed as pairs in your workbook. Circle the one in each pair that the speaker pronounces.

1. lasen   lassen   4. wessen   Wesen

2. Wiesen   wissen   5. Rose   Rosse

3. Riese   Risse   6. Busse   Busen

EXERCISE IV. Zungenbrecher. Try this tongue twister. First listen to the speaker say the entire sentence.

Siegfried Süße sagt sechs sehr böse Sätze zu Sabine Sauer in der Klasse.
(Siegried Süsse says six very nasty sentences to Sabine Sauer in class.)

Now repeat each phrase after the speaker.

Now try it on your own as fast as you can.

LEKTION VIER
Part II

EXERCISE I. In this exercise you will hear sentences containing dative objects. In your workbook write the dative noun or pronoun that you hear. Each sentence will be read twice.

1. _____

2. _____

3. _____

4. _____

5. _____

6. _____

7. _____

8. _____

EXERCISE II. In this exercise you will hear answers to questions. Each one will be given twice. Formulate a question for each of the answers. Then repeat the correct question after the speaker. Use the familiar du-form in questions calling for a you-form.

      Example: Nein, ich habe keinen Kassettenspieler. Nein, ich habe keinen Kassettenspieler.
               Hast du einen Kassettenspieler?

Now begin.

EXERCISE III. In this exercise you will hear quotations appropriate for particular speakers. In your workbook you will find a list of six speakers. Select the appropriate speaker for each quotation, and place the number of the quote in the space provided next to the speaker. For example, if you thought that quotation No.1 were appropriate for ein Polizist you would put the number 1 next to ein Polizist in your workbook. Since that is not the right answer, you can go ahead and see what the correct answer is. Each quote sill be given twice.

eine Frau _____   ein Verkäufer _____   ein Professor _____

ein Polizist _____   ein Student _____   ein Kind _____

EXERCISE IV. After each of the following questions you will hear four responses. Three are correct; one is not. Circle the letter of the incorrect response in your workbook.

1. a)   b)   c)   d)

2. a)   b)   c)   d)

3. a)   b)   c)   d)

4. a)   b)   c)   d)

EXERCISE V. For each of the following situations or quotations you will be given
four responses. One response is correct; three are incorrect. Circle the letter of
the correct response.

1. a)   b)   c)   d)

2. a)   b)   c)   d)

3. a)   b)   c)   d)

EXERCISE VI. In this exercise you will hear some descriptions. After each description
write, in the appropriate space in your workbook, the name of the thing that is being
described. You will hear each description only once.

1. _____

2. _____

3. _____

LEKTION FÜNF
PART I

EXERCISE I. Listen to the entire conversation of Lektion Fünf

Onkel Norbert hat einen Porsche... /

Heiko, ein Student, besucht seinen reichen Onkel. /

Heiko: Ich habe eine Bitte, Onkel Norbert. / Ich muß heute abend nach Dudweiler, / denn unser Dekan hält dort einen Vortrag. / Kannst du mir deinen Wagen leihen? /
Onkel: Was, schon wieder? / Darf ich fragen, was mit deinem Käfer los ist? /
Heiko: Mein VW ist in der Werkstatt. / Die Bremse funktioniert nicht richtig, / und der Anlasser, / und die Gangschaltung ... / Der Mechaniker weiß nicht, / ob er ihn noch reparieren kann. /
Onkel: Verkauf doch das Museumsstück! / Warum gibt dein Vater dir seinen BMW nicht? /
Heiko: Weil ich ein „Rennfahrer" bin! / Und „noch zu jung". / Ich habe meinen Führerschein schon fast ein Jahr! /
Onkel: Deine Mutter ... /
Heiko: Wenn ich ihren Mercedes nur ansehe, wird sie nervös. /
Onkel: Du weißt, daß mein Porsche schon sehr alt ist ... /
Heiko: Selbstverständlich fahre ich vorsichtig und langsam. /
Onkel: Kannst du nicht mit dem Fahrrad fahren? /
Heiko: Bei dem Verkehr? /
Onkel: Na, wenn es unbedingt sein muß ... / Hier ist der Autoschlüssel. /
Heiko: Danke, Onkel! / Und Benzin kaufe ich auch. / An der Tankstelle, wo du Stammkunde bist. /

Now repeat each phrase or sentence after the speaker.

This pronunciation section will review the long a and the short a. A later exercise will practice the German w.

EXERCISE II. First practice the long a and short a. Repeat after the speaker.

haben	hat//	Aale	alle//
raten	Ratte//	Wahn	wann//
Wagen	wackeln//	Tag	Takt//

Now the speaker will pronounce one of the words in each pair printed in your workbook. Circle the word you hear. Remember that a vowel is normally long when it is followed by an h or a single consonant.

1. lasen   lassen
2. kann   Kahn
3. Rasen   Rassen
4. Kamm   kam
5. Mannen   mahnen
6. lahm   Lamm

EXERCISE III. Now put a check mark in the appropriate column, depending on whether you hear a long <u>a</u> or a short <u>a</u> as the speaker says each word.

	long a	*short a*		*long a*	*short a*		*long a*	*short a*		*long a*	*short a*
1.	_____	_____	2.	_____	_____	3.	_____	_____	4.	_____	_____
5.	_____	_____	6.	_____	_____	7.	_____	_____	8.	_____	_____

EXERCISE IV. In this exercise you will practice the German w. Its pronunciation is close to the English v. Repeat after the speaker.

Wagen//   weil//   Welt//   Werkstatt//

wichtig//   Wirtschaft//   Wunder//   wohnen//

Now the w in medial position:

Lawine//   Gewalt//   ewig//   Löwe//   Erwin//   bewegen//   unwichtig//

EXERCISE V. Let's try another <u>Zungenbrecher</u>. First listen as the speaker reads the entire tongue twister.

Wir Wormser Weiber würden weiße Wäsche waschen, wenn wir wüßten, wo warmes Wasser
    wär.
(We women of Worms would wash white linen if we knew where warm water was.)

Now try the entire tongue twister as fast as you can.

LEKTION FÜNF
PART II

EXERCISE I.   Change each of the following direct questions to an indirect question beginning with: <u>Weißt du</u>...? Repeat the correct form after the speaker.

> Example: Wie alt ist sein Wagen?
> *Weißt du, wie alt sein Wagen ist?*

Now begin.

EXERCISE II.   Change each <u>weil</u>-clause given by the speaker to a main clause. Then repeat the correct form after the speaker. Follow the example.

> Example: weil er eine Party gibt
> *Er gibt eine Party.*

Now begin.

EXERCISE III.   Rephrase the statements into <u>warum</u> questions, replacing the definite articles with appropriate possessive adjectives. Repeat the correct form after the speaker.

> Example: Er kann die Großmutter nicht abholen.
> *Warum kann er seine Großmutter nicht abholen?*

Now begin.

EXERCISE IV.   Answer the questions beginning each answer with <u>wenn</u>, and using the material provided by the speaker and printed in your workbook. Then repeat the answer after the speaker.

> Example: Wann gehst du in die Stadt? (ich habe Zeit)
> *Wenn ich Zeit habe, gehe ich in die Stadt.*

1. (ich bin alt genug)

2. (ich habe Zeit)

3. (ich habe Geld)

4. (ich sehe ihn)

5. (ich habe Hunger)

6. (ich kann einen Wagen leihen)

7. (ich habe Glück)

8. (ich muß meinen Wagen reparieren)

9. (sie haben ein Sonderangebot)

10. (ich habe Geburtstag)

EXERCISE V. Woher komme ich? After each description write in your workbook the
name of the country from which the person comes. Each one will be read only once.

No.1: _____

No.2: _____

No.3: _____

LEKTION SECHS
PART I

EXERCISE I. First listen to the conversation of <u>Lektion Sechs</u>.

Wer bezahlt was? /

Telefongespräch. / Petra möchte mit ihrem Freund Ralf sprechen. / Sie wählt die Nummer, / und Ralfs Telefon läutet. /

Ralf: Hier Wagner. /
Petra: Hallo. Ralf, bist du's? /
Ralf: Ja, 'Tag, Petra, was gibt's Neues? /
Petra: Nichts. / Sag mal, warst du gestern im Kino? /
Ralf: Nein, ich hatte nicht genug Geld. / Mein Vater hat den Scheck noch nicht
   geschickt. / Und ich hatte ein Examen. / Hast du etwas von dem Fassbinder-Film
   gehört? /
Petra: Gabi hat mir gesagt, er ist toll. /
Ralf: Was? / Gabi meckert doch sonst immer über alles! /
Petra: Nein, den Film hat sie gar nicht kritisiert. / Sie hat sogar die Schauspieler
   bewundert. /
Ralf: Mensch, / ich werde direkt neugierig. /
Petra: Weißt du was? / Übermorgen habe ich Zeit. / Mein Vater ist verreist. / Ich
   muß meinen Brüdern im Geschäft helfen. / Aber am Freitag können wir vielleicht
   zusammen ins Kino gehen. /
Ralf: Ist das eine Einladung? /
Petra: Du Geizhals! / Also abgemacht, / ich bezahle. / Ich treffe dich beim
   Parkplatz, / wo du letztesmal gewartet hast. /
Ralf: Warum nicht im Café? / Die Drinks bezahle ich natürlich. /
Petra: Ralf, deine Großzügigkeit ist überwältigend! / Also, bis Freitag. /
   Tschüß. /
Ralf: Vielen Dank für den Anruf. /

Now repeat each phrase or sentence after the speaker.

This pronunciation section will review the long <u>o</u> and the short <u>o</u> as well as the
ng-sound.

EXERCISE II. Repeat the word pairs after the speaker.

ohne	noch//	Symbol	sondern//
Motor	toll//	Vortrag	Rolltreppe//
groß	Stock//	oder	ob//
los	oft//	wohnen	sonst//

Now the speaker will say one of the words in each of the following pairs. Circle the one that you hear. Remember that a vowel is generally long if it is followed by an h or by one consonant.

1. Fohlen   vollen   5. Polen   Pollen

2. Lote   Lotte   6. Sohlen   sollen

3. None   Nonne   7. wohnen   Wonnen

4. Bohne   Bonne   8. Zoten   Zotten

EXERCISE III. Put a check mark in the appropriate column to indicate whether you hear a long o or a short o.

	long o short o		long o short o		long o short o
1.	_____ _____	2.	_____ _____	3.	_____ _____
4.	_____ _____	5.	_____ _____	6.	_____ _____

EXERCISE IV. Now you will practice the contrast between the long o and the long a. Repeat after the speaker.

wogen   Wagen//   Ton   getan//

wohl   Wahl//   logen   lagen//

Kohl   kahl//

And now practice the contrast between short o and short a. Repeat the pairs after the speaker.

offen   Affen//   ob   ab//

Lotte   Latte//   Tonne   Tanne//

voll   Fall//

EXERCISE V. The -ng in German is always pronounced like the -ng in English ring, never as in finger or anger. Repeat after the speaker.

langsam//   englisch//   singen//   bringen//   Ding//

gelingen//   jung//   Hunger//   Beleidigung//

Now repeat these phrases and sentences after the speaker.

Bring mir das Ding.//   Ich bekomme langsam Hunger.//

ein junger Engländer//   Die jungen Engländer singen.//

Es muß langsam gelingen.//

EXERCISE VI. Ever heard a German limerick? First just listen.

Ein Cowboy aus Texas sagt: „Mister,

Wo ist denn mein Partner, wo ist er?

Er trinkt sehr gern Bier,

Doch ist er nicht hier."

Der Deutsche sagt: „Cowboy, dort sitzt er!"

Now repeat each line after the speaker.

Now say the entire limerick yourself.

LEKTION SECHS
PART II

EXERCISE I. In this exercise you will hear someone say what people do today. Respond with a statement about the fact that that was not done in the old days. Then repeat the correct form after the speaker. Follow the example.

> Example: Heute verdient man gut.
> *Aber damals hat man nicht gut verdient.*

Now begin.

EXERCISE II. You will hear a question. Respond, beginning each sentence with: Ich weiß nicht, ob... Then repeat the correct form after the speaker. Follow the example.

> Example: Haben sie schwer gearbeitet?
> *Ich weiß nicht, ob sie schwer gearbeitet haben.*

Now begin.

EXERCISE III. Here are answers. Formulate the questions, then repeat the correct form after the speaker.

> Example: Ich weiß nicht, ob er pleite war.
> *War er pleite?*

Now begin.

EXERCISE IV. Raten Sie mal! (Guess!) Wer oder was sind wir? Answer by writing the plural form of the noun in the appropriate space in your workbook. Each description will be given twice.

No.1: _____

No.2: _____

No.3: _____

No.4: _____

EXERCISE V. You will hear a question or a description of a situation. Of the four answers given three are correct, one is wrong. Circle the letter of the incorrect response. You will hear each description twice.

1. a)   b)   c)   d)   2. a)   b)   c)   d)

3. a)   b)   c)   d)   4. a)   b)   c)   d)

EXERCISE VI. Was bin ich? You will hear two descriptions. After each select from the list in your workbook the appropriate answer to was bin ich? and write the answer in the space provided.

    Astronaut(in)

    ein Chauvi (male chauvinist)

    Schauspieler(in)

    Regisseur(in)

    ein Geizhals

1. _____

2. _____

LEKTION SIEBEN
PART I

EXERCISE I. First listen to the entire conversation of Lektion Sieben.

Amerika ist O.K./

Interview. / Ein Austauschstudent kehrt aus den Vereinigten Staaten zurück. / Eine Zeitung schickt einen Reporter zu ihm. /

Reporter: Herr Gerber, / warum wollten Sie im Ausland studieren? /
Jan: Ich wollte die Welt kennenlernen. /
Reporter: Konnten Sie vorher schon gut Englisch? /
Jan: Ja, ich bin Anglist. / Aber anfangs mußte ich gewaltig aufpassen. / Nach zwei Wochen hatte ich dann keine Schwierigkeiten mehr. /
Reporter: Ist es wahr, / daß die Studenten in Amerika viele Prüfungen haben? /
Jan: In einigen Vorlesungen gibt es nur ein Examen, / wie bei uns. / In anderen Klassen / -so nennt man drüben die Vorlesungen / -geben die Professoren einfach zu viele Prüfungen. / Das hat mich verrückt gemacht! /
Reporter: Stimmt es, / daß das akademische Jahr drüben schon im September anfängt? /
Jan: Ja, und es hört Ende Mai oder Anfang Juni auf. / Es gibt also ein Herbst- und ein Frühlingssemester. /
Reporter: Sind Sie in Amerika viel herumgereist? /
Jan: Ja, im Sommer bin ich von Nebraska nach Texas getrampt. / Mit Rucksack und Schlafsack. / Leider mußte ich im August zurückkommen, / weil man mein Visum nicht verlängern konnte. /
Reporter: Möchten Sie wieder in die USA? /
Jan: Totsicher! / Amerika ist O.K. /
Reporter: Herr Gerber, ich danke Ihnen für das Interview. /

Now repeat each phrase or sentence after the speaker.

The pronunciation section of this lesson will review the long u and the short u and will practice the st and sp in initial position.

EXERCISE II. Notice the contrast between the long u and the short u in these word pairs. Repeat after the speaker.

Minute	Mutter//	Uhr	Bus//
genug	Punkt//	gut	Schluß//
tun	Kunst//	du	uns//

Now indicate in your workbook whether you hear a long u or a short u by putting a check mark in the appropriate column.

	long u	*short u*		*long u*	*short u*		*long u*	*short u*		*long u*	*short u*
1.	_____	_____	2.	_____	_____	3.	_____	_____	4.	_____	_____
5.	_____	_____	6.	_____	_____	7.	_____	_____	8.	_____	_____

Now read the following sentences after the speaker.

Du mußt zu uns kommen.//

Warum mußt du Schluß machen?//

Er besucht eine gute Schule.//

Du tust nicht genug für deine Gesundheit.//

EXERCISE III. Zungenbrecher! First listen.

In Ulm und um Ulm und um Ulm herum.
(In Ulm (city), around Ulm, and all around Ulm.)

Now repeat after the speaker.

Now see how quickly you can say it. /

EXERCISE IV. In initial position in the syllable the st is pronounced <u>sht</u> and the
<u>sp</u> is pronounced <u>shp</u>. Repeat after the speaker.

First the st:

Stadt//	Stammkunde//	statistisch//	Status//	stimmen//
stinklangweilig//	Stock//	studieren//	Student//	

Now the sp:

spielen//   Sport//   Gespräch//   sprechen//

Repeat these sentences after the speaker.

Der Student spielt und studiert.//

Statistisch stimmt das.//

Die Studentin studiert in dieser Stadt.//

Das Gespräch war stinklangweilig.//

EXERCISE V. How about two new limericks? Listen to the first one.

Ein Klempner aus Hamburg war gestern

Im Kino mit seinen zwei Schwestern.

Der Film war O.K.

Nachher im Café,

Da meckern sie über den Western.

Now repeat each line after the speaker.

Now the second limerick. Just listen.

Ein Austauschstudent aus Brasilien

Bekommt eine Wurst aus Kastilien.

Er weiß nicht, von wem;

Das ist ein Problem!

Er schickt sie dem Freund in Sizilien.

Now repeat each line after the speaker.

LEKTION SIEBEN
PART II

EXERCISE I. Answer each question, using the past tense of the modal given by the speaker and printed in your workbook. Follow the example, and repeat the correct form after the speaker.

> Example: Warum bist du nicht zurückgekehrt? (wollen)
> *Ich wollte nicht zurückkehren.*

Now begin.

1. (können)   4. (mögen)   7. (sollen)

2. (dürfen)   5. (können)   8. (müssen)

3. (müssen)   6. (dürfen)   9. (sollen)

EXERCISE II. Answer the question using the present tense of können. Then repeat the correct form after the speaker.

EXERCISE III. Answer, omitting the modal, as in the example. Then repeat the correct form after the speaker.

> Example: Du mußt zurückkommen.
> *Ich komme ja zurück.*

New begin.

EXERCISE IV. Rephrase the following sentences as singular familiar commands, omitting sollen. Then repeat the correct form after the speaker.

> Example: Du sollst bald zurückkommen.
> *Komm bald zurück.*

Now begin.

EXERCISE V. Let's see how well you know the noun plurals. You will hear: eine Woche; you will say: zwei Wochen. For each new noun given, add one number, so the next noun will be preceded by drei, then vier, and so on. Repeat the correct form after the speaker.

EXERCISE VI. Ich bin Schauspieler. Ich beschreibe Ihnen drei Szenen aus drei Filmen. On your answer sheet write after each description which of the following type of movie has been described:

    a) ein Dokumentarfilm   d) ein Horrorfilm
    b) eine Seifenoper (soap opera)   e) ein Western
    c) ein Detektivfilm

Szene Eins : _____

Szene Zwei : _____

Szene Drei : _____

LEKTION ACHT
PART I

EXERCISE I. First just listen to the conversation of <u>Lektion Acht</u>.

Können Sie tippen? /

Elisabeth spricht mit ihrer Freundin / über ihre Pläne für die Ferien. /

Ursula: Hast du schon eine Stellung für die Sommermonate gefunden? /
Elisabeth: Nein, ich habe noch keine Stelle bekommen. / Da hat eine Anzeige in der
   Zeitung gestanden: / Sommerbeschäftigung für Studenten. / Zoologischer Garten, /
   muß tierliebend sein, / angenehme Arbeitsbedingungen. /
Ursula: Zoo, das klingt ideal. /
Elisabeth: Nicht? / Ich bin also ins Personalbüro gegangen. / Da hat so ein netter
   Opa gesessen. / Er hat mich gefragt, ob ich tippen kann. /.
Ursula: Das kann doch nicht wahr sein! / Gibt es das heutzutage immer noch? /
   Erzähl mal, / was hast du ihm geantwortet? /
Elisabeth: Ich habe gesagt, nein, leider nicht, / aber ich kann Schreibmaschinen
   reparieren, / habe Erfahrung in Datenverarbeitung / und studiere Physik. /
Ursula: Da ist er sicher vom Stuhl gefallen. /
Elisabeth: Er hat mich ein bißchen pikiert angesehen. / Dann hat er gemeint, / ich
   bin überqualifiziert. /
Ursula: Typisch! / Wie war denn die Bezahlung? /
Elisabeth: Das habe ich nicht herausgefunden. /
Ursula: Gib's nicht auf. / Such weiter. /
Elisabeth: Ich habe heute morgen eine Anzeige gelesen: / Technische Fähigkeiten
   erforderlich. / Vielleicht ist es möglich, / da was zu bekommen. /
Ursula: Ich drücke dir die Daumen. / Dann klappt es sicher. /

Now repeat each phrase or sentence after the speaker.

This pronunciation section will review the long <u>e</u> and the short <u>e</u> and will practice
the sch-sound in combination with other consonants.

EXERCISE II. Note the difference between the long <u>e</u> and the short <u>e</u>. Repeat each
word pair after the speaker.

geht	Bett//	wen	wenn//
Problem	denkt//	schwer	Scheck//
den	denn//	geht	Kette//
steht	Stellung//		

Now indicate with a check mark whether you hear a long <u>e</u> or a short <u>e</u>.

	long e	*short e*		*long e*	*short e*		*long e*	*short e*
1.	_____	_____	2.	_____	_____	3.	_____	_____
4.	_____	_____	5.	_____	_____	6.	_____	_____

EXERCISE III. Now the speaker will pronounce one of the two words in each pair printed in your workbook. Circle the one you hear.

1. wessen   Wesen   4. den   denn

2. Betten   beten   5. steller   stehlen

3. wenn   wen   6. Kelle   Kehle

EXERCISE IV. Now you will practice the sch-sound in combination with w. Remember that the sch is pronounced sh and the w is pronounced v. Repeat after the speaker.

Schweden//   schwer//   Schweiz//   Schwierigkeit//   verschwinden//   Schwester//

Now you will practice the sch in combination with l. Remember to put your tongue behind your upper teeth when you pronounce the German l. Repeat after the speaker.

schlank//   Schluß//   Schlüssel//   Schlafsack//   schlafen//

Now repeat these phrases and sentences after the speaker.

die schlanke Schwester//

Die schlanke Schwester ist verschwunden.//

Er verschwindet nach Schweden.//

Die Schwester hat Schwierigkeiten mit dem Schlüssel.//

EXERCISE V. *Und jetzt ein Zungenbrecher!* First just listen.

Der schlaue Schwabe schläft und schweigt schließlich,

schließlich schläft und schweigt der schlaue Schwabe.
(The sly Swabian is finally asleep and quiet.)

Now repeat each phrase after the speaker.

Und jetzt sagen Sie es bitte sehr schnell.

EXERCISE VI. Now you will have a dictation. First you will hear the entire sentence, then each sentence will be broken up into units, giving you time to write what you hear. Then the entire sentence will be read once again so that you can check what you have written.

Listen to the entire sentence.

Now write.

1. _____

Now the entire sentence again.

Now listen to the next sentence.

Now write.

2. _____

Now listen again and check.

LEKTION ACHT
PART II

EXERCISE I. Respond to the question in the present perfect tense as in the example. Then repeat the correct form after the speaker.

Example: Wolltest du es nicht lesen?
Ich habe es schon gelesen.

Now begin.

EXERCISE II. Ich habe keine Zeit. All of the following invitations have to be turned down because you have an exam tomorrow. Answer each invitation by saying that you have no time to do whatever it is you are being asked to do. Begin each answer with: Ich habe keine Zeit ... Repeat the correct form after the speaker.

Example: Komm mit, wir gehen ins Kino.
Ich habe keine Zeit, ins Kino zu gehen.

Now begin.

EXERCISE III. Answer the question in the present tense using the pattern shown in the example. Then repeat the correct form after the speaker.

Example: Hat er mit ihr gesprochen?
Er spricht nie mit ihr.

Now begin.

EXERCISE IV. In this exercise you will hear ads for jobs. You want to apply for them because you need the money. What do you do? Pick the appropriate response from the four that are given after each ad. Each ad will be heard twice.

Now circle in your workbook the letter of the correct response.

Ad No.1   a)   b)   c)   d)

Now circle the letter of the correct response.

Ad No.2   a)   b)   c)   d)

EXERCISE V. After you have listened to the following selection you will be asked to complete some statements based on the information you hear. The text will be read only once.

Anton schreibt nicht gern Briefe. Aber er weiß, seine Freundin hat ein neues Tonbandgerät. Er schickt ihr also ein Tonband und erzählt ihr über den Sommer:

Now circle the letter of the clause that best completes the sentence that you hear.

1. Anton wollte keine Hamburger verkaufen,

       a) weil er nicht gern Hamburger ißt
       b) weil er meint, das ist kein Job für einen Philosophiestudenten
       c) weil er keine Erfahrung als Verkäufer hat

2. Den Job bei Mercedes-Benz hat er nicht bekommen,

       a) weil er überqualifiziert ist
       b) weil sein Deutsch nicht so gut ist
       c) weil Englisch so einfach ist

3. Den Job im Zoo hat er nicht bekommen,

       a) weil er kein Deutsch spricht
       b) weil er kein Zoologiestudent ist
       c) weil er kein Chinesisch spricht

4. Den Job bei der reichen Dame hat er bekommen,

       a) weil er bei den deutschen Modalverben Fehler macht
       b) weil er nervös wird, wenn er einen Dobermann-Pinscher sieht
       c) weil er deutsch spricht

LEKTION NEUN
PART I

EXERCISE I. First listen to the entire conversation of <u>Lektion Neun</u>.

Blockhütte oder Segelboot? /

Im Wartezimmer beim Zahnarzt. / Herr Fischer sitzt neben einem anderen Herrn. / Sie denken nicht an Zahnschmerzen, / Bohrer und Spritzen, / sondern sie sprechen über den Urlaub. /

Fischer: Waren Sie schon mal am Meer? /
Holzer: Nein, wir fahren im Urlaub immer in die Berge. /
Fischer: Und die Kinder nehmen Sie mit? /
Holzer: Selbstverständlich. / Wir haben eine Blockhütte in einem Bergwald gebaut. / Morgens um sechs wandern wir in den Wäldern herum. / Oder wir machen eine Bergtour vor dem Frühstück / ... Sehr gesund! /
Fischer: Und ans Meer möchten Sie nicht mal? /
Holzer: Vielleicht fahren wir nächstes Jahr mit dem Wohnwagen an die Ostsee, / oder ans Mittelmeer. / Meine Frau behauptet, / sie hat Rheuma / und kann nicht mehr auf die Berge klettern. /
Fischer: Ja, Sonne und warmer Sand sind gut für Rheuma. / Und die Kinder können schwimmen / und am Strand spielen. / Und Sie können unterm Sonnenschirm sitzen und schlafen, / oder segeln. /
Holzer: Ich habe aber kein Segelboot. /
Fischer: Da kann ich Ihnen aushelfen! / Ich muß mein Segelboot verkaufen. / Fast neu. /
Holzer: Ich kann aber nicht segeln. /
Fischer: Das lernt man schnell, / und dann macht es Spaß. /
Holzer: Warum wollen Sie denn Ihr Boot verkaufen? /
Fischer: Ich werde seekrank. / Das habe ich nicht gewußt, / als ich es gekauft habe. /

Now repeat each phrase or sentence after the speaker.

In this pronunciation section you will review the e in final unaccented syllables and practice the German z as contrasted with the voiced s.

EXERCISE II. First you will review the e in final position. Repeat after the speaker.

Bäume//   Reise//   Sonne//   Zelte//   Zähne//   Straße//

Now the el and eln ending. Repeat.

Titel//   Schlüssel//   Segel//   Zettel//   jodeln//   segeln//   behandeln//

Now the en ending. Repeat.

planen//   landen//   kaufen//   Examen//   Süden//   Wagen//

Now the er ending. Repeat.

Bruder//   Klempner//   Verkäufer//   Anlasser//

Schwester//   Tochter//   Zimmer//   Mutter//

And finally the ern ending. Repeat.

Eltern//   meckern//   bewundern//   gestern//

sondern//   verlängern//   klettern//   wandern//

EXERCISE III. Jetzt haben wir wieder mal einen Zungenbrecher. First just listen.

Kleine Kinder kugeln mit den Kugeln gern,

Gern kleine Kinder kugeln mit den Kugeln.
(Little children like to bowl with the balls.)

Now repeat the phrases after the speaker.

Now try to say it as fast as you can.

EXERCISE IV. In this exercise you will practice the German z and the voiced s.
Remember that the z is pronounced ts, and that s before a vowel is pronounced like
an English z. Repeat after the speaker.

Zoo//   Zahn//   zurück//   Zeit//   zeigen//

zu//   Zug//   ziemlich//   Zimmer//

Now repeat each pair after the speaker.

Zelten   selten//   Zoo   so//   Zeit   seit//   Zahl   Saal//

Now circle in your workbook the word in each pair that you hear the speaker say.

1. Zehen   sehen   4. sogen   zogen   7. zurren   surren

2. Seiten   Zeiten   5. zagen   sagen   8. zählen   Sälen

3. selten   zelten   6. Sinn   Zinn

EXERCISE V. Was?? Noch ein Zungenbrecher? Ja, warum nicht! First just listen.

Es saßen zwei zischende Schlangen zwischen zwei spitzigen Steinen und zischten
    dazwischen.
(Two hissing snakes were sitting between two sharp stones and hissing between them.)

Now repeat in phrases after the speaker.

Jetzt sagen Sie es bitte sehr schnell./

LEKTION NEUN
PART II

EXERCISE I. In answer to the question <u>Wo ist Tante Nelly</u>? use, one at a time, each of the words given by the speaker and printed in your workbook. Follow the example, repeating the correct form after the speaker.

> Example: Wo ist Tante Nelly? das Geschäft
> *Vielleicht im Geschäft. Sie geht oft ins Geschäft.*

Now begin.

1. die Stadt   4. das Museum

2. der Garten   5. die Werkstatt

3. das Café   6. der Zoo

EXERCISE II. This time we are looking for <u>Onkel Bruno</u>. Listen to the example. Repeat the correct form after the speaker.

> Example: Wo ist Onkel Bruno? der Tennisplatz
> *Vielleicht auf dem Tennisplatz. Er wollte auf den Tennisplatz.*

Now begin.

1. die Bank   4. der Bahnhof

2. die Party   5. das Land

3. der Parkplatz   6. das Büro

EXERCISE III. Now that we have found <u>Tante Nelly</u> and <u>Onkel Bruno</u>, let's look for the newspaper. Follow the example, and repeat the correct form after the speaker.

> Example: Wo ist die Zeitung? der Stuhl
> *Sie liegt unter dem Stuhl. Schau mal unter den Stuhl.*

Now begin.

1. die Schreibmaschine   4. die Kamera

2. das Bett   5. der Koffer

3. der Schlafsack

EXERCISE IV. Now you will hear statements. After each statement pretend you have not heard the place mentioned and ask a question using <u>wo</u> or <u>wohin</u>, whichever is correct, to find out where. Repeat the correct question after the speaker. Use <u>du</u> when you-questions are called for.

Now begin.

EXERCISE V. Ich möchte mal sehen, wie gut Sie Ihre Verben können. Restate each sentence in the present perfect tense. Then repeat each sentence after the speaker.

EXERCISE VI. Wo war ich auf Urlaub? In this section you will hear three descriptions of places where the speaker spent a vacation. After each description select, from among the places listed in your workbook, which place has been described. Write the name of the place next to the description number in your workbook. The choices are:

    a) Paris
    b) Südamerika
    c) New York
    d) die Schweiz
    e) Afrika

Now listen.

No.1: _____

No.2: _____

No.3: _____

LEKTION ZEHN
PART I

EXERCISE I. First listen to the entire conversation of <u>Lektion Zehn</u>.

Wie knackt man einen Safe? /

Elke und Holger im Lesesaal. / Elke löst Kreuzworträtsel. / Holger liest die Zeitung, / und plötzlich beginnt er zu lachen. /

Elke: Welchen Artikel liest du denn? / Lies mal vor. /
Holger: „Montagnacht versuchte ein Einbrecher / in einer Züricher Bank / einen Safe mit einem Schraubenschlüssel zu öffnen. / Er bemerkte nicht, / daß er eine Alarmvorrichtung berührte. / Die Polizei erreichte die Bank, / als der erfolglose Dieb / gerade aus einem Fenster herauskletterte." / Mit einem Schraubenschlüssel! / Großartig, was? /
Elke: So ein Dummkopf! / Jedes Kind weiß doch, / daß man damit keinen Safe knacken kann. /
Holger: Er sieht wohl nie fern. /
Elke: Hatte dieses Genie was zu sagen? /
Holger: Moment mal ... / ja, hier: „Der Täter erklärte, / daß er Geld brauchte, / um damit seine Miete zu bezahlen." /
Elke: Was für eine Wohnung hat er denn? / Ein Penthaus? /
Holger: Warte ... / „In seiner Brieftasche entdeckte man ein Sparbuch. / Auf seinem Konto waren über 25.000 Schweizer Franken. / Darüber wollte der Täter jedoch nichts sagen / und verlangte einen Rechtsanwalt." /
Elke: Manche Leute kriegen nie genug. / Steht auch drin, / woher er die Kohlen hat? /
Holger: Nein. / Vielleicht ist er sonst nicht so naiv, / wenn er stiehlt. /

Now repeat each phrase or sentence after the speaker.

In this pronunciation section you will review the long ä and short ä, and practice the b, d, and g sounds.

EXERCISE II. First practice the contrast between the long ä and the short ä. Repeat after the speaker.

Währung	Geschäft//	Käfer	Männer//
Täter	Länder//	erzählen	verlängern//
wählt	fällt//	schläft	Nächte//

Remember that the short ä sounds like the short e. Repeat after the speaker.

fällt	Welt//	Gärten	Gerten//
Männer	Kenner//	verlängern	verengen//
Nächte	Rechte//	Fänge	Menge//

Now circle in each pair the word that you hear. Remember that ä followed by two consonants is short.

1. kämen   kämmen   4. Wellen   wählen

2. Vetter   Väter   5. stählen   stellen

3. beten   Betten   6. häkeln   häckeln

Now read these sentences after the speaker.

Er erwähnte, die Männer hatten Pläne.//

Er fällt aus dem Bett.//

Sie fährt spät ins Geschäft.//

EXERCISE III.   In this exercise you will practice the b, d, and g sounds. Remember that these letters are voiced (b,d,g) except in final position where they approach p,t,k respectively.

First the b in medial and, by contrast, in final position. Repeat after the speaker.

aber   ab//   schreiben   schrieb//

bleiben   blieb//   geben   gib//

Now the d in medial and final position. Repeat after the speaker.

wandern   Wand//   Winde   Wind//

Länder   Land//   Freunde   Freund//

Kinder   Kind//

And now the g in medial and final position. Repeat.

Tage   Tag//   mögen   mag//

fragen   frag//   Züge   Zug//

sagen   sag//   Berge   Berg//

The b and g are also unvoiced if they are followed by another consonant. Repeat.

gibt//   bleibt//   schreibt//   freundlich//

kindlich//   sagt//   magst//   möglich//

LEKTION ZEHN
PART II

EXERCISE I. You are given some information, but it is not enough. You want specifics. Form questions, using the correct form of welcher, as in the example. Repeat the correct question after the speaker.

    Example: mit dem Fahrrad
                mit welchem Fahrrad?

Now begin.

EXERCISE II. Change the following sentences to the simple past tense. Then repeat the correct form after the speaker.

EXERCISE III. Tante Irene hört nicht gut. You pretend to be Tante Irene. You hear everything in each sentence except the first part of the compound noun. Follow the example. Repeat the correct question after the speaker.

    Example: Er hat ein Sparbuch gestohlen.
                Was für ein Buch hat er gestohlen?

Now begin.

EXERCISE IV. Using the um+zu+infinitive construction, answer the following questions with the information provided in your workbook and given by the speaker. Repeat the correct form after the speaker.

    Example: Warum geht man in eine Diskothek? Musik hören
                Man geht in eine Diskothek, um Musik zu hören.

Now begin.

1. Filme sehen   4. Geld verdienen

2. Leute kennenlernen   5. die Welt sehen

3. einen Spaziergang machen   6. im Sand liegen

EXERCISE V. For each item in this exercise, you will hear four responses or sentence completions. Three are correct, one is wrong. Circle the letter of the incorrect response.

1.   a)   b)   c)   d)

2.   a)   b)   c)   d)

3.   a)   b)   c)   d)

EXERCISE VI. After hearing the following conversation between Hans Kleinknecht and his lawyer you will be asked some questions.

Der Einbrecher Hans Kleinknecht erzählt seinem Rechtsanwalt, was passiert ist.

Now you will hear some statements. For each statement that is correct put an R for richtig; for each one that is false, put and F for falsch.

_____ a) Letztesmal hat Kleinknecht beim Pokerspiel 50.000 Franken gewonnen.

_____ b) Kleinknecht konnte von seinem Bruder Geld leihen.

_____ c) Joseph wollte ihm nicht helfen.

_____ d) Hans Kleinknecht lernte eine Banksekretärin kennen.

_____ e) Die Sekretärin war ein Dummkopf.

_____ f) Bruder Joseph war ein Dummkopf.

_____ g) Kleinknecht versuchte den Safe mit einem Schraubenschlüssel zu öffnen, weil er die Kombination nicht finden konnte.

_____ h) Der Richter hat Verständnis für Kleinknechts Geschichte.

LEKTION ELF
PART I

EXERCISE I. First just listen to the entire conversation of Lektion Elf.

Kennst du Kafka? /

Zwei Studenten kommen aus der Mensa, / wo sie zu Abend gegessen haben. /

Kai: Am Montag ist meine Semesterarbeit über Kafka fällig. /
Helmut: Mal sehen, wieviel du schon weißt. / Woher ist dieses Zitat: / „Als Gregor
    Samsa eines Morgens aus unruhigen Träumen erwachte, / fand er sich in seinem
    Bett zu einem ungeheuren Ungeziefer verwandelt." /
Kai: Glaubst du, ich kenne „Die Verwandlung" nicht? /
Helmut: Das ist doch ein großartiger Anfang für eine Geschichte. Er will aufstehen,
    und siehe da ... /
Kai: Kafka interessiert dich, was? / Mal sehen, wie gut du seine Werke kennst. /
    „Es war spät abends, als K. ankam ..." /
Helmut: Das kommt mir bekannt vor ... / „Der Prozeß"! /
Kai: Falsch. / Hör zu: / „Das Dorf lag in tiefem Schnee. / Vom Schloßberg war nichts
    zu sehen. / ... Lange stand K. auf der Holzbrücke ..." /
Helmut: Ich hab's, „Das Schloß". /
Kai: Bravo! / Du hast die Preisfrage gelöst! /
Helmut: Ich bin ja schließlich Wiwi und kein Germanist. / Ich werde mal feststellen, /
    was du über das Thema „Sozialprodukt" weißt. / ... /
Kai: Ein andermal, / ich hab's eilig. / Ich muß in die Bibliothek. / Sonst wird meine
    Arbeit nicht fertig. /
Helmut: Schlaf nicht ein. / Du weißt, was dir passieren kann ... /

Now repeat each phrase or sentence after the speaker.

In this pronunciation section you will review the long ö and the short ö. In addition
you will practice the r in combination with other consonants.

EXERCISE II. In this exercise you will practice the contrast between the long ö and
the short ö. Repeat after the speaker.

hören	öffnen//	möglich	Töchter//
schön	Wörter//	nervös	Wörter//
lösen	Dörfer//	mögen	können//
böse//	plötzlich//		

Now indicate whether you hear a long ö or a short ö by putting a check mark in the
appropriate column.

	long ö	*short ö*		*long ö*	*short ö*		*long ö*	*short ö*
1.	_____	_____	2.	_____	_____	3.	_____	_____
4.	_____	_____	5.	_____	_____	6.	_____	_____

EXERCISE III. Now circle in each pair the word that you hear. Remember that ö is long if it is followed by an h or by one consonant.

1. Höhle   Hölle   4. Bögen   Böcken

2. blöken   Blöcke   5. Köller   Köhler

3. hökern   Höckern

EXERCISE IV. In this exercise you will practice the r in combination with other consonants. Repeat after the speaker. First the br:

bringen//   Bremse//   Bruder//   brechen//   brauchen//   bravo//

Now the dr:

drei//   Drink//   drüben//   drücken//   dreißig//   draußen//

Now the gr:

groß//   Grundschule//   grün//   grau//   Griechenland//

Now the kr:

kritisieren//   kriegen//   Kreuzwort//   Kritik//   krank//   Krokodil//

Now the pr:

Professor//   Problem//   Preis//   Prozeß//   protestieren// Prüfung//

produzieren//

And finally the tr:

trinken//   treffen//   tragen//   traümen//   Treppe//   Transport//

trampen//   Traum//

EXERCISE V. Now a tongue twister. First just listen.

Ein krummer Krebs kroch über eine krumme Schraube;

Über eine krumme Schraube kroch ein krummer Krebs.
(A crooked crab crawled over a crooked screw.)

Now repeat each phrase after the speaker.

Nun sagen Sie es bitte sehr schnell.

LEKTION ELF
PART II

EXERCISE I. Wie gut können Sie Ihre Verben? Restate each sentence in the simple past tense. Then repeat each one after the speaker.

EXERCISE II. In each of the following sentences replace man kann by es ist leicht, as in the example. Remember to use zu with the dependent infinitive. Repeat the correct form after the speaker.

    Example: Man kann das feststellen.
             Es ist leicht, das festzustellen.

Now begin.

EXERCISE III. Answer each question negatively, using the future tense, as in the example. Then repeat the correct form after the speaker.

    Example: Hat er es schon getan?
             Nein, aber er wird es bestimmt tun.

Now begin.

EXERCISE IV. Answer each question with the information provided by the speaker and printed in your workbook. Use wenn or als, as appropriate, and repeat the correct form after the speaker.

    Example: Wann besuchst du ihn? (ich habe Zeit)
             Wenn ich Zeit habe.

Now begin.

1. (ich war auf der Party)   4. (ich war ein Kind)

2. (ich habe gegessen)   5. (er verlangt es)

3. (er stand auf der Brücke)

EXERCISE V. Answer the questions, giving the correct day. Repeat the correct form after the speaker.

EXERCISE VI. Wir erzählen Ihnen jetzt drei Szenen aus drei Märchen der Brüder Grimm. Diese Märchen gibt es auch auf englisch. Write the title of each fairy tale, in English, after you have listened to the description.

Szene Eins: _____

Before the next scene you should be introduced to a few words you will hear and do not yet know. These words are printed in your workbook. Take a look at them. die Königin means the queen; töten means to kill; der Spiegel means the mirror; die Schönste means the most beautiful woman. Now listen; then give the English name of the fairy tale.

Szene Zwei: _____

Now a few words before the next scene: backen means to bake and brauen to brew; Stroh means straw.

Szene Drei: _____

LEKTION ZWÖLF
PART I

EXERCISE I. First just listen to the entire conversation of Lektion Zwölf.

Wenn ich ein Optimist wäre ... /

Peter, in Lederjacke, Sturzhelm und Motorradbrille. / Astrid bewundert sein Motorrad. /

Astrid: Was hat dieses tolle Motorrad denn gekostet? /
Peter: Zuviel. / Aber im nächsten Jahr könnte ich es nicht mehr bezahlen, / bei den steigenden Preisen. /
Astrid: Hättest du nicht Lust ... /
Peter: ... Wenn ich ein Optimist wäre, würde ich sagen: / „Es *kann nicht* schlimmer werden." / Ich bin aber ein Pessimist ... /
Astrid: ... und deswegen sagst du: / „Es kann, es kann!" /
Peter: Genau! /
Astrid: ... Und die moderne Wegwerfgesellschaft denkt nicht an die Zukunft. /
Peter: Richtig! /
Astrid: ... Und die Umweltverschmutzung / stört den modernen Europäer gar nicht. /
Peter: Stimmt! / Ich habe gehört, / die neue Mülldeponie soll hierher kommen ... /
Astrid: ... Und das ganze Dorf sollte an der nächsten Demonstration teilnehmen. /
Peter: Was ist denn mit dir los? / Du klingst ja wie eine Schallplatte! /
Astrid: ... Und wenn es nach dir ginge, / würde man die Industrie abschaffen, / und nur Kartoffeln und Gemüse pflanzen. /
Peter: Jawohl! / Ich wollte, ich könnte nach Australien auswandern! /
Astrid: Oder nach Kanada! /
Peter: Du nimmst mich auf den Arm! /
Astrid: Nein, ich habe das schon so oft gehört, / ich kann es auswendig. / Du hast natürlich recht. /
Peter: Wie wär's mit einer Spritztour zur Demo? /
Astrid: Mit dem neuen Motorrad?! / Auf die Barrikaden! /

Now repeat each phrase or sentence after the speaker.

In this pronunciation section you will review the long ü and the short ü, and you will also practice the r in combination with several consonants.

EXERCISE II. Now practice the long ü and the short ü. Repeat each pair after the speaker.

Gemüse	Flüsse//	natürlich	Glück//
über	Müll//	Bücher	fünf//
Büro	müssen//	Führerschein	pünktlich//

Now indicate whether you hear a long ü or a short ü by putting a check in the appropriate column.

	long ü	short ü		long ü	short ü		long ü	short ü
1.	_____	_____	2.	_____	_____	3.	_____	_____
4.	_____	_____	5.	_____	_____	6.	_____	_____

EXERCISE III. Now circle, in each word pair, the word you hear spoken.

1. Hütte   Hüte   4. Füller   Fühler

2. Füßen   Füssen   5. Dünne   Düne

3. Mühle   Müller   6. fühlen   füllen

EXERCISE IV. In this exercise you will practice the r in combination with other consonants. Repeat after the speaker.

First the fr:

fragen//   französisch//   Frau//   Freitag//

Freunde//   Freund//   früher//   Frühstück//

Now the schr:

Schraubenschlüssel//   schreiben//   schreien//   schriftlich//

Now the spr:

Sprache//   sprechen//   Spritze//   Spritztour//

And now finally the str:

Strafzettel//   Strand//   Strahlen//   Straße//

Now read these sentences after the speaker:

Früher schrieb und sprach er mit Freude französisch.//

Am Freitag vor dem Frühstück schrieb er dem Freund einen freundlichen Brief.//

Ich spreche von der Spritztour an den Strand.//

EXERCISE V. Zungenbrecher. First just listen.

Fischers Fritz fischt frische Fische,

frische Fische fischt Fischers Fritz.
(Fischer's Fritz is fishing for fresh fish.)

Now repeat a phrase at a time.

Sagen Sie es jetzt sehr schnell.

LEKTION ZWÖLF
PART II

EXERCISE I. Answer the following questions, using the definite article with the adjective printed in your workbook and given by the speaker. Then repeat the correct form after the speaker. Follow the example.

      Example: Welcher Student ist das? (neu)
                der neue

Now begin.

1. (alt)	5. (klein)	9. (neu)
2. (deutsch)	6. (modern)	10. (deutsch)
3. (teuer)	7. (spät)	11. (amerikanisch)
4. (groß)	8. (groß)	12. (alt)

EXERCISE II. <u>Welche Wünsche hätten Sie?</u> Express your wishes by using the phrases provided in your workbook and given by the speaker. Repeat the correct form after the speaker. Follow the example.

      Example: einen Mercedes haben
                Ich wollte, ich hätte einen Mercedes.

Now begin.

1. keine Arbeit haben	5. alles wissen
2. reich sein	6. nach Deutschland können
3. besser deutsch können	7. ein Motorrad haben
4. ein Optimist sein	

EXERCISE III. Respond to the statements with wishes. Repeat the correct form after the speaker. Follow the example.

      Example: Ich darf über Kafka schreiben.
                Ich wollte, ich dürfte über Kafka schreiben.

Now begin.

EXERCISE IV. Respond again with wishes, this time using <u>er</u> as the subject. Repeat the correct form after the speaker. Follow the example.

      Example: Sie kann das Einmaleins.
                Er wollte, er könnte auch das Einmaleins.

Now begin.

EXERCISE V. This time express wishes, using <u>wir</u> as the subject. Repeat the correct form after the speaker. Follow the example.

    Example: Sie sind glücklich.
              Wir wollten, wir wären auch glücklich.

Now begin.

EXERCISE VI. In your workbook are listed three questions. They are:

    1. Wo wohnt er?
    2. Wohin geht er?
    3. Woher kommt er?

On the tape you will hear prepositional phrases. Each prepositional phrase is an appropriate answer to one of the questions. Decide which of the three questions it can answer, and write the letter of the phrase after the correct question in your workbook. For example, if you hear "x. nach Hause", you will place the letter x next to question No.2 because <u>nach Hause</u> is the appropriate response to that question. Now begin.

EXERCISE VII. Of the four sentence completions you will hear, three are correct. Circle the letter of the <u>incorrect</u> one.

1. a)   b)   c)   d)   2. a)   b)   c)   d)   3. a)   b)   c)   d)

EXERCISE VIII. Listen to the following conversation between the psychiatrist <u>Dr. Freundlich</u> and <u>Herr Fischer</u>. Later you will do an exercise based on this text. <u>The text will be read only once.</u>

Now, based on the text you have just heard, complete each statement given by the speaker by circling the correct choice from among those given.

1. Herr Fischer hat den Butt ins Wasser geworfen,
        a) weil der Butt schon ein alter Fisch war
        b) weil er keinen Prinzen zum Abendessen essen wollte
        c) weil seine Frau nicht gern Fisch ißt

2. Frau Fischer wollte
        a) IBM haben, und sie hat sie auch bekommen
        b) General Motors kaufen, aber die Firma war zu teuer
        c) eine Spritztour nach China machen, aber es hat nicht geklappt

3. Frau Fischer möchte Präsidentin
        a) von Saudi Arabien werden
        b) der USA werden
        c) von General Motors werden

4. Herr Fischer meint, er hat kein psychologisches Problem, sondern
        a) er möchte nur wissen, was er tun soll
        b) er ist Demokrat und seine Frau ist Republikanerin
        c) er muß seiner Frau IBM kaufen

5. Dr. Freundlich meint,
        a) Herr Fischer soll eine neue Frau suchen
        b) Herr Fischer ist ganz normal
        c) daß man Herrn Fischers Problem nicht in einer Stunde lösen kann

LEKTION DREIZEHN
PART I

EXERCISE I. First just listen to the entire conversation of <u>Lektion Dreizehn</u>.

Susanne spielt gefährlich ... /

Nachdem Dieter lange durch die Stadt spaziert ist, / trifft er Gerd vor dem Schaufenster eines Sportgeschäfts. /

Dieter: Tag, Gerd. / Sag mal, hast du Susanne gesehen? /
Gerd: Ich sollte sie am Fußballplatz treffen. / Aber als ich hinkam, war sie schon weggegangen. / Mit Hans, diesem Esel, habe ich gehört. /
Dieter: Was?? / *Ich* hatte eine Verabredung mit ihr. / Ich sollte sie am Eingang zum Schwimmbad treffen. / Aber sie ist nicht erschienen. /
Gerd: Wahrscheinlich hatte sie vergessen, / daß sie mit *mir* eine Verabredung hatte. / Na, die gefällt mir! /
Dieter: Mich hat sie ja auch versetzt. / Wie war denn das Fußballspiel? /
Gerd: Wir haben eins zu fünf verloren. / Als ich kam, / hatte unsere Mannschaft gerade das erste und letzte Tor geschossen. / Das Spiel war schlecht. / Miserabel! / Während der Halbzeit / hat der Trainer mit dem Mittelstürmer gestritten. / Danach wurde es etwas besser. / Aber am Ende des Spiels / stand es doch eins zu fünf. /
Dieter: Unser Torwart ist ein Idiot. / Es gelingt ihm nie, einen Elfmeter zu stoppen. /
Gerd: Es macht mir einfach keinen Spaß mehr. / Ich war ja nur wegen Susanne hingegangen, / wegen dieser dummen Pute, / wegen dieser ... /
Dieter: Nimm's nicht so schwer. / Gehen wir in die Turnhalle. /

Now repeat each phrase or sentence after the speaker.

In this pronunciation section you will practice the contrast between short <u>o</u> and short <u>a</u> and between ck and the hard ch.

EXERCISE II. Notice the contrast between short <u>o</u> and short <u>a</u>. Repeat after the speaker.

gewannen	gewonnen//	warten	Worte//
Dach	doch//	Ball	soll//
kann	konnte//	machte	mochte//
ab	ob//	acht	Tochter//

Now identify the sound you are hearing by placing a check mark in the appropriate column.

	o	*a*		*o*	*a*		*o*	*a*		*o*	*a*
1.	___	___	2.	___	___	3.	___	___	4.	___	___
5.	___	___	6.	___	___						

EXERCISE III. Now circle in your workbook the word in each pair that you hear spoken.

1. schallen   schollen   4. Kamm   komm

2. knallen   Knollen   5. Tanne   Tonne

3. hacken   hocken   6. stapfen   stopfen

EXERCISE IV. Now read these sentences after the speaker.

Bald kommen Onkel Albert, Tante Olga und Tochter Anna.//

Hans soll den Ball doch stoppen.//

Wann kommt Lotte?//

Otto hat alles gewonnen.//

EXERCISE V. Now you will practice the contrast between ck and the hard or back ch. Repeat each word pair after the speaker.

Nacht   nackt//   machen   Macken//

doch   Dock//   flach   Flak//

acht   Akt//   lachen   lacken//

Now indicate in your workbook which of the two sounds you hear by putting a check in the appropriate column.

	ch	*ck*		*ch*	*ck*		*ch*	*ck*
1.	____	____	2.	____	____	3.	____	____
4.	____	____	5.	____	____	6.	____	____

EXERCISE VI. Now circle in each word pair the one you hear.

1. lach   Lack   3. doch   Dock   5. Nachen   Nacken

2. Buch   buk   4. lachen lacken   6. pochen   Pocken

EXERCISE VII. Jetzt lernen Sie das längste Wort in der deutschen Sprache. Sehen Sie es in Ihrem Buch? First just listen.

Hottentottenpotentatenmutterattentäterinnen
(*Female assassins of the mother of a Hottentot potentate*)

Now repeat each section after the speaker.

Hottentotten / potentaten / mutter / attentäterinnen /

Wie schnell können Sie das sagen? In der nächsten Klasse können Sie Ihren Professor überraschen.

LEKTION DREIZEHN
PART II

EXERCISE I. A German visiting you hears some names and titles and doesn't know what they are. So he asks you and you answer, as in the example, using the material provided in your workbook and given by the speaker. Use the word <u>Name</u> or <u>Titel</u>, whichever is appropriate. Repeat the correct form after the speaker.

> Example: <u>The Old Man and the Sea</u>, was ist das? (Roman)
> *Das ist der Titel eines Romans.*

Now begin.

1. (Supermarkt)   6. (Zeitung)

2. (Schauspieler)   7. (Brücke)

3. (Märchen)   8. (Hotel)

4. (Dichter)   9. (Schauspielerin)

5. (Straße)   10. (unser Buch)

EXERCISE II. Using the phrases provided in your workbook and given by the speaker, answer the question as in the example. Repeat the correct form after the speaker.

> Example: Wessen Auto ist das? (sein Bruder)
> *Das ist das Auto seines Bruders.*

Now begin.

1. (ihr Vater)   4. (meine Eltern)

2. (unsere Tante)   5. (sein Freund)

3. (sein Onkel)   6. (dein Bruder)

EXERCISE III. Continue the sequence started in the first sentence. Repeat the correct form after the speaker. Always use complete sentences.

Der Montag ist der erste Tag der Woche.

EXERCISE IV. Answer the question: <u>Wem hat es nicht gefallen</u>? using each of the nouns given by the speaker and printed in your workbook. Repeat the correct form after the speaker.

> Example: meine Freundin
> *Meiner Freundin hat es nicht gefallen.*

Now begin.

1. sein Vater   4. meine Eltern

2. ihr Onkel   5. der junge Mann

3. eure Tante   6. der Student

EXERCISE V.   Respond to the statement according to the example. Repeat the correct form after the speaker.

Example: Er kann nicht kommen.
Es tut ihm leid, daß er nicht kommen kann.

Now begin.

EXERCISE VI.   After hearing the following text you will be asked Richtig oder Falsch questions.   First just listen.

Richtig oder Falsch?   Write R for richtig or F for falsch next to the appropriate letter.

_____ a) Der Fußball ist nur im Westen beliebt.

_____ b) Das Fußballspiel ist in der ganzen Welt beliebt.

_____ c) Das Fußballspiel ist nicht einfach.

_____ d) Nur der Mittelstürmer darf den Ball mit den Händen berühren.

_____ e) Hockey und Golf sind mit Fußball verwandt.

_____ f) Rugby und der amerikanische football haben etwas mit Fußball zu tun.

_____ g) Die Römer spielten Tennis.

_____ h) König Edward glaubte, daß das Fußballspiel zu gefährlich war.

_____ i) In der alten Zeit waren die Tore 6 Kilometer von einander entfernt (apart).

_____ j) Das Wort "soccer" kommt von "to sock" wie in "sock it to them".

_____ k) Das Wort "soccer" kommt von "association football".

LEKTION VIERZEHN
PART I

EXERCISE I. First just listen to the entire conversation of Lektion Vierzehn.

Ein teures Telefongespräch /

*Gabriele Hauser, / eine neunzehnjährige Studentin, / ruft ihren Vater an. /
Nachdem sie ihm ausführlich / über ihre guten Fortschritte beim Studium berichtet
hat, / sagt sie: /*

Gabriele: Du, Paps, / könntest du mir einen kleinen Gefallen tun? / Ich brauche
dringend hundert Mark für ein neues Wörterbuch. /
Vater: Gottseidank willst du keinen großen Gefallen, Gabriele! / Hundert Mark! / Das
ist wohl ein rarer Druck aus Gutenbergs Zeit! / Du bist genauso verschwenderisch
wie dein Bruder. / Und was ist mit deinem eigenen Konto? /
Gabriele: Ich brauche ein technisches Wörterbuch. / Und ich habe mein Konto
überzogen! / Ich mußte mir einen warmen Mantel kaufen. / Sehr schick! /
Vater: Und du hättest auch gern einen schicken Wagen? / Und eine größere Wohnung? /
Gabriele: Nein, Paps. / Mein alter VW läuft noch prima. / Und mit meiner kleinen
Bude bin ich ganz zufrieden. /
Vater: Als ich Student war ... /
Gabriele: Ja, Paps, ich weiß, / in der guten alten Zeit waren die jungen Leute
sparsam. /
Vater: Wenn ich zu meinem Vater gekommen wäre / und hätte um hundert Mark
gebeten ... /
Gabriele:... dann hätte er dir was anderes gesagt, nicht? / Aber du hättest auch
keine hundert Mark gebraucht. /
Vater: Wieso? /
Gabriele: Inflation, Paps, Inflation. / Fünfzig Mark hätten genügt ... /

*So geht es noch eine kleine Weile weiter. / Aber Herr Hauser ist ein
verständnisvoller Vater / und schickt Gabriele am nächsten Tag einen Scheck. /*

Now repeat each phrase or sentence after the speaker.

In this pronunciation section you will practice the contrast between the u and ü
sounds and between the soft or front ch and sch.

EXERCISE II. First the long u and long ü. Repeat.

Buch	Bücher//	Gruß	Grüße//
Bruder	Brüder//	Stuhl	Stühle//
Betrug	betrügen//	Hut	Hüte//
genug	genügen//		

Now the short <u>u</u> and short <u>ü</u>. Repeat.

drucken	drücken//	Wunsch	wünschen//
Sturz	stürzen//	Mutter	Mütter//
Fluß	Flüsse//	jung	jünger//
muß	müssen//		

Now indicate whether you hear an <u>u</u> or <u>ü</u> by making a check mark in the appropriate column.

	u	*ü*		*u*	*ü*		*u*	*ü*
1.	_____	_____	2.	_____	_____	3.	_____	_____
4.	_____	_____	5.	_____	_____	6.	_____	_____

<u>EXERCISE III</u>. First practice the front or soft ch once again. Repeat.

ich//   mich//   reich//   Nächte//   Märchen//   durch//

sicher//   manche//   möchte//   glücklich//   Mechaniker//

Now listen carefully and imitate the difference between the soft ch and sch. Repeat.

Tisch	dich//
deutsch	deutlich//
englisch	ähnlich//
französisch	königlich//

Now you will practice some words that contain both the front ch and the sch sounds. Repeat after the speaker.

Geschichte//   schließlich//   schriftlich//

Taschenrechner//   technisch//   durchschnittlich//

Now circle the word the speaker says in each pair.

1. wischen	wichen	4. brechen	breschen
2. misch	mich	5. Büsche	Bücher
3. Kirsche	Kirche	6. Löcher	Löscher

NAME _____ INSTRUCTOR _____ CLASS _____

EXERCISE IV. Now indicate by a check mark whether you hear ch or sch.

	ch	*sch*		*ch*	*sch*		*ch*	*sch*
1.	____	____	2.	____	____	3.	____	____
4.	____	____	5.	____	____	6.	____	____

LEKTION VIERZEHN
PART II

<u>EXERCISE I.</u> Change the definite article in each phrase to the <u>ein-word</u> indicated in your workbook and given by the speaker, and make any necessary changes in the adjective ending. Repeat the correct form after the speaker.

1. (mein)   6. (ihr)   10. (ein)

2. (ihr)   7. (sein)   11. (ihr)

3. (unser)   8. (ein)   12. (sein)

4. (Ihr)   9. (mein)   13. (unser)

5. (unser)

<u>EXERCISE II.</u> Respond with a wish beginning with: <u>ich wollte</u>, as in the example. Then repeat the correct form after the speaker.

    Example: Hast du ihn gesehen?
          Nein, ich wollte, ich hätte ihn gesehen.

Now begin.

<u>EXERCISE III.</u> <u>Was hättest du getan?</u> You are telling a friend of something that happened, and you want to know what he or she would have done under the circumstances. Follow the example, beginning each time with: <u>Was hättest du getan</u> ... In each case the original statement will be given twice, as in example. Repeat the correct form after it has been given by the speaker.

    Example: Er hat mich versetzt.
          Was hättest du getan, wenn er dich versetzt hätte?

Now begin.

<u>EXERCISE IV.</u> <u>Was bin ich von Beruf?</u> In this exercise you will hear descriptions. After each description write the person's occupation in the space provided.

1. _____

2. _____

3. _____

4. _____

5. _____

6. _____

7. _____

EXERCISE V. Wer war das? You will hear four descriptions of famous people. After each description select, from the list in your workbook, the name of the person that has been described and write it in the appropriate space in your workbook. Here are the names:

a) Mae West
b) Christopher Columbus
c) Marie Curie
d) Thomas Edison
e) Wilhelm Roentgen
f) Johann Gutenberg

Now listen to the descriptions.

1. _____

2. _____

3. _____

4. _____

LEKTION FÜNFZEHN
PART I

EXERCISE I. First just listen to the entire conversation of Lektion Fünfzehn.

Friß die Hälfte! /

Auf einer Silvesterparty. / Bruno, ein Mann im mittleren Alter, / setzt sich auf eine Couch. / Hugo sieht ihn, / ist überrascht,/überlegt sich, womit er die Unterhaltung beginnen soll / und sagt dann: /

Hugo: Bruno! / Ich hätte dich beinahe nicht erkannt! / Irgendwie hast du dich verändert. /
Bruno: Streng dich nicht so an, höflich zu sein. / Ich weiß, ich habe zugenommen. /
Hugo: Und was sagt dein Arzt dazu? / Und deine Frau? / Ich kann mir vorstellen, / daß sie sich auch nicht darüber freut. /
Bruno: Mein Arzt sagt: „FDH! / Nehmen Sie sich zusammen! / Sie müssen unbedingt abnehmen." / Meine Frau sagt: „Trimm dich!" / –Zigarette? /
Hugo: Nein, danke, / *ich* habe das Rauchen aufgegeben! /
Bruno: Schon wieder mal? /
Hugo: Hast du nicht auch aufgehört? /
Bruno: Ja, aber ich kann's einfach nicht lassen. /
Hugo: Das habe ich mir gedacht. / Selbstdisziplin, Bruno, / Willenskraft! / Sieh dir mal die Statistiken über Lungenkrebs an. /
Bruno: Nichts ist schlimmer als ein ehemaliger Raucher! /
Hugo: Nichts für ungut, Bruno, / ich will ja nur dein Bestes. /
Bruno: Ich habe mir vorgenommen, / ab morgen wird es anders: / Sargnägel weg, / FDH / und täglich einen Kilometer Dauerlauf. / Früher bin ich ja auch gern gerannt. / Mit was soll ich anfangen? / Na, mit den Zigaretten, / und dann ... /
Hugo: Prost Neujahr, Bruno. / Du wirst dich wundern, wie leicht es ist! /

Now repeat each phrase or sentence after the speaker.

In this pronunciation section you will practice some vowel contrasts and the pronunciation of -ig in final position.

EXERCISE II. First note the difference between the long o and the long ö. Repeat the pairs.

zogen	zögen//	Sohn	Söhne//
Rom	Römer//	groß	größer//
los	lösen//		

Now the short o and short ö. Repeat.

mochte	möchte//	Schloß	Schlösser//
Wort	Wörter//	konnte	könnte//

Now contrast the long e and the long ö. Repeat.

lesen	lösen//	Sehne	Söhne//
Besen	böse//	Heere	höre//

Now the short e (ä) and the short ö. Repeat.

Mächte	möchte//	Helle	Hölle//
kennen	können//	fällig	völlig//

Now indicate whether you hear a short e (ä) or short ö by putting a check mark in the appropriate column in your workbook.

short e (ä)	short ö	short e (ä)	short ö	short e (ä)	short ö
1. _____	_____	2. _____	_____	3. _____	_____
4. _____	_____	5. _____	_____		

EXERCISE III. Now you will practice the -ig in final position, pronounced ich, as contrasted with the ig in medial position, pronounced ig. Repeat each pair of phrases after the speaker.

ein König	zwei Könige//
wenig Geld	wenige Fehler//
die Antwort ist richtig	die richtige Antwort//
das Problem ist wichtig	ein wichtiges Problem//
das Gas ist giftig	ein giftiges Gas//
der Fluß ist schmutzig	ein schmutziger Fluß//

EXERCISE IV. Now you will have a dictation. Remember that if an l precedes the ich-sound, it is written l i c h, unless the l is part of the preceding word-stem, as in einmalig or eilig. You will hear each word twice. Write it in the appropriate space in your workbook.

1. _____

2. _____

3. _____

4. _____

5. _____

6. _____

LEKTION FÜNFZEHN
PART II

EXERCISE I. Answer the following questions affirmatively, keeping the same tenses. Repeat the correct form after the speaker.

EXERCISE II. Respond to each statement in the first person, as in the example. Repeat the correct form after the speaker.

    Example: Er kann sich das nicht vorstellen.
              Ich kann mir das auch nicht vorstellen.

Now begin.

EXERCISE III. Continue the speaker's statement by adding a familiar singular imperative, as in the example. Then repeat the correct form after the speaker.

    Example: Man muß sich das ansehen.
              Sieh dir das an.

Now begin.

EXERCISE IV. The speaker will give you an infinitive phrase. Use the singular familiar du-form in the present perfect tense to ask a question, as in the example.

    Example: sich wundern
              Hast du dich gewundert?

Now begin.

EXERCISE V. Put the following sentences into the present perfect tense. Then repeat the correct form after the speaker.

EXERCISE VI. Continue the speaker's statement, using können in the past tense, as in the example. Then repeat the correct form after the speaker.

    Example: Er wäre fast ausgewandert.
              Aber er konnte nicht auswandern.

Now begin.

EXERCISE VII. Use the infinitive type of imperative construction in place of the one you hear. Follow the example, and then repeat the correct form after the speaker.

    Example: Nimm den Koffer mit.
              Den Koffer mitnehmen!

Now begin.

EXERCISE VIII. You will hear some irresponsible ads for miracle pills. After each ad you will be asked what the pill is supposed to be for.

Now complete the statement by circling the letter of the correct completion.

No.1: Diese Tablette soll man nehmen, wenn man

        a) Raucher ist
        b) abnehmen will
        c) Schnupfen hat
        d) Angst vor Leuten hat

Select the correct completion.

No.2: Diese Tablette soll man nehmen, wenn

        a) man Husten hat
        b) man Halsschmerzen hat
        c) der Streß zu viel wird
        d) man ein Idiot ist

Now answer the question.

No.3: Was soll Ihnen gelingen, wenn Sie diese Tabletten nehmen?

        a) abzunehmen
        b) aufzupassen
        c) anzurufen
        d) zuzunehmen

LEKTION SECHZEHN
PART I

EXERCISE I. First listen to the entire conversation of <u>Lektion Sechzehn</u>.

Das kann jedem passieren! /

Andrea sitzt im Wartesaal eines Bahnhofs. / Ihr Zug, der um 15:45 Uhr abfahren soll, hat Verspätung. / Verena kommt. / Sie trägt einen riesigen Koffer, / fast so groß wie ein Frachtcontainer. / Sie kommt kaum damit durch die Tür. /

Verena: Hallo Andrea! / Daß ich dich ausgerechnet hier treffe! / Fährst du auch nach Düsseldorf? /

Andrea: Tag Verena; / nein, zu meinem Onkel in Kassel. /

Verena: Ich habe in Düsseldorf einen besseren Job gefunden. / In der Forschungsabteilung der größten Reklameagentur! / Der Traumjob, den ich schon immer wollte. /

Andrea: Ich gratuliere! /

Verena: Danke. / -Dein Onkel, / ist das der gutaussehende ältere Mann, / der voriges Jahr bei euch war? /

Andrea: Nein, das war der älteste Bruder meiner Mutter. / -Fährst du mit dem Intercity? /

Verena: Nein, mit dem früheren D-Zug. / -Ich brauche wirklich einen größeren Koffer. / Das ist der größte, den ich habe. /

Andrea: Er platzt gleich. /

Verena: Um Gotteswillen, / es ist schon geschehen! /

Andrea: Du hast schon immer die meisten Sachen mitgeschleppt. / Sogar mehr als Alice. / Erinnerst du dich noch, als wir... /

Verena: Andrea, das kann jedem passieren! / Was nun? / Eine Tragetasche! / Vielleicht gibt's eine am Kiosk. / Ah, dort geht's zur U-Bahn, / dort ist bestimmt ein Kiosk. / Bin gleich zurück! /

Andrea: (resigniert) Ich bin mal gespannt, ob sie den Zug nicht verpaßt! /

Now repeat each phrase or sentence after the speaker.

In this pronunciation section you will practice the contrast between <u>ü</u> and <u>i</u> as well as the sp and st combination.

EXERCISE II. Listen to the contrast between long <u>ü</u> and <u>i</u>. Repeat after the speaker.

Züge	Ziege//	Süden	sieden//
kühl	Kiel//	Stühle	Stiele//
Tür	Tier//		

Now the short <u>ü</u> and short <u>i</u>. Repeat.

brüllen	Brillen//	Müller	Miller//
Stücken	sticken//	Künden	Kinder//

Now the u, ü and i. Read after the speaker.

Mutter	Mütter	Mitte//		Zug	Züge	Ziege//
Kuli	kühl	Kiel//		Gruß	Grüße	Grieß//
Mull	Müller	Miller//		Hut	Hüte	hielte//

Now indicate whether you hear ü or i.

	ü	i		ü	i		ü	i
1.	___	___	2.	___	___	3.	___	___
4.	___	___	5.	___	___

EXERCISE III. Now you will practice the st and sp. First, the st. Remember that in initial position st is pronounced sht . Repeat.

Stadt//   studieren//   stehen//   Straße//   Streß//   Steuer//

st after a prefix or in a compound noun is also pronounced sht. Repeat.

bestimmt//   verstehen//   Großstadt//   Frühstück//   Austauschstudent//

The st in medial or final position is pronounced st. Repeat.

gestern//   Leistung//   protestieren//   System//

Angst//   Kunst//   fast//   fest//

Now the sp. Remember that in initial position the sp is pronounced shp. Repeat.

Sport//   Spiel//   Spaß//   Sprache//   sprechen//   Spritze//

After a prefix or in compound nouns, sp is also pronounced shp. Repeat.

versprechen//   Gespräch//   Schauspieler//   Beispiel//   Fremdsprache//

In final and medial position, sp is rather rare. It is pronounced sp. Repeat.

Wespe//   Kaspar//   Knospe//

LEKTION SECHZEHN
PART II

EXERCISE I. Answer each question negatively using the adjective provided in the comparative form. Repeat the correct form after the speaker. Follow the example.

> Example: Hast du eine jüngere Schwester? (alt)
> *Nein, eine ältere.*

Now begin.

1. (klein)   4. (groß)

2. (interessant)   5. (spät)

3. (früh)   6. (jung)

EXERCISE II. Answer affirmatively, using a superlative, as in the example. Repeat the correct form after the speaker.

> Example: Ist er ein guter Mechaniker?
> *Ja, der beste, den es gibt.*

Now begin.

EXERCISE III. Now you will hear answers for which you will state the questions. Use a relative clause each time. Follow the example. Then repeat the correct form after the speaker.

> Example: Ja, von dem Film habe ich dir erzählt.
> *Ist das der Film, von dem du mir erzählt hast?*

Now begin.

EXERCISE IV. Now the speaker will give you the time on the twenty-four system. You tell what your watch would say. Repeat the correct form after the speaker.

> Example: Es ist dreizehn Uhr zwanzig.
> *Es ist zwanzig nach eins.*

Now begin.

EXERCISE V. Was bin ich? You will now hear descriptions of businesses or places. After each description write the name of the place or business in the appropriate space in your workbook.

1. _____

2. _____

3. _____

EXERCISE VI. <u>Welche Sprache muß ich lernen?</u> In each of the following passages a prospective tourist tells about the country he or she wants to visit. After the passage select the language the tourist wants to learn from the list in your work-book, and write it in the appropriate space. The languages are:

a) französisch   e) italienisch
b) englisch   f) arabisch
c) deutsch   g) japanisch
d) schwedisch   h) spanisch

1. _____

2. _____

3. _____

4. _____

LEKTION SIEBZEHN
PART I

EXERCISE I. First listen to the entire conversation of Lektion Siebzehn.

Sie sind doch keine Geheimagentin, oder...? /

In einer Raststätte an der Autobahn. / Eine Amerikanerin, / Lektorin bei einem amerikanischen Verlag, / unterhält sich mit ihrem deutschen Tischnachbarn. / Nach einer Weile fragt sie: /

Elaine: Wie komme ich am schnellsten nach Bad Mergentheim? /
Jens: Nach Bad Mergentheim, / hm, da muß ich mal überlegen. / Moment mal, / ich habe eine Landkarte im Handschuhfach. /
Elaine: Aber bitte, bemühen Sie sich nicht ... /
Jens: Macht nichts, / ich warte sowieso auf meinen Wagen. / Er wurde geschmiert / und muß gewaschen und gewachst werden. / Ich bin hinter einem Lastwagen mit Sand hergefahren. / Total verstaubt! /

(Später)

Jens: Also, es wäre am besten, / wenn Sie über Langenburg fahren würden. / Es dauert ein wenig länger, / aber die Landschaft ist schöner. / Diese Strecke über Blaufelden ist die kürzere, / aber nicht sehr aufregend. / Und da ist mehr Verkehr. /
Elaine: Ich glaube, ich fahre lieber über Langenburg. / Dann komme ich eben etwas später als geplant. /
Jens: Werden Sie von jemand erwartet? /
Elaine: Ja, eine geschäftliche Verabredung. / Mit einem Lyriker aus der DDR. /
Jens: Ein internationales Treffen, was? / Sie sind doch keine Geheimagentin, oder ...? /
Elaine: (lacht) Nein, mit der CIA habe ich nichts zu tun! / Ich bin von meinem Verlag hergeschickt worden. / Ich soll einiges mit ihm besprechen. /
Jens: Na denn, gute Reise! / Und viel Erfolg. /

Now repeat each sentence or phrase after the speaker.

In this pronunciation section you will practice contrast between ö and ü, the consonant clusters pf and ps and stress on final ie- syllables.

EXERCISE II. First the long ö and the long ü. Repeat the pairs.

Römer	rühmen//	lögen	lügen//
fröhlich	früh//	Töne	Düne//
zöge	Züge//		

Now the short ö and short ü. Repeat the pairs.

Stöcke	Stücke//		flösse	Flüsse//
Schlösser	Schlüssel//		völlig	füllig//
Wörter	würde//			

Which do you hear, ö or ü? Check the appropriate column in your workbook.

	ö	ü		ö	ü		ö	ü
1.	____	____	2.	____	____	3.	____	____
4.	____	____	5.	____	____	6.	____	____

EXERCISE III. Which word in each pair do you hear? Circle the correct one.

1. München	Mönchen		4. zöge	Züge
2. Hölle	Hülle		5. Güsse	gösse
3. Köhl	kühl		6. Schüsse	schösse

EXERCISE IV. Most nouns ending in -ie have the stress on the ie. Repeat.

Biologie// Geometrie// Geologie// Astronomie// Psychologie// Zoologie//

Geographie// Psychiatrie// Kategorie// Astrologie// Zeremonie//

EXERCISE V. Now you will practice the pf combination. Repeat.

Kopf// Pfennig// Pfeffer// Pferd// Pfund// pflanzen//

Now the ps. Both letters must be pronounced. Repeat.

Psychologie// Psychiater// psychologisch// Psychoanalyse// Pseudonym//

EXERCISE VI. This will be a dictation. Write what you hear. Distinguish between single s and double s.

1. _____		4. _____
2. _____		5. _____
3. _____		6. _____

LEKTION SIEBZEHN
PART II

EXERCISE I. Respond as in the example using the information provided by the speaker and printed in your workbook. Use the present perfect tense of the passive voice. Repeat the correct form after the speaker.

      Example: Wann wurde es bemerkt? (gleich danach)
                Gleich danach ist es bemerkt worden.

Now begin.

1. (gestern)   4. (am Montag)

2. (nachts)   5. (1492)

3. (letzte Woche)   6. (letztes Jahr)

EXERCISE II. Answer each question negatively, using <u>man</u> instead of passive voice. Each question will be given twice. Repeat the correct form after the speaker has given it. Follow the example.

      Example: Ist er gesehen worden?
                Nein, man hat ihn nicht gesehen.

Now begin.

EXERCISE III. Complete the following statements, using a comparative, as in the example. Repeat the correct form after the speaker.

      Example: Er spricht schnell.
                Er spricht schnell, viel schneller als ich.

Now begin.

EXERCISE IV. The speaker will make a statement about <u>Karl</u>; you continue using <u>Inge</u> and <u>Tina</u> as your subjects, and giving the comparative and superlative, as in the example. Repeat the correct form after the speaker.

      Example: Karl hat es schwer.
                Aber Inge hat es schwerer, und Tina hat es am schwersten.

Now begin.

EXERCISE V. After the following text you will be asked some questions. First some vocabulary clues: <u>die Idee</u>, plural <u>die Ideen</u>, means idea; <u>eine Tasse Kaffee</u> means a cup of coffee.

Now listen.

Now circle the item that correctly completes each statement that you hear.

1. Auf dem Schild in der Mensa stand,

        a) daß die zweite Tasse Kaffee weniger kostete als die erste
        b) daß die zweite Tasse Kaffee mehr kostete als die erste

2. Der Trick der Studenten war, zu sagen,

        a) daß es die zweite Tasse Kaffee war
        b) daß sie Coca Cola statt Kaffee trinken würden

3. Herr Schmidt hatte Magenschmerzen,

        a) weil er zu viel Kaviar gegessen hatte
        b) weil er zu oft in weniger teuren Restaurants gegessen hatte

4. Bei dem ersten Arzt

        a) war der zweite Besuch teurer als der erste
        b) war der erste Besuch teurer als der zweite

5. Mit seinem Trick wollte Herr Schmidt

        a) Schlaftabletten bekommen
        b) Geld sparen

6. Der erste Arzt

        a) bemerkte den Trick
        b) bemerkte den Trick nicht

7. Wenn Herr Schmidt keinen Trick versucht hätte,

        a) hätte sein erster Besuch 30 anstatt 100 Mark gekostet
        b) hätte sein zweiter Besuch 100 Mark gekostet

LEKTION ACHTZEHN
Part I

EXERCISE I. First just listen to the entire conversation of <u>Lektion Achtzehn</u>.

Ich glaube, ich lasse mich scheiden! /

In einer Pension im Schwarzwald. / Es ist elf Uhr morgens und es regnet. / Frau
Kappel sitzt am Fenster und liest alte Zeitungen; / Herr Kappel sitzt im Sessel
und starrt an die Wand. /

Er: Schon drei Tage miserables Wetter, / kalter Regen, / grauer Himmel! / Mir
    stinkt's! /
Sie: Auf Regen folgt Sonnenschein. /
Er: Du mit deinen blöden Bauernweisheiten! /
Sie: Du hast ja behauptet, / nur im Schwarzwald gäbe es noch unberührte Natur. / Jetzt
    hast du deine unberührte Natur. /
Er: Warum liest du denn die alten Zeitungen? /
Sie: Hast du etwas Besseres vorzuschlagen? /
Er: Nein, aber vielleicht ... /
Sie: ... na also! /
Er: Unterbrich mich doch nicht. / Hast du nicht heute morgen gesagt, / wir hätten
    uns schon ewig nicht mehr richtig unterhalten? /
Sie: Habe ich etwa unrecht? /
Er: Ich bin halt so beschäftigt. / Und am Wochenende bin ich immer müde. /
Sie: Stimmt! /
Er: Oder du bist auf Geschäftsreise. /
Sie: Na und? / Soll ich vielleicht sagen, / ich kann leider nicht, / mein Mann sagt, /
    ich soll mich mit ihm unterhalten? /
Er: Weißt du, / wann wir das letztemal im Kino waren? / Vor vier Monaten! /
Sie: Das ist mir nichts Neues. / Und hier gibt's nicht mal ein Kino. / Lauter
    unberührte Natur! /
Er: Beate, du bist mal wieder unausstehlich! /
Sie: Ich bin ...?? / Arthur, ich glaube, / wenn morgen die Sonne nicht scheint, /
    lasse ich mich scheiden! /

Now repeat each phrase or sentence after the speaker.

In this pronunciation section you will practice the contrast between <u>ei</u> and <u>eu</u> (<u>äu</u>)
as well as some consonant combinations with r.

EXERCISE II. First practice the <u>ei</u>. Repeat after the speaker.

nein//   Freitag//   leider//   schreiben//   gleich//   Zeit//   Freiheit//

Now the <u>eu</u>. Repeat.

deutsch//   neun//   Freund//   Häuser//   Steuer//   läuft//   Leute//

Now contrast the ei and eu (äu). Repeat each pair after the speaker.

nein	neun//	zeigen	zeugen//
Feier	Feuer//	breit	bereut//
leiten	läuten//	Meiler	Mäuler//
Streit	streut//	leichter	Leuchter//

Now indicate, by a check mark in the appropriate column, which sound you hear.

	ei	*eu (äu)*		*ei*	*eu (äu)*		*ei*	*eu (äu)*
1.	_____	_____	2.	_____	_____	3.	_____	_____
4.	_____	_____	5.	_____	_____	6.	_____	_____

EXERCISE III. Now you will practice some consonant combinations with r. Repeat. First str-:

Strafzettel//   Strand//   Straße//   Strecke//   Streit//   Streß//

Now the spr-:

Sprache//   sprechen//   spricht//   Spritze//   Gespräch//

Now the -rt:

hört//   Wort//   schmiert//   starrt//   kehrt//   spart//   fährt//

Now the -rl:

gefährlich//   natürlich//   jährlich//   ausführlich//

And finally the -rz:

kurz//   März//   herzlich//   Sturzhelm//   Arzt//

EXERCISE IV. Now the last tongue twister of the semester. First listen.

Auf dem Türmchen	*(On the little tower*
sitzt ein Würmchen	*sits a little worm*
mit dem Schirmchen	*with a little umbrella*
unterm Ärmchen.	*under its little arm;*
Kommt ein Stürmchen,	*comes a little storm and*

wirft das Würmchen	*throws the little worm*
mit dem Schirmchen	*with its little umbrella*
unterm Ärmchen	*under its little arm*
von dem Türmchen.	*from the little tower.)*

Now repeat each line after the speaker.

Können Sie das jetzt ganz schnell sagen?

LEKTION ACHTZEHN
PART II

EXERCISE I. Answer each question negatively and using the adjective supplied by the speaker and printed in your workbook. Follow the example. Repeat the correct form after the speaker.

>   Example: Trinkst du gern englisches Bier? (deutsch)
>   *Nein, deutsches.*

Now begin.

1. (italienisch)   6. (warm)

2. (französisch)   7. (spanisch)

3. (langweilig)   8. (europäisch)

4. (leicht)   9. (deutsch)

5. (lang)

EXERCISE II. Answer each question with an indirect quotation beginning with: er sagte. Then repeat the correct form after the speaker. Follow the example.

>   Example: Ist er beschäftigt?
>   *Er sagte, er wäre beschäftigt.*

Now begin.

EXERCISE III. Rephrase the following questions as indirect quotations, beginning with: er fragte, as in the example. Then repeat the correct form after the speaker.

>   Example: Hat er schon Pläne für den Sommer?
>   *Er fragte, ob er schon Pläne für den Sommer hätte.*

Now begin.

EXERCISE IV. Listen to each description and then select the correct response in each case.

1. a)   b)   c)

2. a)   b)   c)

EXERCISE V. Listen to this story from the Middle Ages. Later you will be asked questions. Just one vocabulary item before you begin: Paradies is German for paradise.

Now circle the letter of the item that correctly completes each statement.

1. Der Student kam aus

        a) Paris
        b) aus dem Paradies
        c) von einer Party

2. Der Bruder der Frau

        a) wohnte in Paris
        b) war letztes Jahr gestorben
        c) war ein schlechter Mensch

3. Der Student sagte,

        a) er kenne den Bruder nicht, und er wohne nicht im Paradies
        b) er kenne Karl gut, und es ginge Karl schlecht
        c) er habe Karl nie im Paradies gesehen

4. Die Frau gab dem Studenten Geld und Essen,

        a) weil er ihr leid tat
        b) weil er versprach, er würde es ihrem Bruder im Paradies geben
        c) weil der Student so ein netter Mensch war

5. Der Bauer sagte seiner Frau,

        a) er hätte dem Studenten das Pferd gegeben, so daß er
           schneller ins Paradies käme
        b) sein Pferd wäre von dem Studenten gestohlen worden
        c) sein Pferd wäre im Wald verschwunden/

Practical Math in Context

Book 4
Budgeting & Banking

SADDLEBACK PUBLISHING · INC.

Development: Frishman Co
Authors: Lucia McKay, Ph.D. and Maggie Guscott
Design and Production: The Format Group, LLC
Cover Art: IQ Design

SADDLEBACK PUBLISHING, INC.
Three Watson
Irvine, CA 92618-2767
Web site: www.sdlback.com

ISBN 1-56254-758-5

Printed in the United States of America

10 09 08 07 06 9 8 7 6 5 4 3 2 1

Table of Contents

Unit 5: Rental Budgeting

Unit 6: Self-Employment

Unit 7: Going on a Trip

Unit 8: Keeping the Books

To the Student

Welcome to *Budgeting & Banking!* This is Book 4 of the *Practical Math in Context* series.

The goal of this book and the other books in this series is to build your confidence and practical math skills. You will use these math skills in everyday situations throughout your life.

You solve problems and make mathematical decisions every day. You compare products and make choices about what to buy. You work to earn money. You decide what to spend and how much to save.

Practical Math in Context gives you strategies to solve everyday math problems in a variety of ways. It strengthens your skills and gives you practice with many different math topics. Each of the six books presents topics you are likely to encounter in everyday life. Each book includes problems that involve estimation, equations, mental math, calculators, and critical thinking. Each book includes additional topic-specific skills such as graphing, averages, statistics, ratios, and measurement.

Each unit begins with a preview lesson, which models and explains the types of problems you will encounter in the unit. Then there are five lessons, at least one of which is usually a game. Each unit ends with a review of the unit concepts. There are illustrations and graphic art throughout.

Here is a list of the titles of the other books in the *Practical Math in Context* series:
Book 1: Everyday Life
Book 2: Home & School
Book 3: On the Job
Book 5: Smart Shopping
Book 6: Sports, Hobbies, & Recreation

With review and practice, you will build your math skills and learn to approach everyday mathematical situations with confidence! *Practical Math in Context* will help you become a successful problem solver!

Unit 1 — *Paying Your Way*

Preview

How You Will Use This Unit

Paying your way involves many different things. Sharing day-to-day costs and budgeting for special items are just two examples. You probably also consider saving some of the money you make. You may also want to compare services from banks. As you compare options and make choices, you will often use math. The math skills you use include mental math and estimation, basic operations and equations, statistics, and ratios and proportions.

What You Will Do in This Unit

In this unit, math steps demonstrate how to solve problems. These steps can help you answer questions such as these:

You share an apartment with a friend, and share equally the cost of rent, utilities, and food. How much money do you budget for these expenses each month?

Out of your weekly income, you budget $20 toward new windsurfing equipment. How much do you have toward your new equipment after six weeks?

You keep $1,000 in your checking account. When this grows to $1,500, you transfer $500 to savings. What is the percent increase in your checking account just before you transfer funds?

Your bank offers free checking when you maintain a minimum daily balance of $2,000. When you do not maintain this balance, the bank charges a $5 monthly service charge, and a $0.05 transaction charge. What is the fee if your daily balance is $800, and you write 15 checks?

What You Can Learn from This Unit

When you complete this unit, you will have used mathematics to work problems related to paying your way. These problems are similar to those that may actually occur in your daily life.

Lesson 1

Sharing Day-to-Day Costs

Example Milan and Dale share a student apartment. They share equally the cost of rent, utilities, food, and miscellaneous living expenses. Milan draws a circle graph to show their total costs for this month.

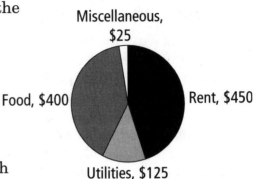

a. What fraction of the total costs is the rent?

b. What dollar amount does each student budget for these expenses per month?

Solve

Step 1: First, find the total expenses by adding.
$450 + $125 + $400 + $25 = $1000

Step 2: Then, write the rent as a fraction of the total. Simplify the fraction by dividing out the common factors.

$$\frac{\$450}{\$1000} = \frac{9}{20}$$

Step 3: Underline the sentence that tells how Milan and Dale handle apartment costs.

They share equally the cost of rent, utilities, food, and miscellaneous living expenses.

Step 4: Divide to find x, the amount of the two equal shares of the costs.

x = total cost ÷ 2
= $1,000 ÷ 2
= $500

Answer the Question

Step 5: a. The rent is $\frac{9}{20}$ of the total cost.
b. Each student budgets $500 each month.

✏️ Now try these problems.

1. Milan and Dale share equally the costs of rent, utilities, food, and other living expenses equally. Their rent increases to $549. They reduce their other shared costs to $366.

a. What fraction of the total is this increased rent?

b. What amount does each student budget for these expenses per month?

Answer: a. The rent is _____ of the total.

       b. Each student budgets $_____.

2. Melissa pays a car insurance premium of $160 each month. She starts to carpool to work. She informs her car insurance company of the change. The company takes 5% off her car insurance premium. How much is her monthly car insurance premium now? Circle the bills and write the number of those bills under each, to represent this amount.

_____   _____   _____   _____

3. Jo-emma rents a house. She makes an agreement with the owner about the garden. The owner buys the plants, and Jo-emma plants and waters them. The owner saves $100 a month for a gardener. The owner reduces Jo-emma's rent each month by this amount. This represents a 20% savings each month on Jo-emma's rent. What is the amount Jo-emma actually pays each month for rent?

    A $160   **B** $200   **C** $400   **D** $500

4. Ruben budgets $20 a week for lunch. On Monday, Alex and Melvyn invite him to go to lunch with them. Ruben's lunch costs $5.75. Alex's lunch costs $6.25. Melvyn's lunch costs $6.00. They split the total bill equally between them. How much does Ruben have left for lunches for the rest of the week?

Answer: $_____

☆ *Challenge Problem*
You may want to talk this one over with a partner.

Can you use the same sequence of symbols, in the same order, to make each equation correct? Choose from these symbols: +, −, ×, ÷, (). Write an equation to support your answer.

$$4 \_\_ 4 \_\_ 4 \_\_ 4 \_\_ 4 = 1 \qquad 5 \_\_ 5 \_\_ 5 \_\_ 5 \_\_ 5 = 1 \qquad 6 \_\_ 6 \_\_ 6 \_\_ 6 \_\_ 6 = 1$$

_____

_____

Lesson 2

Budgeting for Special Items

Example Out of her weekly income of $480, Carmen budgets $20 toward new windsurfing equipment.

a. What percent of her weekly income is the amount she budgets?

b. She plans to continue to budget this amount each week. How much will she have toward her windsurfing equipment after six weeks?

Solve

Step 1: Underline the sentence that tells the amount Carmen budgets of her income.

Out of her weekly income of $480, Carmen budgets $20 ...

Step 2: Write an equation that gives the budgeted amount as a percent of her income.

$$\text{Percent} = \frac{20}{480} \times 100\%$$
$$= 4.167\%$$

Step 3: Use a proportion to find the amount x that Carmen has after six weeks.

First, use words to write the proportion.

$$\frac{\text{amount in one week}}{\text{one week}} = \frac{\text{amount after six weeks}}{\text{six weeks}}$$

Second, write the proportion using numbers.

$$\frac{20}{1} = \frac{x}{6}$$

Step 4: Solve for x.

$$x = 20 \times 6$$
$$x = 120$$

Answer the Question

Step 5: a. Carmen budgets 4.167% of her weekly income.
b. After six weeks, she has $120 toward her windsurfing equipment.

✐ Now try these problems.

1. Out of his monthly income of $1,200, Chaz budgets $60 for a digital camera.

   a. Chaz budgets _____% of his monthly income for a digital camera.

---

b. He plans to continue to budget the same amount each month towards the camera. Which equation gives the amount he will have after six months?

A $\frac{x}{60} = \frac{1}{6}$ **B** $\frac{x}{6} = \frac{60}{1}$ **C** $\frac{x}{1} = \frac{6}{120}$ **D** $\frac{x}{6} = \frac{1}{1,200}$

2. As a book illustrator, Ravenna takes about four hours to create one finished drawing. She likes to create at least 15 drawings per week. Ravenna budgets her time so that she has Sundays off. This week she completes four drawings on Monday and two on Tuesday. How can she budget her time for the rest of the week and meet her goals? Fill in a number of working hours for each day.

Monday	Tuesday	Wednesday	Thursday	Friday	Saturday	Sunday
		____ hours	____ hours	____ hours	____ hours	____ hours

3. Veronica budgets $19.95 a month for a new E-zine she reads. Her monthly expenses total $760 per month before this new expense. Her income is $800 per month. How much money will she have left over each month after this new budget item?

Answer: $_____

4. Dimitri buys a car for $3,600. He agrees to pay for it in equal monthly installments over two years. His car insurance is $1,600 per year. He pays it in equal monthly installments. Write a set of steps to calculate the change in Dimitri's monthly expense budget.

Answer: _____

☆ *Challenge Problem*
You may want to talk this one over with a partner.

Ask a friend to pick (without telling you) the number of times a week that they would like to have dinner out (more than once, less than 10). Then give them these directions: Multiply this number by 2. Add 5. Multiply by 50. If they have already had their birthday this year, add 1753. If they haven't, add 1752. Add 1 if this year is 2004. Add 2 if this year is 2005. Add 3 if this year is 2006 … and so on. Now subtract the four digit year that they were born. Ask your friend what the final three-digit number is.

You can decode this final number! The first digit is the number of times your friend chose to eat out. The next two digits is the age of your friend! See if you can figure out why this always works.

_____

_____

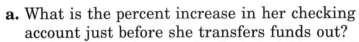

Lesson 3

Saving, a Little at a Time

Example Roe keeps $1,000 in her checking account. When this grows to $1,500, she transfers $500 to her savings account.

  a. What is the percent increase in her checking account just before she transfers funds out?

Roe keeps $3,000 in her savings account. When this account has the same percent increase, she transfers the excess to an investment account.

  b. What amount does her savings account reach just before she transfers out funds?

  c. How much money does she transfer out?

Solve

  Step 1: Underline the sentence that tells how much Roe keeps in her checking account.

  <u>Roe keeps $1,000 in her checking account.</u>

  Step 2: To find the percent increase in Roe's checking account, first subtract to find the amount of the increase.

  $1,500 − $1,000 = $500

  > Percent of change
  > (increase or decrease)
  > equals
  > $\frac{\text{amount of change}}{\text{original amount}}$

  Step 3: Next, find the percent by comparing the amount of change to the original amount.

  $\frac{50}{1,000} \times 100\% = 50\%$

  Step 4: Now, use the same percent to calculate the amount of increase for her savings account.

  50% of $3,000 = $1,500   Find 50% of the amount she keeps in that account.

  $3,000 + $1,500 = $4,500   Add this increase.

Answer the Question

  Step 5: **a.** Roe's checking account has increased by 50% when she transfers out funds.
  b. Roe's savings account grows to $4,500.
  c. Then she transfers out $1,500.

✏️ Now try these problems.

  1. Monty keeps $800 in his checking account. When this grows to $1,000, he transfers $200 to his savings account.

  a. When Monty's checking account increases by _____%, he transfers funds out.

Monty keeps $2,000 in his savings account. When this grows by the same percent increase, he transfers the excess to an investment account.

b. What amount is in his savings account when he transfers out funds?

c. How much money does he transfer out?

Answer: Monty's savings account grows to $_____.

Then he transfers $_____ out.

2. To save money, Donna separates her essential expenses from her optional expenses. On her telephone bill, the essential service charge expense is about $20.00 a month. Her optional long-distance calls average about $50 per month. She reduces her optional expenses by 20%. How much does she save per month?

    A $5   **B** $10   **C** $20   **D** $50

3. During the first year of their marriage, Dawn and Jeff save $1,000. With $600, they buy a three-year Certificate of Deposit (CD). With the remaining money they buy a used sewing machine and a chain saw. Dawn uses the sewing machine to make gifts. She spends $300 less on buying gifts. Jeff uses the chain saw to cut up logs. He spends $250 less on their heating bill. Circle the numbers that represent savings. Draw squares around the numbers that represent expenses.

    $600 $400 $300 $250

4. Eduardo earns $25,000 a year this year. He estimates that he will get an 8% increase in salary each year. He plans to save 10% of his income each year. Complete the chart. How much can he save in 3 years?

Year	Income	Year's Savings	Accumulated Savings
1	$25,000	10% of $25,000 = $	$
2	1.08 × $25,000 = $	$	$
3		$	$

☆ Challenge Problem
You may want to talk this one over with a partner.

You count the change you have been saving. You have exactly enough for the hubcaps that cost $98. You have four five-dollar bills, 21 one-dollar bills, 141 quarters, 69 dimes, and a lot of nickels.
How many nickels do you have?   **Answer:** _____

(Lesson 4)

→ *Using Bank Services*

Example Marta's bank offers free checking when she maintains a minimum daily balance of $2,000. When she does *not* maintain a minimum daily balance of $2,000, the bank charges a fee. The fee includes a monthly service charge of $3, and a 10-cent charge for each check or withdrawal transaction. Marta does *not* maintain a daily balance of $2,000. Write an equation for the bank fee for one month.

> **For daily balances less than $2,000, bank fees will be charged:**
> *Monthly service fee: $3.*
> *Charge per check or withdrawal transaction: 10 cents each.*
>
> **Banking Services**
>
> Gold Standard
> Bank & Trust Co.

Solve

Step 1: Use *f* for the bank fee for one month.

Use *t* for the number of check or withdrawal transactions in one month.

Write an expression for the charge for *t* transactions.

Charge for *t* transactions = $0.10 × *t*   10 cents for each transaction.

Step 2: Now, write an equation for the bank fee, *f*, for the month.

$f = (\$0.10 \times t) + \$3$ Add the $3 monthly service charge.

Answer the Question

Step 3: The equation for the bank fee for one month is:
$f = (\$0.10 \times t) + \$3$.

✏ Now try these problems.

1. Cody's bank offers free checking when he maintains a minimum daily balance of $2,500. When he does *not* maintain this minimum daily balance, the bank charges a fee. The fee includes a $4 monthly service charge and a $0.05 transaction charge. Cody maintains a daily balance of $2,000. Which equation gives Cody's bank fee for one month?

   A $f = \$0$ **C** $f = (\$0.05 \times t) + \$4$

   B $f = (\$0.04 \times t) + \$5$ **D** $f = \$4$

2. Jere does *not* maintain the required $1,500 minimum daily balance at her bank. This month, she writes 21 checks, and makes two withdrawal transactions. Her bank charges her a

---

Unit 1 • Paying Your Way   8   Budgeting & Banking

monthly charge of $3.50, and 10 cents per transaction. The bank across the street charges a flat fee of $5 per month, with no restrictions. Which bank suits Jere's banking needs better? Why?

Answer: _____

_____

3. Fia's bank offers Internet banking services. She checks the status of her checking account on-line. Her rent check for $525, that she just mailed, has not cleared yet. Will she have enough in her account to pay her $745 credit card bill in full, after the rent check clears? Write an equation and find the amount in her account if she pays these two bills.

Deposits: $1,312.50
Checks paid: $27.97, $52.70, $345.59
Withdrawals: $200, $200, $300
Current balance: $1,483.82

Answer: _____ (Yes/No) _____ = $_____

4. Here are the yearly rates for a $1,000 Certificate of Deposit (CD) at Elton's bank:

Interest earned on a $1,000 CD	180 days: 0.65% interest	1 year: 0.75% interest

Elton considers withdrawing his $1,000 CD after 180 days. How much *more* interest can Elton earn if he leaves the CD in the bank for one year?

$1 $3.25 $4.25 $7.00

☆ Challenge Problem
You may want to talk this one over with a partner.

You have a bank debit card and a bank credit card. There is no charge for the debit card. But you can *not* exceed the $2,000 that you have in your checking account without incurring a charge. There is a 16% interest charge on any unpaid balance in your credit card account. But you have a $5,000 credit limit with this card. You have an outstanding balance of $2,200 against this card. You want to purchase a $1,500 sofa for your apartment. Which card do you use? Why?

_____

_____

_____

_____

Lesson 5

A Jigsaw Puzzle Game (for One or More Players)

The goal of this game is to build a three-by-three square. First, you look at the nine pieces. Then, you put them together so that the answers on adjacent edges of the small squares are the same.

Materials

Nine small squares (on the next page)

Directions

1. Mix up the nine small square pieces and place them face up on a flat surface. Players arrange themselves so they can see all the pieces.

2. Player 1 picks two pieces where the answer to the expression on one side of a square is equal to the answer to the expression on one side of the other square. Player 1 places the pieces so that these two matching sides are together.

3. Player 2 then takes a turn, and adds a piece to one of edges of the two pieces. (Remember that the answer on each side of the touching edges must be the same.)

4. Players take turns adding *or replacing* a piece in the puzzle.

5. The game is over when the nine pieces fit together in a three-by-three square, and the answers to the expressions on adjacent edges are equal.

6. For a more complex game, cut two sets of the small squares, mix them up, and try to build two squares at the same time. Alternatively, two teams can compete to build their own square. The winning team is the team that finishes first.

Before you play the game, try these warm-up problems.

1. Nate looks at the expressions on several of the *It All Adds Up!* squares. Which expression is equal to this expression: $1^2 + 2^2 - 4$? (Recall that any number to the zero power is equal to 1.)

    A 1   B $2^0 - 3$ C $\sqrt{4}$ D $\sqrt{25}$

2. When all nine pieces fit together, how many of the small squares have unmatched answers on more than one side? Explain your answer.

    Answer: _____

Game Squares for *It All Adds Up!*

Copy this page and cut apart the squares to make a set of nine game pieces.

$\sqrt{16} + 3^2$ $\frac{1}{5}$ of 75 $\frac{1}{6}$ of 120 $70 \div \sqrt{4}$	$10 - \sqrt{1}$ 0.025×120 5×9 4^2	$11 - 3$ 9% of 100 $7 \times \sqrt{25}$ $1^2 + 2^2 - 4$
$3^3 - 11$ $3 \times 7 - 1$ 18% of 50 $13 + 8$	3×5 $2^2 + 3$ $\sqrt{25} \times 2^2$ $2^2 \times 3$	$\frac{1}{8}$ of 88 $\frac{1}{2}$ of 10×3^2 $(3 \times 6) - 3$ $1 + 7$
6×0.5 $\sqrt{49}$ 100^0 $85^0 + 10^1$	$40 - \sqrt{25}$ 50% of 40 $\frac{1}{7}$ of 49 $(2^2 \times 3^2) \div 4$	20% of 60 4×5 $\frac{1}{3}$ of 9 $4^2 - 3$

Review

Review What You Learned

In this unit you have used mathematics to solve many problems. You have used mental math and estimation, practiced basic operations, solved equations, and used statistics, ratios, and proportions.

These two pages give you a chance to review the mathematics you used and check your skills.

✔ Check Your Skills

1. Korey and Joe share a student apartment. They share equally the cost of rent, utilities, food, and miscellaneous living expenses. Korey draws a circle graph to show their total costs for this month.

   a. What fraction of the total is the rent?

   b. What amount does each student budget for these expenses per month?

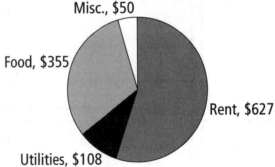

Misc., $50
Food, $355
Rent, $627
Utilities, $108

   Answer: a. _____

   b. _____

   If you need to review, return to lesson 1 (page 2).

2. Out of his monthly income of $1,900, Seb budgets $125 for new kiteboarding equipment.

   a. Seb budgets _____% of his monthly income for kiteboarding equipment.

   b. He plans to continue to budget $125 each month toward this equipment. Which equation gives the amount he has after three months?

   A $\frac{x}{125} = \frac{1}{3}$ **C** $\frac{x}{1} = \frac{125}{3}$

   B $\frac{x}{3} = \frac{125}{1}$ **D** $\frac{x}{3} = \frac{1}{125}$

   If you need to review, return to lesson 2 (page 4).

3. Arno keeps $1,000 in his checking account. When this grows to $2,000, he transfers $1,000 to his savings account.

    a. What is the percent increase in his checking account just before he transfers funds out? Circle the percent inside the circle.

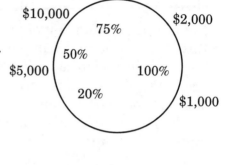

Arno keeps $5,000 in his savings account. When this grows by the same percent increase, he transfers the excess to an investment account.

    b. How much does his savings account grow to before he transfers funds out? Circle the dollar amount outside the circle.

If you need to review, return to lesson 3 (page 6).

4. Brenda's bank offers free checking when she maintains a minimum daily balance of $1,000. When she does *not* maintain this minimum daily balance, the bank charges a fee. The fee includes a $5 monthly service charge, and a $0.05 transaction charge. Brenda maintains a minimum daily balance of $800. Which equation gives Brenda's bank fee for one month?

    A $f = \$5 \times t + \$0.05$ **C** $f = \$0.05 \times t + \$800$

    B $f = \$0.05 \times t + \$200$ **D** $f = \$0.05 \times t + \$5$

If you need to review, return to lesson 4 (page 8).

Write Your Own Problem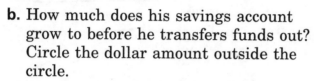

Choose a problem you liked from this unit. Write a similar problem using a situation and related facts from your own life. With a partner, share and solve these problems together. Discuss the mathematics and compare the steps you used. If you need to, rewrite or correct the problems. Write your edited problem and the answer here.

Buying Large Items

Preview

How You Will Use This Unit

Buying large items involves many different things. Buying a home or a car are just two examples. You probably also consider other large expenses such as college and insurance. As you compare options and make choices, you will often use math. The math skills you use include mental math and estimation, basic operations and equations, statistics, and ratios and proportions.

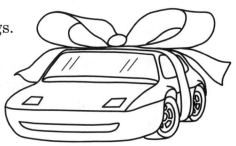

What You Will Do in This Unit

In this unit, math steps demonstrate how to solve problems. These steps can help you answer questions such as these:

A car salesperson offers you two payment plans. You can pay for your car in 12 months. Or, with $1,000 down, you can pay $25 less and pay for the car in 8 months. What is the price of the car?

You want to borrow $35,000 to buy a house. For a 30-year loan at an 8% interest rate, your monthly payments will be about 0.7% of the loan. About how much are your monthly payments?

You are going to technical school. To cover your expenses, you borrow $4,000 for two years at 8.5% interest rate, compounded annually. How much will you owe at the end of the second year?

You spend $133 of your monthly income of $1,250 on health insurance. Beth spends the same fraction of her monthly income of $1,440 on health insurance. How much does she spend on health insurance each month?

What You Can Learn from This Unit

When you complete this unit, you will have used mathematics to work problems related to buying large items. These problems are similar to those that may actually occur in your daily life.

Lesson 1

Example Angelina visits several car dealerships, and finally decides on which used car to buy. The salesperson offers her two 0%-interest payment plans. She writes notes of these details.

i. With no down payment, she pays for the car in twelve equal monthly installments.

ii. With a down payment of $1,200, she pays $40 less per month over ten months.

But what is the price of the car?

Solve

Step 1: Write an equation for the first payment plan. Use p for the price of the car. Use x for the amount she pays each month.

$12x = p$ 12 months at x dollars per month gives the total.

Step 2: Now, write an equation for the second payment plan.

$\$1,200 + 10(x - \$40) = p$ Down payment + 10 months of (x less $40) is the total.

Step 3: Solve this system of two equations to find the value of p.

$x = \dfrac{p}{12}$ Use the first equation to write x in terms of p.

$\$1,200 + 10(\dfrac{p}{12} - \$40) = p$ Substitute $\dfrac{p}{12}$ for x in the second equation.

$\$1,200 + \dfrac{10}{12}p - \$400 = p$ Apply the Distributive Property to multiply 10.

$\$800 = p - \dfrac{5}{6}p$ Combine terms and simplify.

$\$800 = \dfrac{1}{6}p$ Think of p as $\dfrac{6}{6}p$ and subtract.

$6(\$800) = 6(\dfrac{1}{6}p)$ Multiply each side by the denominator.

$\$4,800 = p$ Simplify.

Answer the Question

Step 4: The price of the car is $4,800.

✏ Now try these problems.

1. Calvin visits several car dealerships, and finally decides which used car to buy. The salesperson offers him two 0%-interest payment plans. He notes these details.

---

i. With no down payment, he pays for the car in twelve equal monthly installments.

ii. With a down payment of $750, he pays $25 less per month over ten months.

What is the price of the car?

Answer: The price of the car is $_____.

2. The motorbike that Faye likes has a price tag of $16,900. She makes a table to show various 0%-interest payment plans to pay off the bike. Which entries are not correct? Circle each incorrect entry. What error did Faye make?

0%-interest plans	Pay off in 1 year	Pay off in 2 years	Pay off in 3 years
$1,000 down payment	$1,325/month	$662.50/month	$441.67/month
$2,000 down payment	$1,241.67/month	$620.83/month	$413.89/month
$5,000 down payment	$1,158.33/month	$579.17/month	$386.11/month

Answer: _____

3. Brett looks at a new truck that costs $26,000. He reads that a new vehicle goes down in value each year by an amount equal to 17% of the original price. What is the value of the truck at the end of three years?

　　A $12,339　　　B $12,740　　　C $14,866　　　D $17,911

4. Danna shops for a used car. One car with basic accessories and no alarm system, costs $5,400. Exactly the same car but with all the accessories and an alarm system, costs $1,200 more. Danna's $1,600 annual insurance cost will go down by 9% with an alarm system. She plans to pay off the car in one year. Fill in the cost details for each car. Which car would you buy? Why?

Car 1: Car cost:　$5,400　　　　**Car 2:** Car cost:　$_____

　　　　　Insurance: $_____　　　　　　Insurance: $_____

　　　　　Total cost: $_____　　　　　　Total cost: $_____

Answer: _____

☆ *Challenge Problem*
You may want to talk this one over with a partner.

You buy a used car for $4,300 that you will pay for by credit card. You pay $1,000 down. You plan to pay off the car in monthly installments over 3 years. The bank that issued your credit card charges an annual interest rate of 19.8%. Each month the bank charges interest on unpaid balances. You make no more purchases. How much interest do you pay at the end of the first month?　　$_____

Example Tandy thinks about buying a house that is valued at $75,000. He can make a $10,000 down payment. He will need to borrow the rest

from a mortgage company. His uncle gives him a good rule to use for a rough approximation of his monthly payments. For a 30-year loan at an 8% interest rate, his monthly payments will be about 0.7% of the amount he borrows. What is an approximation of Tandy's monthly payments by this rule?

Solve

Step 1: Compute the amount that Tandy will owe on a $75,000 house, after he puts $10,000 down.

$75,000 − $10,000 = $65,000

Step 2: Now, use his uncle's rule to find an approximation for one monthly payment.

$$\text{One monthly payment} = 0.7\% \text{ of } \$65,000$$
$$= \frac{0.7}{100} \times \$65,000$$
$$= \frac{7}{1,000} \times \$65,000$$
$$= \$455$$

Answer the Question

Step 3: Tandy can expect his monthly payments to be approximately $455.

✐ Now try these problems.

1. Claudette is buying a house that is valued at $35,000. She can make a $5,000 down payment. She needs to borrow the rest. She uses the following rule for a rough approximation of her monthly payments: For a 30-year loan at an 8% interest rate, the monthly payment is about 0.7% of the amount. What is an approximation of Claudette's monthly payment by this rule?

   Answer: Claudette can expect her monthly payment to be

   approximately $_____.

2. Gene can make a $20,000 down payment on a house valued at $70,000. He estimates his monthly payments for a 30-year loan on the remainder to be about 0.7% of the amount he borrows. He

asks his realtor about a 15-year mortgage. His realtor says that if Gene can afford $100 more each month, he can afford a 15-year mortgage. What is an approximation of Gene's monthly payment for a 15-year mortgage?

A $140 **B** $350 **C** $450 **D** $490

3. Mort asks his bank representative about getting a mortgage loan. His bank representative tells him that they use 28% of his gross salary to estimate the monthly payment he can afford on a loan. Mort's gross salary, including bonuses and before taxes, is $24,000. One rule says that the monthly payments on a 30-year loan at an 8% interest rate is about 0.7% of the loan amount. What size loan can Mort get? Use d for the loan. Use p for his monthly payment. Fill in the blanks to find the answer.

$p \approx$ _____% × ($24,000 ÷ 12)   bank's estimate of monthly payment

$\approx$ $_____

$p \approx 0.7\%d$ rule's estimate of monthly payment

so $d \approx p \div 0.7\%$

$d \approx$ $_____ $\div 0.7\%$ substitute the bank's value for p

so $d \approx$ $_____   the approximate size of the loan Mort can get

4. Jassica's bank charges 1% of any mortgage loan as a fee. Jassica gets a $60,000 mortgage. Shade the number of squares that represents the fee she must pay if all 100 squares together represent $10,000.

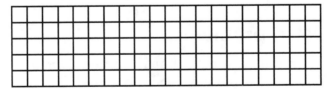

☆ Challenge Problem

You may want to talk this one over with a partner.

Eduardo and Malika's house is assessed at a value of $65,000. Compute the total real-estate taxes they pay, given the tax-rate table.

Taxing Body	Tax rate	Taxes owed
State	0.02%	
County	0.62%	
Town	0.44%	
School District	1.47%	
Library	0.12%	
TOTAL ANNUAL TAXES		

College Costs

Example Linden is going to a dental technical college. To cover his expenses, he borrows $5,000 for three years at 7.5% interest rate per year, compounded annually. Make a table that shows how much he owes at the end of each year.

Solve

Step 1: First, define these four column headings for the table.

Year, Balance at start of year, Interest due, Balance at end of year.

Step 2: For year 1, calculate the interest due and the balance at the end of the year.

year 1:
interest due = 7.5% of $5,000   yearly interest rate
                                        × original loan.

             = 0.075 × $5,000

             = $375

balance at   balance at start
end of year = $5,375   + interest due

Step 3: Repeat the process for years 2 and 3.

year 2:
interest due = 7.5% of $5,375   rate × balance at
                                        start of year 2

             = $403.13

balance at   balance at start of
end of year = $5,778.13   year 2 + interest

year 3:
interest due = 7.5% of $5,778.13

             = $433.36

balance at   balance at start of
end of year = $6,211.49   year 3 + interest

Answer the Question

Step 4:

Year	Balance at start of year	Interest due	Balance at end of year
1	$5,000	$375	$5,375
2	$5,375	$403.13	$5,778.13
3	$5,778.13	$433.36	$6,211.49

✏ Now try these problems.

1. Melody is going to a fashion merchandising school. To cover her expenses, she borrows $4,000 for two years at 8.5% yearly interest rate, compounded annually. How much will she owe at the end of the second year?

    A $340   **B** $4,340   **C** $4,680   **D** $4,708.90

2. Marissa loans her nephew $3,000 for a 3-month trip to Europe. She charges him 5% yearly simple interest for the two years that he owes her the money. Draw a pie chart that relates these three amounts: the interest, the original loan and the total amount he owes after two years.

3. Asami wins a scholarship for $6,000 to be used for enrichment courses. The first year she uses $2,500. She invests $2,000 in a bank and earns 2% simple interest annually. She loans the rest to a friend for one year at 5% simple interest. At the end of the first year, how much can she expect to have available to take more courses? Arrange these pieces of the puzzle to create an equation that gives this amount. Fill in the blank puzzle piece with that amount.

    | $2,000 | = | + | 1.02 | $____ |

    | 1.05 | × | $1,500 | × |

    Answer: _____

4. Before going to technical school, Rubin works at a computer store. For three years, he puts $1,500 into a savings account at the first of each year. His savings account earns 5% simple interest per year. At the end of each year, he takes out the interest and puts it into a special envelope. Which expression gives the total amount he will have at the end of three years in his account and his envelope?

    A $3(1,500 \times 1.05) + 2(\$1,500 \times 1.05) + (\$1,500 \times 1.05)$

    B $3(1,500 \times 0.05) + 2(\$1,500 \times 0.05) + (\$1,500 \times 0.05)$

    C $\$1,500 + 5(1,500 \times 0.05) + (\$1,500 \times 1.05)$

    D $\$4,500 + 6(1,500 \times 0.05)$

☆ Challenge Problem
You may want to talk this one over with a partner.

One report says it will cost about $237,000 (including inflation) to raise a child born in 1999, over the next 17 years. (These costs include food, shelter, and other necessities.) Does this mean that the costs in the first year in high school will be $13,941? Explain your answer.

_____

_____

Lesson 4

What Do You Owe?

♟ A Board Game (for Two or More Players)

The goal of this game is to be the first player to reach 25 points or more. First, you take the top flowchart card. Then you apply a number to the flowchart and calculate the answer.

Materials

Flowchart cards (on the next page; players can make up more), and two number cubes

Directions

1. Shuffle flowchart cards, and place them, face down, in the center of the table. Sit with players around the table. One player records player scores.

2. Player 1 tosses the number cubes and adds the two numbers. Player 1 then takes the top flowchart card. This player uses the sum in the flowchart as the value of *INPUT,* and calculates the *OUTPUT.* Other players check the answer. If the answer is correct, the player gets 2 points. If it is incorrect, the first player who calculates the correct value for *OUTPUT* gets 1 point. The flowchart card is discarded to a separate deck.

3. Player 2 then takes a turn. This player can choose to toss the number cubes again, or to use player 1's *OUTPUT* as the next *INPUT* value. Player 2 takes one card from the flowchart card deck and calculates the *OUTPUT.*

4. Players take turns taking a flowchart card, applying a number, and calculating the *OUTPUT.* Replace the flowchart card deck with the shuffled discard deck.

5. The game is over when one player's score is equal to or greater than 25 points.

✎ Before you play the game, try these warm-up problems.

1. Toni tosses the number cubes and gets 9. Her flowchart card says to multiply by 2. If the result is greater than or equal to 40, multiply by $\frac{1}{8}$ for the *OUTPUT.* Otherwise multiply by 2 again, until the result is greater than or equal to 40, and then multiply by $\frac{1}{8}$ for the *OUTPUT.* What is Toni's *OUTPUT?*

2. Andy starts with Toni's *OUTPUT.* His flowchart card says to add 16. If the result is greater than 24, multiply by 40%. In both cases, then divide by 2. What is his *OUTPUT?*

   A 2   **B** 3.5   **C** 5   **D** 10

Flowchart cards for *What Do You Owe?*

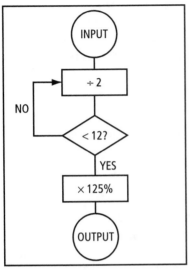

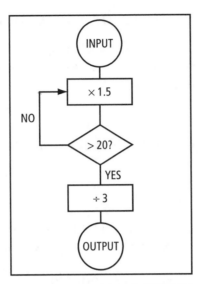

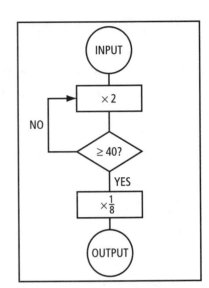

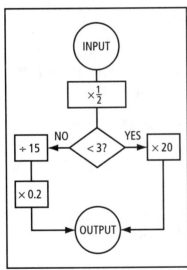

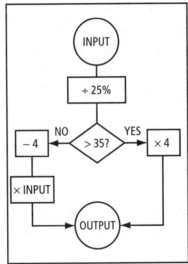

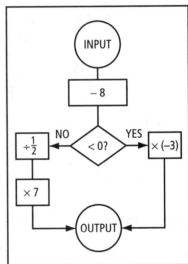

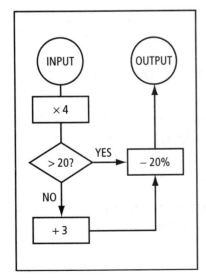

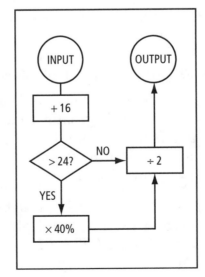

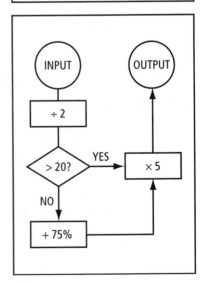

Lesson 5

Example Talaitha spends $260 of her monthly income on health insurance. She earns $34,320 per year. Annika spends the same fraction of her monthly income on health insurance. She earns $22,440 per year. How much does Annika spend on health insurance each month?

Solve

Step 1: First, find what fraction of Talaitha's monthly income she spends on health insurance. Calculate her income per month. Then find the fraction.

$34,320 \div 12 = $2,860$

$\frac{\$260}{\$2,860} = \frac{1}{11}$ health insurance payment as a fraction of monthly income

Step 2: Now, find the same fraction of Annika's income.

$\frac{1}{11}$ of $22,440 = $2,040$ This is Annika's *annual* health insurance.

$2,040 \div 12 = 170

Answer the Question

Step 3: Annika spends $170 on health insurance each month.

✐ Now try these problems.

1. Reed spends $133 of his monthly income on car insurance. He earns $14,364 per year. Luther spends the same fraction of his monthly income on health insurance. He earns $17,280 per year.

   a. What fraction of his monthly income does Luther spend on health insurance?

   b. How much does Luther spend on health insurance each month?

   Answer: a. Luther spends _____ of his monthly income on health insurance.

            b. Luther spends $_____ per month on health insurance.

2. For $500, Cat can buy insurance for her new house. But this insurance does not include insurance against water damage from broken pipes. For $1,600 she can buy insurance that does cover water damage. Suppose she buys the policy that does not include

insurance against water damage. Now suppose she goes three years without water damage, and puts the difference in a savings account. How much does Cat save?

A $1,500   **B** $3,300   **C** $4,800   **D** $6,300

3. Jerilee buys a basic health insurance policy. The company offers a rider costing $24 per month that will pay for office visits. Her doctor's office tells her that the average cost for a visit is $80. Usually Jerilee visits the doctor twice a year. Answer the questions, and state your conclusion.

Answer: a. For the office visit rider, Jerilee pays $_____ this year.

b. For two office visits (without the rider) she pays $_____.

c. Jerilee would have saved money by _____ (buying/ not buying) the office visit rider.

4. Davis buys a new bike for $285. It has a 5-year guarantee. Twelve months later it is stolen from the garage. Davis makes an insurance claim based on a fraction of the bike's original price. This fraction is equal to the time left on the guarantee divided by the total years of the guarantee. Make a table to show the value of the bike after 1, 2, 3, 4, and 5 years. Circle the value of the bike that Davis can expect the insurance company to pay.

Years after purchase	Time left on guarantee / total years	Value
1		
2		
3		
4		
5		

☆ Challenge Problem
You may want to talk this one over with a partner.

You have basic car insurance that does not include towing. Last year, your truck broke down twice, and you paid $50 and $110 to get towed. For an extra $18 per year you can add towing coverage to your policy. The insurance company will then pay up to $75 per towing. Would you pay the extra $18 to add towing coverage to your policy? Explain your answer.

_____

_____

Review What You Learned

In this unit you have used mathematics to solve many problems. You have used mental math and estimation, practiced basic operations, solved equations, and used statistics, ratios, and proportions.

These two pages give you a chance to review the mathematics you used and check your skills.

✔ Check Your Skills

1. Audrey finally decides which car to buy. The salesperson offers her two 0%-interest payment plans. These are the details.
   i. With no down payment, she pays for the car in twenty-four equal monthly installments.
   ii. With a down payment of $2,500, she pays $50 less per month over twenty months.

   Write two equations to find the price of the car. What does Audrey pay per month with no down payment? What is the price of the car?

   Answer: _____ _____

       Audrey pays $_____ per month with no down payment.

       The price of the car is $_____.

   If you need to review, return to lesson 1 (page 15).

2. Moneya is buying a house that is valued at $45,000. She can make a $5,000 down payment. She needs to borrow the rest from a loan company. For a 30-year loan at an 8% interest rate, her monthly payments will be about 0.7% of the amount she owes. Which expression gives an approximation of Moneya's monthly payments?

   A $0.7 \times \$40,000$ **C** $0.007 \times \$40,000$

   B $0.07 \times \$40,000$ **D** $0.0007 \times \$40,000$

   If you need to review, return to lesson 2 (page 17).

3. Brody is going to technical school. To cover his expenses, he borrows $6,000 for two years at 6.5% yearly interest rate, compounded annually. He makes a table that shows how much

he will owe at the end of each year. Are his figures correct? Make any necessary changes.

Year	Balance at start of year	Interest incurred	Balance at end of year
1	$6,000	$390	$6,390
2	$6,390	$830.70	$7,220.70

If you need to review, return to lesson 3 (page 19).

4. James spends $142.92 of his monthly income on car insurance. He earns $14,292 per year. Hal spends the same fraction of his monthly income on car insurance. He earns $16,500 per year.

   a. Draw a diagram to show what fraction of his monthly income Hal spends on car insurance.

   b. How much does Hal spend on car insurance each month?

   Diagram a.

   Answer: b. Hal spends $_____ on car insurance each month.
   If you need to review, return to lesson 5 (page 23).

5. Kay buys a basic health-insurance policy. The company offers a rider for office visits for $15 per month. The average cost for an office visit is $75. She usually visits the doctor three times a year.

   Kay would save money by _____ (buying/not buying) the office visit rider.

   If you need to review, return to lesson 5 (page 23).

Write Your Own Problem ✍🏻

Choose a problem you liked from this unit. Write a similar problem using a situation and related facts from your own life. With a partner, share and solve these problems together. Discuss the mathematics and compare the steps you used. If you need to, rewrite or correct the problems. Write your edited problem and the answer here.

_____

_____

_____

_____

_____

Unit 3

Unplanned Expenses

Preview

How You Will Use This Unit

Unplanned expenses may involve many different things. Unexpected changes in rent, bills, medical or dental care, and unexpected repairs are some examples. Unanticipated gifts and weekend trips are other examples. As you handle unplanned expenses, you will often use math. The math skills you use include mental math and estimation, basic operations and equations, statistics, and ratios and proportions.

What You Will Do in This Unit

In this unit, math steps demonstrate how to solve problems. These steps can help you answer questions such as these:

Last winter, your electricity bill was $85 per month. In the summer, this amount doubled. You now budget the maximum amount each month. How much do you budget for November?

You go online to look for the prescription drug that your doctor recommends. The drug costs $56. Priority mail is free for orders over $49, and $8.99 for second-day service. How much less do you pay if you order by priority mail?

You get another heel dent in your sailboard. Last week, you got a heel dent repaired for $300. You think that this one is only half as bad as the last one. What can you expect to pay this time?

You buy a cake, a card, and a CD for a friend's birthday. The cake costs one third of the money in your wallet. The CD costs as much as the cake. The card costs one quarter the cost of the cake. What fraction of the money that you start with do you have after buying everything?

What You Can Learn from This Unit

When you complete this unit, you will have used mathematics to work problems related to unplanned expenses. These problems are similar to those that may actually occur in your daily life.

Example Last summer, Charlene's average electricity bill was about $99 per month. During the winter, her average electricity bill was about $150 per month. She had to borrow money to pay for this unexpected increase. Charlene now budgets each month the higher average monthly amount. She also budgets for the recent 5% increase in electricity rates. How much does she budget for electricity for next July?

Solve

Step 1: Underline the words that tell you the higher average amount that Charlene paid per month for electricity last year.

... her average electricity bill was about $150 per month.

Step 2: Underline the sentence that tells you about any changes in electricity rates.

She also budgets for the recent 5% increase in electricity rates.

Step 3: Calculate the monthly amount that Charlene budgets for this year, including the increase.

105% of $150 = 1.05 × $150
= $157.50

Step 4: Draw a conclusion about what Charlene will budget for electricity in July.

$157.50   She budgets the same amount each month.

Answer the Question

Step 5: Charlene budgets $157.50 for electricity in July.

✏ Now try these problems.

1. Last year, Alfonso's average telephone bill was about $65 per month. Since he moved away to tech school, his average telephone bill increased to about $110 per month. Last month, he had to borrow money to cover this unexpected increase. He now budgets the higher amount per month to cover his telephone bill. What is his annual budget for telephone use now?

   Answer: Alfonso's annual budget for telephone use is $_____.

2. Libby is surprised to see a bank charge of $17.20 on her bank statement this month. The bank says that she did not maintain a minimum daily balance of $2,000. This means that she must pay a $3 service fee plus 10 cents for each transaction. There is also a fee of $12 for a lost check on which she stopped payment.

    a. How many transactions did she have this month? Circle that amount.

      10   22   30   52   172

    b. How much did it cost her to have her daily balance fall below $2,000? Draw a rectangle around that amount.

    $3 $3.10 $5.20 $12 $17.20

3. This month, the air conditioning costs Melvyn an extra $75 to run. Last month, his telephone bill cost him an extra $120. The month before that, he paid $45 to replace a lost contact lens. Imagine you are Melvyn. On average, how much would you put aside per month for unexpected expenses like these? Explain your answer.

    A $45   **B** $75   **C** $80   **D** $120

Explanation: _____

4. Each September, Berta renews her rental contract. This year her rent goes up by 10% from the previous year's $545 per month. Each box represents $54.50. Shade the number of boxes that show her new rent.

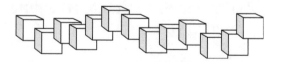

☆ *Challenge Problem*
You may want to talk this one over with a partner.

You and your friend each have a number. These two numbers add to 5, 10, or 21. You have 7. You ask if your friend knows your number. Your friend replies, No. What number does your friend have? How do you know that number?

_____

_____

_____

Lesson 2 → Doctors, Dentists, & Veterinarians

Example Pierce goes online to look for the diabetes testing kit that his doctor recommends. He finds a website that lists the kit. It costs $74 and weighs 2 lbs. He consults the table of shipping rates on that website. How much *less* does he pay for 5–7 day priority mail than for next-day service?

Shipping Rates	
5–7 day priority mail/UPS Ground	Free (for orders over $49)
5–7 day priority mail/UPS Ground	$3.99 (for orders under $49)
Second-day service	$8.99 + $1.50 per lb over 1 lb
Next-day service	$14.99 + $3.00 per lb over 1 lb

Solve

Step 1: Underline the line in the table that tells the rate for next-day service. Then find the exact rate that Pierce would pay for this service.

<u>Next-day service $14.99 + $3.00 per lb over 1 lb</u>

Pierce would pay $17.99   His order weighs 2 lbs.

Step 2: Pierce's order is over $49. Find the line for 5–7 day priority mail when an order is that size.

<u>5–7 day priority mail/UPS Ground   free (for orders over $49)</u>

Step 3: Write an expression for the difference in rates.
$17.99 – $0 = $17.99

Answer the Question

Step 4: Pierce pays $17.99 less for 5–7 day priority mail than for next-day service.

✏ Now try these problems.

Use the shipping rates table above.

1. Chase goes online to look for the prescription drug that her veterinarian recommends. The website lists the drug for $25, and the package weighs less than 1 lb. She consults the table of shipping rates. How much *more* does she pay for next-day service than for second-day service?

Answer: Chase pays $_____ more for next-day service than for second-day service.

2. Carolee has to go out of town unexpectedly. She asks her veterinarian if he knows of a cat-sitting service. The veterinarian says his assistant will make a pet visit twice a day for $10 per day. Carolee pays him $50. How many visits does he make?

     A 5   **B** 10   **C** 15   **D** 20

3. Philo cracks his tooth in an accident on the exercise equipment at school. The dentist charges him $110 for X-rays and $650 for a cap on the tooth. The charge is $35 for a final check-up. Philo pays the total bill in equal monthly installments over the next six months. How much does Philo pay in each installment? Complete the following expression to show this amount.

($110 + $_____ + $_____) ÷ ____ = $_____

4. Shelley goes to the hospital emergency room for a stomach problem. The visit costs her $135. Her insurance deductible is $2,000. So far, she has paid $1,365 of this deductible. Circle the drawing that shows the percent of her deductible left after she pays the $135 bill.

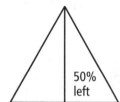
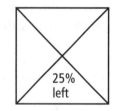

☆ *Challenge Problem*
You may want to talk this one over with a partner.

Look at the figure below that shows the first 5 rows of a number triangle. Find the mean of the first and last term for each row. Write this mean to the right of each row. Predict the mean of the first and last term for row 100.

Answer: The mean of the first and last term for row 100 is _____.
        Explain your reasoning.

_____   1   _____

                                   3 5   _____

_____   7 9 11 _____

                               13 15 17 19 _____

_____ 21 23 25 27 29 _____

_____

Lesson 3

Careful Spending

♟ A Board Game (for Two or More Players)

The goal of this game is to cross out two numbers in each row and each column, until each row and column is left with four numbers that add to 10. First, you check numbers in a row and in an intersecting column. Then you cross out the number at the intersection, as long as this moves you one step closer to the goal of the game.

Materials

Game board (on the next page) and pencils

Directions

1. Give each player a pencil. Sit with players around the game board.

2. Following these two rules, player 1 crosses out one number on the board:
   (i) Four or more numbers must remain in the row and in the column after the number is crossed out.
   (ii) Check the sum of the uncrossed-out numbers in each row and each column. It must be possible for the four numbers remaining at the end of the game to add to 10.

3. Players take turns testing and checking numbers on the board. Each player crosses out one number to approach the goal of the game.

4. The game is over when the goal of the game is achieved: (a) the four numbers remaining in each row add to 10 and (b) the four numbers remaining in each column add to 10.

✎ **Before you play the game, try these warm-up problems.**

1. Paulette crosses out the 7 in row 4, column 2. Which numbers can be crossed out in row 4 or column 2 to satisfy the rules of *Careful Spending*?

   Answer: _____ in row 4, and _____ in column 2.

2. Ralph follows Paulette's move. He crosses out the 1 in row 1, column 2. Sara follows Ralph. What number can she cross out to satisfy the rules of *Careful Spending*?

   A 5 in row 1, column 5   **C** 2 in row 1 column 1

   B 4 in row 1, column 6   **D** 2 in row 1, column 3

Game Board for *Careful Spending*

2	1	2	2	5	4
5	1	1	6	2	3
3	3	5	1	3	1
1	7	6	1	1	2
2	5	1	4	1	3
4	1	2	4	2	3

Lesson 4 ➝ *Unplanned Repairs*

Example Alton blows out his windsurfer sail during the beach festival. *On-the-Spot Repairs* advertises that they can repair sails inexpensively and overnight. Alton's friend Court says that the cost of sail repair is approximately proportional to the size of the sail. Court's sail is $\frac{2}{3}$ the size of Alton's sail. Court paid $300 to have his sail repaired. What can Alton expect the approximate cost of his repair to be?

Solve

Step 1: Use x for the size of Alton's sail. Write a ratio that compares the size of Alton's sail to Court's sail.

Alton's ÷ Court's $x \div \frac{2}{3}x$ which simplifies to
$$1/(\tfrac{2}{3}) \text{ or } \tfrac{3}{2}$$

Step 2: Underline the words that tell you how size and cost of repair are related.

... the cost of sail repair is <u>approximately proportional to the size of the sail.</u>

Step 3: Write a ratio to compare Alton's repairs (y) to Court's repairs.

Alton's ÷ Court's $\dfrac{y}{\$300}$

Step 4: Write a proportion by setting the two ratios equal.

$$\frac{\text{A's size}}{\text{C's size}} = \frac{\text{A's cost}}{\text{C's cost}} \quad \text{so} \quad \frac{3}{2} = \frac{y}{\$300}$$

Step 5: Solve the proportion for y, the cost of repairing Alton's sail.

$\dfrac{3}{2} = \dfrac{y}{\$300}$ Cross multiply.

$2y = \$300 \times 3$

$2y = \$900$ Divide each side by 2.

$y = \$450$

Answer the Question

Step 6: Alton can expect the cost of his repair to be about $450.

Now try these problems.

1. A storm damages Jody's computer. She pays $180 to have it repaired. She also buys a surge protector. The cost of the surge protector is $\frac{1}{5}$ of the total bill (repairs and protector). Complete this equation you could use to solve for the cost of the surge protector, x.

    _____ / _____ = $\frac{1}{5}$

2. The garage tells Ryanna that they can replace the bug shield catch on her car for $130. The bug shield is an optional accessory. Ryanna has the bug shield removed at no cost. She sells the bug shield to her brother for $20. How much does she save? Explain your answer.

    Answer: _____

3. Tyson pays $85 to get his truck towed to the nearest repair shop. The shop keeps the truck for 2 days, and charges him $150 to make the repair. A rental car would cost about $45 per day. Tyson has insurance to cover the cost of a rental car, but not to cover towing. How much does the problem with his truck cost him per day?

    A $117.50   **B** $162.50   **C** $235   **D** $280

4. On the coldest day of the year, Verity's furnace breaks. The repair costs her $520. Verity's emergency fund has $350 in it. She adds $25 to the fund each month. The repair shop allows her to pay $100 right away, and $50 per month without interest. Complete the table and fill in the blanks.

Month		0	1	2	3	4	5	6	7	8	9	10	11
Balance of repair bill	$520	$420											
Emergency fund	$350												

    a. It takes Verity _____ months to pay off the bill.

    b. Verity has $_____ left in her emergency fund when the repair bill is paid off.

☆ *Challenge Problem*
You may want to talk this one over with a partner.

You drive an old car. You have an unexpected fender-bender accident. A local body shop gives you a quote of $250 to replace the fender. A friend tells you to take the car to the local vocational tech school. They pound out the fender and repaint it. They charge $20. What sort of donation do you make to the school?

_____

_____

Lesson 5 → *Gifts, Flowers, & Unexpected Trips*

Example Lena promises to pick up a cake for her best friend's birthday party. The cake costs one third of the money that she has in her wallet. She buys a birthday card that costs one fourth of the cost of the cake. She also buys a gift of a CD that costs as much as the cake. What fraction of the money that Lena starts out with does she have after buying everything?

Solve

Step 1: Use x for the amount of money that Lena has in her wallet when she starts out. Write an expression for the cost of the cake.

$\frac{1}{3}x$ one third of the money

Step 2: Next, write expressions for the cost of the card and the cost of the CD.

Card: $\frac{1}{4}\left(\frac{1}{3}x\right)$ one fourth of the cost of the cake which simplifies to $\frac{1}{12}x$

CD: $\frac{1}{3}x$ equal to the cost of the cake

Step 3: Now, write an expression for the money that Lena has left over afterwards.

$x - \left(\frac{1}{3}x + \frac{1}{12}x + \frac{1}{3}x\right)$ Find the common

$x - \left(\frac{4}{12} + \frac{1}{12} + \frac{4}{12}\right)x$ denominator for the fractions and add.

$x - \frac{9}{12}x$

$x - \frac{3}{4}x$

$\frac{1}{4}x$

Answer the Question

Step 4: Lena has $\frac{1}{4}$ of the money she starts out with after buying everything.

✐ Now try these problems.

1. Faulkner buys paper, tape, and glue for his project. The paper costs one half of the money in his wallet. The tape and the glue each costs one third of the cost of the paper. Faulkner also picks up cookies for half the cost of the tape.

a. What fraction of the money that Faulkner starts out with does he have afterwards?

b. This line represents the money that Faulkner starts out with. Mark distances on the line, one after the other, to show the fraction that each purchase represents.

Answer: a. Faulkner has _____ of the money that he starts out with.

b. └───┘

2. Marisela decides to buy gift items when she sees them on sale. This way, she has gifts ready for birthdays, and she also saves money. On Saturday, she buys items marked with these sale prices: a book for $5.98, a game for $9.99, and a candle for $4.59. These prices are half of the normal price. How much does she save?

   A $6.85   **B** $10.28   **C** $20.56   **D** $41.12

3. On Tuesday morning, Javier's boss asks Javier to go to a meeting in town. The company pays for Javier's mileage and lunch. Javier stays in town and eats supper with friends. He spends $12.75. He usually spends $5 for lunch out and $4 to prepare supper. How much more or less than usual did he spend for this special day? Explain your answer.

   Answer: He spent $_____ _____ (more/less).

4. Ane reviews last year's pattern of unplanned expenses. She spent about $18 per month on flowers, except for two months when she spent $72.50 and $59.50. She expects this pattern to continue. What is the average (mean) amount that she should budget per month for flowers next year? Complete this expression to show the amount.

   Answer:

   ($18 × _____ + _____ + _____) ÷ _____ = $_____

☆ Challenge Problem
You may want to talk this one over with a partner.

You go online and find that you can send a gift plant overnight, direct from the growers. One choice is a Chinese Elm Bonsai tree, delivered, for only $43. The normal price for this kind of plant is $64.50. What fraction of the normal price is the advertised price? Explain why, in your opinion, you often pay less for things over the Internet.

_____

_____

Review

Review What You Learned

In this unit you have used mathematics to solve many problems. You have used mental math and estimation, practiced basic operations, solved equations, and used statistics, ratios, and proportions.

These two pages give you a chance to review the mathematics you used and check your skills.

✔ Check Your Skills

1. Last winter, Caylor's average electricity bill was about $85 per month. During the summer, his average electricity bill was about $175 per month. Caylor now budgets the higher monthly amount each month. He also allows for the recent 4% increase in electricity rates. How much does he budget for electricity this November?

   Answer: $_____.

   If you need to review, return to lesson 1 (page 28).

2. Nancy goes online to look for medication that her doctor recommends. She finds a website where it costs $79, and the package weighs less than 1 lb. She consults the table of shipping rates for the website. How much *less* does she pay for 5–7 day priority mail than for second-day service? Fill in the blanks with the data. Answer the question.

Shipping Rates	
5–7 day priority mail/UPS Ground	Free (for orders over $49)
5–7 day priority mail/UPS Ground	$3.99 (for orders under $49)
Second-day service	$8.99 + $1.50 per lb over 1 lb
Next-day service	$14.99 + $3.00 per lb over 1 lb

   Answer: Nancy would pay $_____ for 5–7 day priority mail.

   OR she would pay $_____ for second-day service.

   Nancy would pay $_____ less for 5–7 day priority mail.

   If you need to review, return to lesson 2 (page 30).

3. Linden gets another heel dent in his sailboard. Last week, *On-Time Repairs* repaired a heel dent for him for $300. Linden thinks that this new dent is only half as bad as last week's dent. He expects

the cost of the new repair to be roughly proportional to the previous one. What can he expect to pay to get this new heel dent repaired?

A $75 **B** $150 **C** $300 **D** $450

If you need to review, return to lesson 4 (page 34).

4. Delfino buys sandwiches, chips, and drinks for the team after the ball game. The sandwiches cost one half of the money he has in his wallet. The chips and the drinks each cost one quarter of the cost of the sandwiches. What fraction of the money that Delfino starts out with, does he have after buying everything? Draw and label a diagram to show this amount as part of the whole.

If you need to review, return to lesson 5 (page 36).

Write Your Own Problem

Choose a problem you liked from this unit. Write a similar problem using a situation and related facts from your own life. With a partner, share and solve these problems together. Discuss the mathematics and compare the steps you used. If you need to, rewrite or correct the problems. Write your edited problem and the answer here.

_____

_____

_____

_____

_____

_____

_____

_____

Credit Card Budgeting

Preview

How You Will Use This Unit

Credit card budgeting involves many different things. Understanding how a credit card works and what the fine print really says, are two examples. Paying bills by credit card and using credit card services are others. As you compare options and make choices, you will often use math. The math skills you use include mental math and estimation, basic operations and equations, statistics, and ratios and proportions.

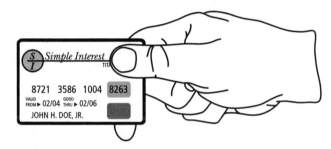

What You Will Do in This Unit

In this unit, math steps demonstrate how to solve problems. These steps can help you answer questions such as these:

You buy a keyboard for $455 and charge it on your credit card. The card company charges 1.9% monthly interest on unpaid balances. After a first payment of $25, what do you owe?

Your credit card offers frequent-flyer miles for an annual fee of $50. Your goal is a 20,000 mile ticket. You charge about $2,500 each year. How much will your ticket cost in annual fees alone?

The closing date for one credit card is the 25th of the month. The closing date for another card is the 15th of the month. You make a purchase on the 7th of the month. Which card allows you use of the money longer?

On May 16th you mail $20 of your $156.50 balance to the credit card company. The closing date is the 16th. Payments not received by that date will cause a late fee. Late fees are $20 on balances up to $150 and $35 on balances over $150. How much do you now owe?

What You Can Learn from This Unit

When you complete this unit, you will have used mathematics to work problems related to credit card budgeting. These problems are similar to those that may actually occur in your daily life.

Lesson 1

How Credit Cards Work

Example Jose buys a boom box for $350 and charges it on his credit card. At the end of the first month, he makes a $50 payment. The credit card company charges 1.5% monthly interest on unpaid balances. After Jose's $50 payment is deducted, interest is computed on the unpaid balance.

a. How much interest does the credit card company charge Jose?

b. This interest is added to the unpaid balance. How much does Jose now owe?

State Bank Credit Card Services			ACCOUNT NAME José Lopez	
PREVIOUS BALANCE	PAYMENTS RECEIVED	NEW PURCHASES	INTEREST	UNPAID BALANCE
$100	$100	$350	$0	$350
DATE OF PURCHASE	ITEM			PRICE
10/1/03	Boom box			$350

Solve

Step 1: First, find the amount that Jose has left to pay after his first month's payment.

$350 − $50 = $300

Step 2: Next, underline the sentence that tells the interest rate that the credit card company charges on unpaid balances.

The credit card company charges 1.5% monthly interest on unpaid balances.

Step 3: Now, find the interest on Jose's unpaid balance.

1.5% of $300
0.015 × $300
$4.50

Step 4: To find how much money Jose owes at the end of the first month, add.

$300 + $4.50 = $304.50   Add the interest to the unpaid balance.

Answer the Question

Step 5: a. The credit card company charges Jose $4.50 interest.
b. He now owes $304.50.

✎ Now try these problems.

1. Kelly buys a new outfit for $212, and charges it on her credit card. At the end of the first month, she makes the minimum payment of

$10. The credit card company charges 2.1% monthly interest on unpaid balances. After Kelly's $10 payment is deducted, interest is computed on the unpaid balance. How much does Kelly owe?

Answer: Kelly now owes $_____.

2. Mae buys an entertainment center on sale for $325, and charges it on her credit card. The credit card company charges 1.8% monthly interest on unpaid balances. Mae pays $50 per month to the credit card company.

   a. Make a table to show how many months it takes for Mae to pay off her purchase.

Month	1	2	3	4	5	6	7	8	9
Payment	$50								
Amount owed									

   b. How much does she pay for the entertainment center?

   Answer: b. Mae pays $_____ for the entertainment center.

3. Duke's bank charges 1.5% monthly interest for a bank credit card. Duke uses his credit card frequently and makes monthly payments every month. But, for a whole year, his unpaid balance stays above $1000. Which estimates the interest that he pays on his unpaid balance over one year?

   A $0.015 \times 12 \times \$1,000 = \$180$ **C** $0.15 \times 12 \times \$1,000 = \$1,800$

   B $0.015 \times \$1,000 = \$15$ **D** $0.15 \times \$1,000 = \$150$

4. The Ellis family has four card holders on one credit card account. The company charges an annual fee of $10 per credit card holder. The company also charges 1.4% monthly interest on unpaid balances. The family's unpaid balance stays at about $1,500, from month to month. About how much does the Ellis family pay for their credit over one year? Show your calculations.

   Answer: _____

☆ *Challenge Problem*
You may want to talk this one over with a partner.

One credit card company charges 12.5% annual interest on unpaid balances. A second credit card company charges 8% annual interest on unpaid balances. The second credit card company charges an annual fee of $35. (The first company charges no fee.) How low does an unpaid balance have to go for the second company's low interest advantage to disappear? Explain your answer.

♠ A Card Game (for Two or More Players)

The goal of this game is to make sets of four equivalent cards. First, a player opens a set with a percent (%) card. Then players build on to that set with equivalent forms of that percent.

Materials

Card deck (on the next page)

Directions

1. Deal six cards to each player. Place the remaining deck of cards face down.

2. Player 1 starts by placing a percent card (a card with a % on it) from their hand face up on the table. Then player 1 draws the top card from the deck to replace the one put down. If player 1 does not have a percent card, the turn passes to the next player, until a player can open a set.

3. Players take turns playing one card per turn (and drawing a replacement card). A player may play a card on any open set or start another set (with another percent card). To play a card on an open set, that card must show an equivalent form of the opening percent card. Any number of sets can be open at once.

4. The player who plays the fourth card on an open set wins the set, and scores 5 points. A wild card may be used in place of any card except a percent (%) card. A player may later replace a wild card on the table with an equivalent card in the set.

5. When the card deck is gone, play continues as long as a player can play a card. The player who goes out first scores 10 points. The winner is the player with the greatest number of points.

✐ Before you play the game, try these warm-up problems.

1. One set is open with the cards 25%, $\frac{25}{100}$, and 0.25. You have the following cards: $\frac{30}{100}$, $\frac{17}{20}$, 0.2, $\frac{1}{4}$, 0.8, and 30%. Which card would you put down and why?

   Answer: _____

2. Zion has a card with $\frac{5}{8}$ on it. On what percent card can he play this card?

   A 20%   **B** 30%   **C** 62.5%   **D** 80%

Card Deck for *Percents*

The card deck is made up of sets of four cards. Each set contains equivalent forms of a percent. (For example, 20%, $\frac{20}{100}$, $\frac{1}{5}$, 0.2, as shown in the card set below.)

Make 13 (or more) sets of four cards for different percent values. Make 2 wild cards. For example, make cards for the following sets of equivalent forms:

1.5%	$\frac{1.5}{100}$	$\frac{3}{200}$	0.015	45%	$\frac{45}{100}$	$\frac{9}{20}$	0.45
5%	$\frac{5}{100}$	$\frac{1}{20}$	0.05	50%	$\frac{50}{100}$	$\frac{1}{2}$	0.5
10%	$\frac{10}{100}$	$\frac{1}{10}$	0.1	62.5%	$\frac{62.5}{100}$	$\frac{5}{8}$	0.625
12.5%	$\frac{12.5}{100}$	$\frac{1}{8}$	0.125	75%	$\frac{75}{100}$	$\frac{3}{4}$	0.75
20%	$\frac{20}{100}$	$\frac{1}{5}$	0.2	85%	$\frac{85}{100}$	$\frac{17}{20}$	0.85
25%	$\frac{25}{100}$	$\frac{1}{4}$	0.25	90%	$\frac{90}{100}$	$\frac{9}{10}$	0.9
30%	$\frac{30}{100}$	$\frac{3}{10}$	0.3				

20%	$\dfrac{20}{100}$	$\dfrac{1}{5}$	**0.2**

Make two wild cards:

Lesson 3

Example Denna charges her new bicycle on her credit card. The bike is on sale for $175. (The regular price is $256.) She makes no more purchases with her credit card. At the end of each month she pays $40. The credit card company charges her 1.5% monthly interest on the unpaid balance. Does she save money by buying the bike on sale with her credit card?

Solve

Step 1: Underline the sentences that tell you what Denna pays for the bike and what she pays at the end of each month.

The bike is on sale for $175.
At the end of each month she pays $40.

Step 2: Make a table to show her monthly unpaid balance until the balance is cleared.

End of Month	Denna pays	Remaining Unpaid Balance
1	$40	($175 − $40) × 1.015 = $137.03
2	$40	($137.03 − $40) × 1.015 = $98.49
3	$40	($98.49 − $40) × 1.015 = $59.37
4	$40	($59.37 − $40) × 1.015 = $19.66
5	$19.66	$0

Step 3: Find the total Denna pays for the bike on her credit card. Compare this to the regular price of the bike.

$40 × 4 + $19.66 = $179.66   This is less than the regular price of $256.

Answer the Question

Step 4: Yes, Denna saves money by buying the bike on sale with her credit card.

✎ Now try these problems.

1. Louie charges his new saxophone on his credit card. The saxophone is on sale for $315. (The regular price is $499.) He makes no more purchases with his credit card. At the end of each month he pays $75. The credit card company charges him 2.0% monthly interest on his unpaid balance.

a. Does he save money by buying the saxophone on sale with his credit card?

b. What is the difference between what he pays and the regular price?

Answer: a. _____ (Yes/No). Louie _____ (saves/does not save) money by buying the saxophone with his credit card.

  b. The difference is $_____.

2. *All*Insured* charges Alton $1,596 per year, or $140 per month for car insurance. Alton decides to pay monthly, by credit card. He makes no more purchases with his credit card. At the end of each month he pays $50. The credit card company charges him 1.5% monthly interest on his unpaid balance.

   a. Complete the table to show Alton's unpaid balance at the end of each month.

End of month	1	2	3	4	5	6
Unpaid balance						
End of month	7	8	9	10	11	12
Unpaid balance						

   b. Alton continues to need car insurance. What is happening to his credit card debt?

   Answer: b. _____

3. The closing date for Vandana's *Diamond* credit card is the 10th of each month. The closing date for her *MyCharge* credit card is the 25th of each month. Each card offers a grace period of 30 days. She makes a purchase on the 5th of the month. Which card allows her money to stay in the bank longer? Why?

   A *Diamond;* payment due in 5 days

   B *Diamond;* payment due in 35 days

   C *MyCharge;* payment due in 20 days

   D *MyCharge;* payment due in 50 days

☆ *Challenge Problem*
You may want to talk this one over with a partner.

You plan to go to a conference in just over three months from now. When you pay 3 months in advance, the cost is $285. But you will have to pay by credit card. Your credit card charges 2.1% monthly interest. This month you would make a $10 payment. Next month you would pay the balance in full. When you pay 2 months in advance, the cost is $325. By then you would be able to pay in full. Which method of payment would you use? Why?

Example Marius gets a credit card that offers frequent-flyer miles. The annual fee is $50. He will earn one mile for every dollar he charges on his credit card. He reads that it takes about 25,000 miles to earn a free round-trip ticket anywhere in the United States. On average, Marius spends $5,000 in credit card charges per year. How much will it cost him in annual fees alone to earn a free round-trip ticket in the United States?

Solve

Step 1: Underline the sentence that tells you how many frequent-flyer miles Marius earns per dollar on his credit card.

He will earn one mile for every dollar he charges on his credit card.

Step 2: Write a proportion for dollars and miles. He must spend $25,000 to earn the trip.

$\frac{\$1}{1}$ frequent-flyer mile $= \frac{\$25,000}{25,000}$ frequent-flyer miles

Step 3: Now, find the number of years it will take to earn 25,000 frequent-flyer miles.

$\frac{\$25,000}{\$5,000} = 5$ years   Divide by the dollars he charges per year.

Step 4: Calculate the annual fees he will pay for this number of years.

$5 \times \$50 = \$250$

Answer the Question

Step 5: It will cost Marius $250 in annual fees to earn a free round-trip ticket, in addition to the $25,000 he spends over the 5 years.

✏ Now try these problems.

1. Este gets a credit card that offers frequent-flyer miles. The annual fee is $80. She will earn two miles for every dollar she charges on her credit card. Her goal is to earn 16,000 miles for

a round trip she wants to take. On average, Este spends $4,000 in credit card charges per year. How much will it cost her in annual fees to earn this free round-trip ticket?

Answer: It will cost Este $_____ in annual fees to earn a free roundtrip ticket.

2. Felicia gets a credit card that offers frequent-flyer miles. The annual fee is $40. She will earn one mile for every dollar she charges on her credit card. How much must she charge to earn 12,000 frequent flyer miles in one year? Besides annual fees, list factors that may make a free frequent-flyer ticket not quite "free."

Answer: _____

_____

_____

3. Some credit card companies offer protection plans. With a protection plan, your balance is paid off if you lose your job or have an accident and can't work. Corbin's credit card has a monthly fee for this service. The fee is 73 cents per $100 of unpaid balance. For the last 12 months, Corbin has maintained his unpaid balance at $1,000. How much has he paid for this service over the year?

   A $7.30   **B** $87.60   **C** $120   **D** $876

4. Peter's credit card company sends him a check for $2.50 in the mail. When he cashes it, he will start earning 1 point for every credit card dollar he spends. One point is worth 1% of $1. He can start redeeming his points after 2,500 points. The maximum number of points he can accumulate is 60,000 points per year.
   a. Circle the minimum dollar amount that he can redeem.
   b. Draw a square around the maximum dollar amount that he can redeem in one year.

$2.50 $10 $25 $27.50 $250 $600 $2,500 $6,000

☆ *Challenge Problem*
You may want to talk this one over with a partner.

For every $2 you spend with your credit card, you get the same number of cents back. How much must you spend to get back $2?

Answer: $_____

Lesson 5

Reading the Fine Print!

Example On March 21st, Savannah mails a $50 payment on her $1,205 balance to the credit card company. The closing date is the 20th of each month. Payments not received by that date will cause a late fee to be added to the account balance. The credit card company also charges 1.5% monthly interest on unpaid balances. What will Savannah owe after her $50 payment is received?

Unpaid Balance	Late Payment Fee
Up to $149.99	$20.00
$150 up to $1,199.99	$28.00
$1,200 and over	$40.00

Solve

Step 1: Determine whether Savannah will owe a late fee. Compare the date when Savannah pays her bill to the credit card closing date.

She mails $50 on March 21st. March 20th is the closing date. So she owes a late fee.

Step 2: Determine what late fee Savannah owes.

$1,200 and over	$40.00

Step 3: Calculate the interest on an unpaid balance of $1,205.

$1,205 × 1.5% = $18.08

Step 4: Calculate the new unpaid balance after the $50 payment is received.

$1,205 + $40 + $18.08 − $50 = $1,213.08

Answer the Question

Step 5: Savannah will owe $1,213.08 *after* her $50 payment is received.

✏ Now try these problems.

1. On July 15th, Robb mails $10 of his $155 balance to the credit card company. The closing date is the 15th of each month. Payments not received by that date will cause a late fee to be added to the account balance. Late fees are $15 on balances up to $150; $25 on balances over $150. The credit card company also charges 1.8% monthly interest on unpaid balances. Complete the table to show what Robb will owe after his $50 late payment is received.

Original Unpaid Balance	Late Payment Fee	Interest Owed	Payment	New Unpaid Balance

2. In the fine print, Ziggy reads that the over-the-credit-limit fee is $27.00 per month. He charges a weight-lifting machine that puts him over the top of his $1,500 credit limit. His next credit card payment is late, *but* it brings him below his limit. Circle the over-the-credit-limit fee that he owes.

$0 $27 $54 $1,500 $1,527 $1,554

3. Jann is consolidating her debts. She makes balance transfers from three credit card accounts to her *OneStop* account. The fine print says that there is a transaction fee for each transfer. The fee is 3% of the amount of the transfer, and not less than $5 nor more than $50. Complete the table to show the transaction fee for each transfer.

Balance	$1,239.00	$1,770.00	$92.12
Transaction Fee			

4. Caris' credit card company sends him 12 "convenience checks." He doesn't see that the transaction fee for using a check is 5% of the amount of the check (and not less that $5). Of the three checks he writes, one is for $10.99. The other two are over $100 each. His transaction fee for all three is $20.45. What do the two other checks add to?

A $200   B $210.99   C $309   D $409

☆ *Challenge Problem*
You may want to talk this one over with a partner.

You and a friend compare credit cards. One card has an annual fee of $80, a low interest rate, and several services (such as frequent-flyer airline mileage and discounts from numerous merchants). The other card has no annual fee, a higher interest rate, and only a few basic services (such as balance transfers). Which card suits you best, and why?

_____

_____

Review What You Learned

In this unit you have used mathematics to solve many problems. You have used mental math and estimation, practiced basic operations, solved equations, and used statistics, ratios, and proportions.

These two pages give you a chance to review the mathematics you used and check your skills.

✔ Check Your Skills

1. Kathianne buys a used guitar for $245, and charges it on her credit card. At the end of the first month, she makes a payment of $25. The credit card company charges 1.9% monthly interest on unpaid balances. After Kathianne's $25 payment is deducted, interest is computed on the unpaid balance. Write an expression that shows how much Kathianne now owes.

   Answer: _____

   If you need to review, return to lesson 1 (page 41).

2. Jamie charges her new surfboard on her credit card. The surfboard is on sale for $199. (The regular price is $245.) She makes no more purchases with her credit card. At the end of each month, she pays $25. The credit card company charges her 2.2% monthly interest on her unpaid balance. Complete the table to show what she owes at the end of each month.

End of month	1	2	3	4	5	6	7	8	9
Unpaid balance									

   a. How long does it take her to pay?

   b. Does she save money by buying the surfboard with her credit card? If so, how much?

   Answer: a. It take Jamie _____ to pay.

   　　　　b. She _____ (saves/does not save) $_____ by buying the surfboard with her credit card.

   If you need to review, return to lesson 3 (page 45).

3. The closing date for Di's *Thistle* credit card is the 25th of each month. The closing date for her *FirstCharge* credit card is the 15th of each month. Each card offers a grace period of 30 days.

She makes a purchase on the 7th of the month. Which card allows her money to stay in the bank longer? Why?

 A *Thistle;* payment due in 18 days

 B *Thistle;* payment due in 48 days

 C *FirstCharge;* payment due in 8 days

 D *FirstCharge;* payment due in 38 days

If you need to review, return to lesson 3 (page 45).

4. Preston gets a credit card that offers frequent-flyer miles. The annual fee is $65. He will earn one mile for every dollar he charges on his credit card. He reads that it takes 20,000 miles to earn a free round-trip ticket anywhere in the United States. On average, Preston spends $2,500 in credit card charges per year. Write an expression to find the cost in annual fees alone to earn a round-trip ticket in the United States.

Answer: _____ = $_____

If you need to review, return to lesson 4 (page 47).

5. On November 15th, Tobias mails $100 of his $247.50 balance to the credit card company. The closing date is the 16th of each month. Payments not received by that date will cause a late fee to be added to the account balance. Late fees are $21 on balances up to $200 and $35 on balances over $200. The credit card company also charges 2.1% monthly interest on unpaid balances. Fill in the table to show how much Tobias owes in the two payment cases.

Payment	Original Unpaid Balance	Payment received by closing date	Late Payment Fee	Interest Owed	New Balance after payment
On-time	$247.50	Yes			
Late	$247.50	No			

If you need to review, return to lesson 5 (page 49).

Write Your Own Problem ✐

Choose a problem you liked from this unit. Write a similar problem using a situation and related facts from your own life. With a partner, share and solve these problems together. Discuss the mathematics and compare the steps you used. If you need to, rewrite or correct the problems. Write your edited problem and the answer here.

_____

_____

Unit 5

Rental Budgeting

Preview

How You Will Use This Unit

Rental budgeting involves many different things. You can rent almost anything: a house, a vehicle, tools or other equipment. You probably consider the length of time you rent, the cost of renting or buying, and the possibility of renting to own. As you compare options and make choices, you will often use math. The math skills you use include mental math and estimation, basic operations and equations, statistics, ratios, and proportions.

What You Will Do in This Unit

In this unit, math steps demonstrate how to solve problems. These steps can help you answer questions such as these:

You have a job in a new town. You rent an apartment for $525 per month. Your rent increases by 5% each year. What is the total amount of rent that you pay over five years?

You rent a car for one day while you are out of town. The company charges a daily rate plus a per-mile charge. The agent tells you the cost for 100 and 200 miles. Later, you wonder what the per-mile charge is, and what the daily rate is. What are these amounts?

You need a saw to cut down a tree in your yard. You find one that costs $189. You also find that you can rent one for $15 per day. How many uses make buying a better deal than renting?

The sticker price of a car is $17,499. You can lease it for $449 per month for two years. Then you have an option to buy it for $359 per month over three years. How much does this plan cost?

What You Can Learn from This Unit

When you complete this unit, you will have used mathematics to work problems related to rental budgeting. These problems are similar to those that may actually occur in your daily life.

Lesson 1

Houses & Apartments

Example Chuy gets a job as building inspector working for the city. He rents an apartment for $754 per month. It is now five years later. His rent has increased by 5% each year since he moved in.

APARTMENT FOR RENT

a. How much has Chuy paid in rent over these five years?

b. What is his average (mean) rent per month over this time?

Solve

Step 1: Calculate Chuy's rent for each year over the five-year period.

Year 1: $754 per month
Year 2: $754 × 105% = $791.70 per month
Year 3: $791.70 × 105% = $831.29 per month
Year 4: $831.29 × 105% = $872.85 per month
Year 5: $872.85 × 105% = $916.49 per month

Step 2: Next, calculate the total amount he has paid over this period. (Remember to multiply by 12 for the number of monthly payments per year.)

($754 + $791.70 + $831.29 + $872.85 + $916.49) × 12 = $49,995.96

Step 3: Now, find his average monthly rent over the five year period.

$49,995.96 ÷ 60 = $833.27   Divide by the number of months in 5 years.

Answer the Question

Step 4: a. Chuy has paid $49,995.96 in rent over the five years.

b. His average rent per month over this time is $833.27.

✏ Now try these problems.

1. Wendi gets a job as park ranger for the local state park. She rents an apartment for $512 per month. Her rent increases by 7% each year over the four years that she lives there.

a. How much does Wendi pay in rent over these four years?

b. What is her average (mean) rent per month over this time?

A $2,273.25; $454.65   C $35,332.56; $588.88

B $27,279.00; $568.31   D $73,740.84; $1,536.27

2. Garth and Denise buy a house near the beach which they plan to rent to tenants. The realtor says their mortgage payments, plus utilities, will be about $1,145/month. She also says that they can rent the house for $1,200 per month during the six summer months, and $600 per month during the rest of the year. Suppose they rent the house out every month. Does the house pay for itself? If not, how much *more* money do Garth and Denise have to pay beyond the rent?

   Answer: Rental house income = $_____ (summer) + $_____ (winter)

   Total income from the house = $_____

   Mortgage payments plus utilities for one year = $_____

   The house _____ (does/does not) pay for itself.

   Garth and Denise have to pay $_____ per year beyond the rent.

3. *YourMiniStore* quotes Glenn a fee of $75 per month for a 500 cubic-foot storage unit. The unit is 10 feet from floor to ceiling.

   a. Draw a diagram to show possible dimensions for the floor of the unit.

   b. How much will Glenn pay per square foot of floor?

   Answer a.

   b. Glenn will pay $_____ per square foot.

☆ *Challenge Problem*
You may want to talk this one over with a partner.

You and your friend find an interesting problem in a book. Each letter stands for a digit. (Be careful, a letter may substitute for more than one digit!) What digit does each letter stand for? What code solves the problem? Explain your answer.

3	F	F
N	S	3
O	3	Z	E

_____

_____

_____

Example Ilene wants to rent a car for one day. The car rental agency charges a daily rate plus a per-mile charge. She asks how much it would cost to drive 100 miles, 160 miles, and 225 miles. The agent gives her the answers and she writes them in her notes. Later, her brother asks her what the per-mile charge is and what the daily rate is. What are these amounts?

Notes:
100 miles: $41
160 miles: $51.80
225 miles: $63.50

Solve

Step 1: Underline the sentence that tells you how the rental company charges.

The car rental agency charges a daily rate plus a per-mile charge.

Step 2: Use x for the daily rate. Use y for the per-mile charge. Write an equation for the first line of data that Ilene wrote in her Notes.

$$\$41 = x + 100y \qquad \text{first equation}$$

Step 3: Now, write an equation for the second line of data in Ilene's Notes. (You only need two equations to solve for two variables.)

$$\$51.80 = x + 160y \qquad \text{second equation}$$

Step 4: Use these two equations to solve for x and y.

$x = 41 - 100y$	first equation (rewritten with x on the left)
$51.80 = (41 - 100y) + 160y$	Substitute this expression for x in second equation.

$$51.80 = 41 + 60y$$
$$51.80 - 41 = 60y$$
$$10.80 = 60y$$
$$0.18 = y$$

$x = 41 - 100(0.18)$	Substitute this value of y in first equation.

$$x = 23$$

Answer the Question

Step 5: The per-mile charge is $0.18. The daily rate is $23.

➭ Now try these problems.

1. Mitchell rents an electric car for one day to tour the city. *Electri*City* charges a daily rate plus a per-mile charge. Mitchell asks how much

it would cost to drive 50 miles and 100 miles. The agent tells him $27.50 and $40. Later, he wonders what the per-mile charge is and what the daily rate is. Write two equations that you could solve together to find the answers.

Answer: _____ and _____

2. Jake's band calls ahead to rent a minibus. The company quotes $60 per 24-hours. The company says they won't charge for the next day if the bus is back less than an hour after it is due. The band has budgeted $240 for a minibus, and cannot afford any more. They pick the minibus up at 2 p.m. on Monday. What is the latest possible time by which they must deliver the minibus back? Mark the time on the calendar.

October 20	
20 Monday *2 p.m. Pick up minibus*	**23** Thursday
21 Tuesday	**24** Friday
22 Wednesday	**25/26** Saturday/Sunday

3. Angelisa rents a car for two days. The company quotes a daily rate of $24.99 per day. When she gets the bill, the charge is $109.98. This is more than twice the daily rate. The company gives her three reasons. There is an $8 fee for being able to pick the car up on airport property. The rate goes up by $10 per day on weekends. They charged $32 to fill the gas tank. On which two days did Angelisa rent the car?

    A Monday, Tuesday   **C** Friday, Saturday

    B Wednesday, Thursday   **D** Saturday, Sunday

4. Brice and Ryan are going away to the same technical college. They each plan to rent a truck at $19.99 per day for two days to move their stuff. They find out that they will both move over the same weekend. So they rent the next largest truck for $29.99 per day and share the cost. Suppose each of them would have spent $39.98 moving independently. How much do they each save by sharing the larger truck for the same length of time?

Answer: $_____

☆ *Challenge Problem*

You may want to talk this one over with a partner. You and your family plus the family down the road are going on a trip. You can rent two cars or one minivan for yourselves and all your luggage. Which would you rent and why?

_____

_____

Lesson 3

Tools

Example Diego needs a power drill to help his mother do several things in her new home. He prices power drills and finds one that costs $79.99. He also finds a rental shop that rents power drills for $5 per day. How many times would Diego have to use the power drill to make buying a better deal than renting?

Solve

Step 1: Find how many rental days are contained in the purchase price.

$79.99 ÷ $5 = 15.998   Divide the cost of purchase by the rental fee.

Step 2: Now, write an inequality to show the number of days for which renting would be *more* than the cost of purchase.

16 × $5 > $79.99   Sixteen rentals at $5 each ($80) would cost more than buying.

Answer the Question

Step 3: Diego would have to use the power drill for 16 days to make buying a better deal than renting.

Now try these problems.

1. Marci and Luis, with their six-month old daughter, visit Marci's grandparents. At *Second*Time*Around*, Marci's grandmother finds a crib and a high chair for $178. Marci says it would be cheaper to rent these items at $15 a weekend. How many weekend visits would make buying a better deal than renting?

    Answer: _____ weekend visits would make buying a better deal than renting.

2. Dane finds a rental shop that rents brush chippers at $150 per day. He asks his neighbors if they would be interested in sharing the rent for a day. Out of twelve neighbors, five say *Yes,* two say *Maybe,* and the others say *No.* What is the per-person rental cost if Dane can convince the neighbors who said *Maybe* to say *Yes*?

    A $12.50   **B** $15   **C** $18.75   **D** $25

Unit 5 • Rental Budgeting   **58**   Budgeting & Banking

3. Hilde buys a party tent for $650. She rents it at $20 a time to neighbors who want to hold outdoor parties. She wants to know how quickly she can start to make money by renting out the tent.

a. Fill in the table to show how quickly Hilde can pay off the tent.

b. Circle the number of times she must rent it per month to start making money within the year.

Number of times per month that Hilde rents out the tent	Number of months before she starts making money
1	
2	
3	
4	

4. Mihaly rents equipment to clean the carpet and repaint his apartment before moving. He wants to get his deposit of $285 back. The rental cost of the equipment adds to $9 per hour. He picks it up at 8 a.m. and delivers it back at 4 p.m. The materials cost him $45. His time is worth $11 per hour. In your opinion, was it worth the effort? Explain.

Answer: _____

_____

☆ *Challenge Problem*
You may want to talk this one over with a partner.

You paint all the outside surfaces of this $3 \times 3 \times 3$ cube made of small cubes. Do any of the small cubes have *no* painted surfaces? If so, how many? _____
Fill in the table to show the number of cubes for each number of painted surfaces.

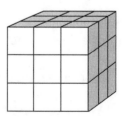

# of painted surfaces on a small cube	0	1	2	3	4	5	6
# of cubes							

What is the total number of small cubes in the large cube? _____
Check that the total of your second row in the table equals this number.

♠ A Card Game (for Two or More Players)

The goal of this game is to make a chain of rental domino cards. First, a player puts down a domino card. Then players add other domino cards to continue the chain.

Materials

Rental domino cards (on the next page), two number cubes

Directions

1. Place the domino cards face down on the playing area. Each player picks up seven cards. Players toss the number cubes until one player tosses a double. This player becomes player 1 and starts the game. Player 1 places a domino card, face up, on the table. Player 1 then picks up a domino card from the remaining face down cards to replace the one played.

2. Player 2 examines cards for a match in the chain. A match occurs when one of these four things happens:
   - A card matches the dollars on an open end of the rental chain. (For example, 5 days at $20 results in, or matches, $100.)
   - You can make the dollar value on a card match the result of a calculation with the time and dollars on an open end of the rental chain. (For example, $4 can be the daily rate if you pay $20 over 5 days. Or 5 days at $20 per day could be a total of $100.)
   - The time period on a card matches the time period in the rental chain. (For example, one month matches four weeks.)
   - A wild card (*) can be used anywhere because it matches anything.

3. Player 2 puts down a card, at right angles to, or in line with, one of the open ends. Player 2 then picks up a card from the remaining cards to replace the one used. If player 2 cannot make a play, then that player misses a turn.

4. Players take turns placing cards. When all the cards are used, players continue with the cards in their hands until one player has no more cards. The winner is the first player without any cards.

✏️ Before you play the game, try this warm-up problem.

1. You have these cards. 2 hours — $5; 5 hours — $4; 10 hours — $1; 2 weeks — $70; 4 weeks — $140; 4 weeks — $2,048; 3 months — $210. Which card can you use on the sample *Chain of Rentals*?

   Answer: _____

Sample *Chain of Rentals*

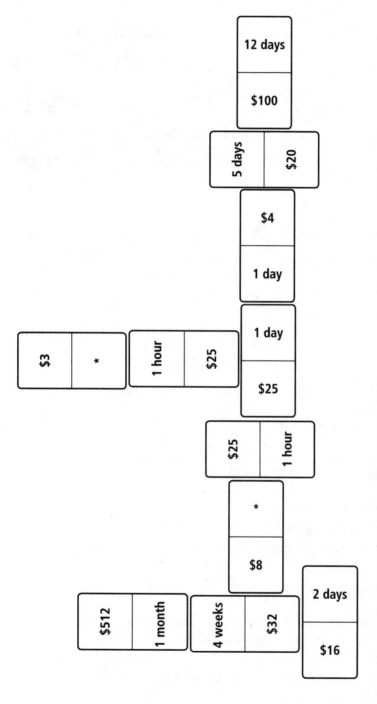

Rental domino cards:

Make cards with the following time/dollar combinations:

1 hour — $3	1 day — $5
1 hour — $5	1 day — $4
1 hour — $25	1 day — $15
2 hours — $5	1 day — $25
5 hours — $4	1 day — $35
5 hours — $25	2 days — $16
10 hours — $1	3 days — $48
24 hours — $15	5 days — $20
36 hours — $40	12 days — $100
48 hours — $30	15 days — $360
72 hours — $20	32 days — $16

1 week — $105	2 weeks — $70
1 week — $128	3 weeks — $75
1 week — $245	4 weeks — $32
1 week — $360	4 weeks — $2,048
2 weeks — $32	4 weeks — $140

1 month — $512	2 months — $720
1 month — $1,220	2 months — $50
1 month — $1,440	3 months — $210

Make these wild cards:

* — $3	* — 1 hour
* — $8	* — 1 day
* — $100	* — 1 week
* — $360	* — 1 month
* — $1,200	* — *

You can make more rental domino cards to extend the game.

Lesson 5

Example Aria wonders whether to buy or lease a new car. The sticker price of the car is $16,893. She can lease the car for $369 per month for two years. At the end of the lease, she can then buy the car, and pay $435.79 per month for three years.

a. How much does this plan cost?

b. How much *more* does the plan cost than the sticker price?

Solve

Step 1: Find the cost of leasing the car for two years.

$369 × 24 = $8,856   Multiply cost per month by 24 months.

Step 2: Next, find the cost of buying the car at the end of the lease.

$435.79 × 36 = $15,688.44   Multiply cost per month by 36 months.

Step 3: Now, add to find the total cost of the plan. Then, calculate the difference between the cost of the plan and the sticker price.

$8,856 + $15,688.44 = $24,544.44

$24,544.44 − $16,893 = $7,651.44

Answer the Question

Step 4: a. The plan costs $24,544.44.
 b. This is $7,651.44 more than the sticker price.

✏ Now try these problems.

1. Zak wonders whether to buy or lease a new car. The sticker price of the car is $20,499. He can lease the car for $405 per month for two years. At the end of the lease, he can buy the car, and pay $452.59 per month for three years. Write an expression and find the difference between the plan cost and the sticker price.

Answer: _____ = _____

2. Cason can lease a car or he can buy it outright. On the lease plan, he will pay $295 per month for two years, then buy the car for $12,540. On the purchase plan, he will pay $464.56 per month

over four years. How much does each plan cost? Which plan do you prefer and why?

Answer: Lease plan costs $_____.

Purchase plan costs $_____.

_____

_____

3. Kota and Jeff put down $7,500 on a $75,000, old Mediterranean-style home. Their mortgage payment is $1,075 per month. They live in one part of the house. They rent out three other sections of the house for $475 per month each. They are saving for a $15,000 down payment on their dream home. Suppose nothing changes. How long will it take them to save the down payment from this rental income (after they use the rental income to pay the mortgage)?

A About 1 year   C About $3\frac{1}{2}$ years

B About $2\frac{1}{2}$ years   D Exactly 5 years

4. The rent-to-own business grew from 2,000 to 7,000 stores in one decade.

   a. What was the mean rate of growth per year?

   b. Suppose this rate of growth continued. How many stores would there be in five more years? Draw a diagram to show this data.

   Answer: a. The mean rate of growth over the decade was _____ stores per year.

         b.

☆ Challenge Problem
You may want to talk this one over with a partner.

In a certain arithmetic sequence, the value of (3 × third term) is equal to the value of (6 × sixth term). What is a simple arithmetic sequence that satisfies this condition? In your sequence, what is the value of (9 × ninth term)?

_____

_____

Unit 5 — Review

Review What You Learned

In this unit you have used mathematics to solve many problems. You have used mental math and estimation, practiced basic operations, solved equations, and used statistics, ratios, and proportions.

These two pages give you a chance to review the mathematics you used and check your skills.

✔ Check Your Skills

1. Sasha gets a job as a teacher's aide at the local high school. He rents an apartment for $625 per month. It is now three years later. His rent has increased by 10% each year since he moved in.

   a. How much is Sasha's rent per month in each of these three years?

   Answer: Year 1 – Sasha's rent is $_____ per month.

   Year 2 – Sasha's rent is $_____ per month.

   Year 3 – Sasha's rent is $_____ per month.

   b. What is the total amount that Sasha pays in rent over this three year period?

   Answer: $_____

   c. What is his average (mean) rent per month over this time?

   Answer: $_____

   If you need to review, return to lesson 1 (page 54).

2. Dessa rents a car for one day while she is out of town at a conference. *TodaysWheels* charges a daily rate plus a per-mile charge. Dessa asks how much it would cost to drive 150 miles and 250 miles. The agent tells her $50 and $60. Later, she wonders what the per-mile charge is and what the daily rate is. What are these figures?

   Answer: The per-mile charge is $_____.

   The daily rate is $_____.

   If you need to review, return to lesson 2 (page 56).

3. Aspen needs a sewing machine to sew curtains for her new apartment. She prices sewing machines and finds one that costs $99 on sale. She also finds a rental shop that rents sewing machines for $15 per day. How many days would Aspen have to use the sewing machine to make buying a better deal than renting? Explain how to find this number.

Answer: _____

_____

If you need to review, return to lesson 3 (page 58).

4. You wonder whether to buy or lease a new car. The sticker price of the car is $17,499. You can lease the car for $449 per month for two years. At the end of the lease, you can buy the car, and pay $359 per month for three years. How much *more* does the plan cost than the sticker price?

    A $6,201   **C** $7,401

    B $7,281   **D** $23,700

If you need to review, return to lesson 5 (page 62).

Write Your Own Problem ✎

Choose a problem you liked from this unit. Write a similar problem using a situation and related facts from your own life. With a partner, share and solve these problems together. Discuss the mathematics and compare the steps you used. If you need to, rewrite or correct the problems. Write your edited problem and the answer here.

_____

_____

_____

_____

_____

_____

_____

Unit 6

Self-Employment

Preview

How You Will Use This Unit

Self-employment involves many different things. Starting up and managing your income and expenses are two examples. You probably also consider insurance costs and taxes. You may also think about getting a loan. As you compare options and make choices, you will often use math. The math skills you use include mental math and estimation, basic operations and equations, statistics, and ratios and proportions.

What You Will Do in This Unit

In this unit, math steps demonstrate how to solve problems. These steps can help you answer questions such as these:

You budget $100 to have business cards printed for your catering business. A local print shop gives you a quote of $75 for a box of 500. There is an additional charge of $10 for every 100 cards over 500. How many cards can you have printed?

You make and sell a mix to make a dip for chips. For every dollar you spend to make your chip mix, only 20 cents goes toward the ingredients. You charge $4 for a packet of mix that costs you $2 to make. You charge $6 for a packet that is 50% larger. How much profit do you make?

You join an association for self-employed people. You used to pay $195 per month for health insurance. Now you pay $167 per month. How much do you save per year?

You have a line of credit at your bank. During the low season, you borrow $4,722 against this line of credit. During the high season you pay the loan back. What is the mean extra income that you must make per month during the high season to pay back this loan?

What You Can Learn from This Unit

When you complete this unit, you will have used mathematics to work problems related to self-employment. These problems are similar to those that may actually occur in your daily life.

Example Franco budgets $100 to have business cards printed for his delivery business. A local print shop gives Franco a quote of $59 for a box of 500 cards in two colors. This charge includes a $9 setup charge. There is an additional charge of $12 for each set of 100 cards over 500. (The shop only prints cards in blocks of 100.) How many cards can Franco have printed?

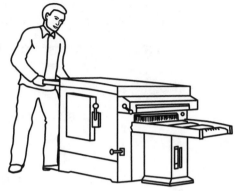

Solve

Step 1: First, subtract the quote for 500 cards from Franco's budgeted money.

$100 − $59 = $41

Step 2: Next, calculate how many additional sets of 100 cards Franco can afford.

$41 ÷ $12 = 3.42
3 sets   The print shop only prints cards in blocks of 100.

Step 3: Now, calculate the total number of cards that Franco can have printed.

500 + 300 = 800   500 for $59; 300 at an additional $12 per 100 over 500

Answer the Question

Step 4: Franco can have 800 cards printed.

✏️ Now try these problems.

1. Pia budgets $500 to have brochures printed. A local print shop gives her a quote of $350 for 1,000 brochures. This charge includes a $10 setup charge. There is an additional charge of $20 for each set of 50 brochures over 1,000. How many brochures can Pia have printed?

   Answer: Pia can have _____ brochures printed.

2. Teryn is trying to keep the start-up costs down for her landscaping business. She wants to print 200 color flyers to pass around the neighborhood. A local printer gives her a quote of $45

to print 50 color flyers. The cartridges for her color printer she would need cost $79.50. A ream of 500 sheets of paper costs $12.99. What is the amount of money she might save by printing the flyers herself? What are your assumptions?

Answer: Cost of 200 flyers printed by local printer =

_____

Cost of supplies for printing the flyers herself =

_____

Amount of money she saves = $_____

Assumptions: _____

3. Mari's start-up costs include setting up an office. Her uncle loans her $230 to buy an old desk and chair, $1,205 for a computer, $565 for office equipment, and $250 for supplies. Mari agrees to pay back the loan in equal monthly installments over one year. How much should she budget per month to cover these expenses?

A $46.88   C $562.50

B $187.50   D $2,250

4. Lark plans to take a one-week vacation. She wants to get ahead on her work hours before she goes. On average, over four weeks, she works 150 hours. Her goal is to work the same number of hours during the four-week period that includes her vacation. How many *more* hours must she work per week for each of the three weeks to meet her goal?

Answer: _____ hours

☆ *Challenge Problem*
You may want to talk this one over with a partner.

You decide that a color printer is the most important part of your graphic arts system. You find exactly the right printer for $350. But you only have $300. You put the money into a savings account with a 6% annual interest rate, compounded monthly. About how much money will be in the account at the end of a year? Explain your process.

_____

_____

_____

Example Waverly makes and sells bread pudding. Out of every dollar she spends to make the pudding, 20 cents pays for the ingredients. The rest covers the electricity, insurance, purchasing, and advertising. Waverly charges $7 for a slice of bread pudding that costs her $5 to make. She charges $10.50 for a portion that is 50% larger. The non-food expenses for the larger portion are the same as for the smaller slice.

a. How much do the *extra* ingredients cost?

b. How much profit does Waverly make when she sells the larger portion of bread pudding?

Solve

Step 1: Underline the sentence that tells how much money goes toward ingredients.

Out of every dollar she spends …, 20 cents pays for the ingredients.

Step 2: Underline the sentence that tells the cost to make a $7 slice of bread pudding.

Waverly charges $7 for a slice of bread pudding that costs her $5 to make.

Step 3: Use a proportion to find the cost of the ingredients for a $7 slice of pudding. Use x to represent that cost.

$\frac{\$0.20}{\$1.00} = \frac{x}{\$5}$

So $x = \$1$ The ingredients for a slice cost $1.

Step 4: Next, calculate the cost of the *extra* ingredients for a $10.50 portion of pudding.

$\$1 \times \frac{1}{2} = \$0.50$ A portion that is 50% larger uses 50% more ingredients.

Step 5: Now, calculate the profit that Waverly makes on the $10.50 portion of pudding.

$\$10.50 - (\$5 + \$0.50) = \$5$ Remember that the non-food expenses stay constant.

Answer the Question

Step 6: a. The extra ingredients cost $0.50.

b. Waverly makes $5 profit when she sells the larger portion.

✐ Now try these problems.

1. Out of every dollar Cameron spends to make a special mix for a chip dip, he spends 20 cents on ingredients. The rest pays for electricity, purchasing, packaging, and advertising. Cameron charges $3 for an 8-ounce packet of mix, which costs him $2 to make. He charges $4.50 for a packet that is 50% larger. The non-food expenses stay constant.

   a. How much do the *extra* ingredients cost?

   b. Make a table to show his profit for larger and larger packets of his special mix.

   c. What assumption(s) do you make?

   Answers: a. The extra ingredients cost $_____.

   b.

Packet size	Sale price	Cost to make mix	Profit
8 ounces	$3	$2	
12 ounces	$4.50		
16 ounces	$6		
20 ounces	$7.50		

   c. Assumption(s): _____

2. Saharah sets up a fruit stand on two opposite corners of an intersection. Two other fruit stand operators set up one fruit stand each on the other two corners. Which math does Saharah use to explain that she should get more business than the other two operators? Explain.

   A geometry   **C** probability

   B algebra   **D** measurement

   Explanation: _____

3. Trista's band makes a CD. They earn 1.5% royalties on the sale of the CD. The band earns $4,829.10 in royalties. Suppose the CDs sell for $12.50 each. About how many CDs have been sold?

   Answer: _____

☆ *Challenge Problem*
You may want to talk this one over with a partner.

The vertical line in a dollar sign separates the **S** into four segments. You draw 100 vertical lines close to each other through the **S**. How many segments have you separated the **S** into? How do you figure this out? Write an expression for the number of segments.

_____

_____

_____

Example Serena joins an association for people who are self-employed. Annual membership fees for the association are $90. Before joining, she paid $270 per month for health insurance. Now she pays $195 per month for the same coverage through the association.

a. How much money does she save per year, after paying her membership fee?

b. She has a deductible of $2,000. What is the most that she will pay in health costs in one year? Include the fee and monthly insurance premiums in her total costs.

Solve

Step 1: Underline the sentences that tell you how much Serena paid per month before, and then through the association.

Before joining the association, she paid $270 per month for health insurance. Now she pays $195 per month ... through the association.

Step 2: Find the difference in payments per month.

$270 − $195 = $75

Step 3: Now, calculate how much she saves per year, after she pays her fee.

($75 × 12) − $90 = $810   She saved $75 per month. She pays a $90 fee.

Step 4: Suppose Serena has over $2,000 in medical bills. Write the maximum amount of these bills that she will pay. Add insurance premiums and member's fee.

$2,000 + ($195 × 12) + $90 = $4,430

Deductible + premiums + member's fee

Answer the Question

Step 5: a. Serena saves $810 per year, after her member's fee.

b. The maximum amount that she will pay in health costs in one year is $4,430.

Now try these problems.

1. Jon joins an association for self-employed people. The cost of membership is $120 per year. He used to pay $275 per month for health insurance with another organization. Now he pays $220 per

month for the same coverage, through the association. How much money does he save per year, after paying his membership fee?

A $540   **B** $660   **C** $780   **D** $2,100

2. Chad owns a fitness consulting business. He pays $215 per month for health insurance premiums. Since he is self-employed, he cannot deduct these premiums as a business expense. Instead, he pays an additional 15.3% tax on the premiums. Write an expression for the amount of tax that Chad pays per year because of this. Find the amount.

Answer: _____ = _____

3. Dustin is a carpenter. Vendors and customers visit him in his workshop. He pays $50 per year for $2,000,000 liability insurance. This protects him in case visitors slip or hurt themselves in his shop. His deductible is $3,000.

   a. How much does he pay per year in insurance premiums?

   b. What is the maximum amount of money that he might pay in one year?

Answer: a. $_____   **b.** $_____

4. Kenetti runs a babysitting service. In her first year of operation, her gross income is about $13,500. Of this, she pays 15% federal income tax, 5% state income tax, and 6.1% social security tax. Circle the column that shows what she pays for each of these taxes.

Federal Income Tax	$202.50	$2,025	$20,250
State Income Tax	$675	$675	$1,012.50
Social Security	$1,006.50	$823.50	$1,006.50

☆ *Challenge Problem*
You may want to talk this one over with a partner.

Look at this sequence of figures. How many dots will be in the *fifth* figure of the sequence? What do you have to do to create each figure from the previous figure?

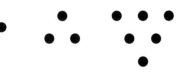

_____

_____

_____

_____

Example Miguel has a line of credit at his bank. His credit limit is $5,000. During the low season, he writes three checks against his line of credit to cover operating expenses. During the four months of the high season, he pays the loan back in equal installments. What is the mean (average) *extra* income that he must make per month during the high season to pay back the loan?

Checks written against bank loan:	
Rent:	$1,050
Utilities:	$875
Supplies:	$521

Solve

Step 1: First, add the checks written against the bank loan.

$1,050 + $875 + $521 = $2,446   This is the amount Miguel must pay back.

Step 2: Underline the sentence that tells the number of months to pay back the loan.

During the four months of the high season, he pays the loan back in equal installments.

Step 3: Now, calculate the amount of each monthly installment.

$2,446 ÷ 4 = $611.50

Answer the Question

Step 4: The mean (average) *extra* income that Miguel must make per month during the high season to pay back the loan is $611.50.

✐ Now try these problems.

1. Cammie has a line of credit at her bank. Her credit limit is $6,000. During the low season, she writes four checks against her loan, to cover operating expenses. The checks are for $435, $291, $719, and $103. During the six-months of the high season, she pays the loan back in equal installments. What is the mean *extra* income that she must make per month to pay back the loan?

   Answer: Cammie must make an extra $_____ per month during the high season.

2. Jesicanne is a graphic artist. Before she starts a project, she asks for payment of half the fee. When a customer agrees to her

design, she is paid another quarter of the project fee. Today a customer agreed to the design she made, and paid her $525. What percent of the total project fee is not yet paid?

A 0%   **B** 25%   **C** 50%   **D** 75%

3. Luis gets a long-term loan of $12,000 to finance new sound-recording equipment. The fixed annual interest rate is 2%, and the repayment term is 5 years. Each year he pays back one fifth of the original loan plus interest on the unpaid balance. How much does Luis pay each year over the period of this loan? Complete the table to show his yearly installment and the interest paid at the end of each year.

End of year	Installment	Interest
1		
2		
3		
4		
5		

4. Through the Small Business Administration, Gaea gets a loan of $9,450 for her new gardening business. She agrees to pay the principal back in equal installments. The monthly interest rate (simple interest) is 1.5%. The term of the loan is one year.

   a. How much principal does she pay each month? How much interest does she pay each month?

   b. How much does Gaea pay in total for her loan, including principal and interest?

   Answer: a. _____

   b. _____

☆ *Challenge Problem*
You may want to talk this one over with a partner.

You have a small business. At times, your income does not cover your expenses. Before going to your bank for a loan, you look for ways to improve your cash flow. What are some ways in which you might do this?

_____

_____

Lesson 5

Making the Numbers Work

♠ A Card Game (for Two or More Players)

The goal of this game is to combine five numbers to get a specified number. You look at the numbers on the cards in your hand. Then you insert operations and grouping symbols to get the specified number. Your expression must use all of the cards in your hand.

Materials

Card deck for *Making the Numbers Work* (on the next page), paper and pencil for each player

Directions

1. Shuffle the cards and deal five cards to each player. Place the next card face up on the the table. Place the rest of the card deck face down, in the center of the table. Players sit around the table.

2. Players look at the cards in their hands. You can use any operation, including +, −, ×, ÷ to combine your five cards. You can also use grouping symbols such as ( ), [ ], and { }, to create expressions. The goal is to use all five of your cards in one expression to equal the number in the center. For example, the five numbers, 3, 5, 6, 7, and 10, can be combined to equal 2 by writing them like this: $(7 − 6) + [3 − (10 ÷ 5)]$.

3. The first player to write an expression that equates to the number on the card in the center of the table wins 3 points. The second and third players who create *different* expressions that also equal that number win 2 points and 1 point. Then put all the players' cards and the card in the center of the table in a discard stack.

4. Deal five more cards to each player, and place the next card face up, in the center of the table. When the deck is all dealt, replace it with the shuffled discard stack. The game goes on until one player has 15 points, or as long as the players choose to continue. The winner is the player with the most points.

✏ Before you play the game, try these warm-up problems.

1. Tracey has 3, 10, 19, 21, and 24 in her hand. What expression can she make that equals 20?

   Answer: _____

2. Jerome has 2, 5, 7, 10, and 18. What expression can he make that equals 20?

   Answer: _____

Card Deck for *Making the Numbers Work*

Make 3 cards for each of the numbers 1 through 10.
Make 2 cards for each of the numbers 11 through 17.
Make one card for each of the numbers 18 through 25.

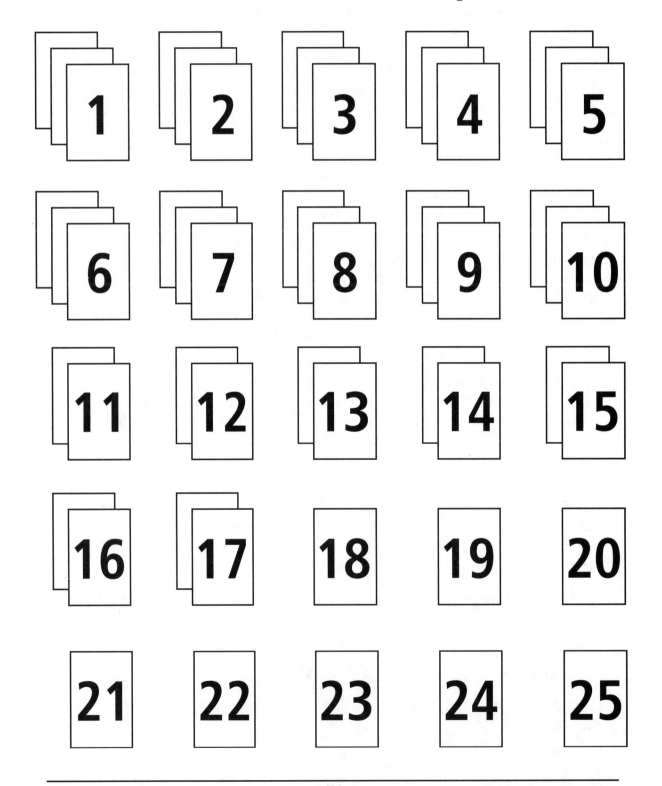

Review What You Learned

In this unit you have used mathematics to solve many problems. You have used mental math and estimation, practiced basic operations, solved equations, and used statistics, ratios, and proportions.

These two pages give you a chance to review the mathematics you used and check your skills.

✔ Check Your Skills

1. Darryl budgets $100 to have flyers printed for his fishing guide. A local print shop charges him $85 for 100 flyers. This charge includes a $7 setup charge. There is an additional charge of $8 for every 10 flyers over 100.

   a. How many flyers can Darryl have printed?

   b. How much *more* money would Darryl need to get one more set of 10 flyers?

   Answer: a. _____ **b.** _____

   If you need to review, return to lesson 1 (page 67).

2. Craig mixes and sells packets of special healthy trail mix. For every dollar he spends to make his trail mix, only 20 cents goes toward the ingredients. The rest pays for electricity, purchasing, packaging, and advertising. Craig charges $4 for an average packet of trail mix, which costs him $2 to produce. He charges $6 for a packet that is 50% larger. The non-food expenses stay constant.

   a. How much do the extra ingredients cost?

   A $0.20   **B** $0.40   **C** $0.50   **D** $1.00

   b. Write an equation to give his profit on the $6 packet of trail mix. Find the amount.

   Answer: b. An equation that gives his profit is

   _____ = _____

   If you need to review, return to lesson 2 (page 69).

3. Loren joins an association for self-employed people. The cost of membership is $95 per year. She used to pay $180 per month for

health insurance with another organization. Now she pays $155 per month for the same coverage, through the association.

a. How much money does she save per year, after paying her membership fee?

b. Her deductible is $2,000. What is the maximum amount that she might pay in one year? Circle the entry in the table that shows the correct amounts.

Money saved per year	Maximum amount that she will pay in one year for health costs
$205	$3,955
$300	$2,300
$395	$1,605

If you need to review, return to lesson 3 (page 71).

4. Cason has a line of credit at his bank. His credit limit is $4,000. During the low season, he borrows $3,840 against this line of credit to cover operating expenses. During the four months of the high season, he pays the loan back in equal installments. What is the mean (average) *extra* income that he has to make per month during the high season to pay back this loan?

    A $320   **B** $640   **C** $960   **D** $1,920

If you need to review, return to lesson 4 (page 73).

Write Your Own Problem ✎

Choose a problem you liked from this unit. Write a similar problem using a situation and related facts from your own life. With a partner, share and solve these problems together. Discuss the mathematics and compare the steps you used. If you need to, rewrite or correct the problems. Write your edited problem and the answer here.

Preview

How You Will Use This Unit

Going on a trip involves many different things. Making reservations and renting special equipment are two examples. You probably also consider sources for cash, such as ATMs. You may also think about the impact on your budget. As you compare options and make choices, you will often use math. The math skills you use include mental math and estimation, basic operations and equations, statistics, and ratios and proportions.

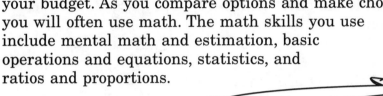

What You Will Do in This Unit

In this unit, math steps demonstrate how to solve problems. These steps can help you answer questions such as these:

You plan a 10-day cruise. The cruise costs $635. The round-trip plane ticket to get to the cruise ship costs $152. You spread the cost over 12 months. What is the monthly cost?

You have a ticket for flight 91. The ticket costs $250. Usually 4% of the ticketed passengers don't show up. The airline offers you a $200 voucher to give up your seat because the airline overbooked its seats. What percent of a future trip, at the same price, do you save?

You rent ski equipment for your week of skiing. The rent is $305. If you take your own equipment, the airline tickets will only cost $40 more each way. What is the difference in cost?

Today, the exchange rate for dollars to English pounds sterling is $1.6272 to £1. How many pounds sterling can you get for $250?

What You Can Learn from This Unit

When you complete this unit, you will have used mathematics to work problems related to going on a trip. These problems are similar to those that may actually occur in your daily life.

Lesson 1

Example Tasha is planning a 7-day, 6-night vacation. Her round-trip plane ticket costs $756. Her hotel room costs $97 per night. She allows $150 for items that she would not buy at home. Suppose she spreads the cost of her vacation equally over 12 months. What is the effect on her budget each month?

Solve

Step 1: Find the cost of Tasha's hotel room.

$97 × 6 = $582   She plans to stay for 6 nights.

Step 2: Next, find the total cost of the vacation.

$582 + $756 + $150 = $1,488   Add the room, ticket, and other items.

Step 3: Now, find the cost per month over 12 months.

$1,495 ÷ 12 = $124

Answer the Question

Step 4: The effect on Tasha's budget is to increase expenses by $124 per month.

✐ Now try these problems.

1. Aaron plans a 14-day, 13-night vacation. The hotel costs $85 per night. The round-trip plane ticket costs $234. He allows $500 for other items. Suppose he spreads the cost of the vacation equally over 6 months. What is the effect on his budget each month?

   Answer: The effect on Aaron's budget is _____.

2. Canda puts the cost of the hotel on her credit card so she can delay paying the cost. The hotel costs $399.54. The credit card company charges 1.8% monthly interest on unpaid balances. How much does she owe at the end of the month?

   A $399.54   **C** $471.46

   B $406.73   **D** $1,016.46

---

3. Ankit plans to go away for a month's vacation. He looks at his average expenses over the past six months. He will leave his car behind, but he will maintain his apartment. About how much (to the nearest $50) of his typical expenses can he safely apply to his month's vacation? Explain.

Average Expenses over last 6 months	
Rent	$465
Utilities	$125
Telephone	$55
Cable TV	$25
Car payment	$205
Gas for car	$110
Food	$350
Clothes	$75
Entertainment	$60

Answer: _____

_____

4. Shonda looks for ways to save money for her trip. She does not take her car. Her auto insurance company allows her to suspend the collision and liability parts of her insurance. They tell her she will save 3% on her $1,200 premium. Suppose each square represents $\frac{1}{100}$ of her auto insurance premium.

a. Shade the squares that represent 3%.

b. Shonda has $_____ extra for her trip.

☆ Challenge Problem
You may want to talk this one over with a partner.

You and a friend need to save $200 each for a ski trip over the holidays. You start with $46 and get a job that pays $7 per hour. Your friend starts with $21.50, and gets a job that pays $8.50 per hour. Write an expression for the number of hours that each of you must work to save $200. Who has to work more hours, and by how much?

Answer: You have to work _____ hours.

Your friend has to work _____ hours.

_____

_____

_____

Lesson 2

Currency Translations

♠ A Card Game (for Two or More Players)

The goal of this game is to translate numbers between one system and another. First, you pick a card. Then you translate and check.

Materials

Currency Translation cards (starter deck on the next page), paper and pencils

Directions

1. Shuffle cards, and put the deck face down in the center of the table. Give each player paper and pencil to write their answers. Players sit around the table.

2. Player 1 takes the top card of the deck. Place it face up on the table. Player 1 then names a base between 2 and 10, other than the base on the card. For example, 12_5 names a number in base 5. The number 12_5 means $(1 \times 5^1) + (2 \times 5^0)$. This number is equal to 7 in our decimal system, or 7_{10}. For example, player 1 might say "base 3." All the players then translate the number shown into base 3. Because $12_5 = 7_{10}$, which equals $(2 \times 3^1) + (1 \times 3^0)$, 12_5 becomes 21_3.

3. Players compare their answers. Players with the correct answer get 2 points.

4. Players take turns turning over the top card from the deck and naming a base. When the card deck is gone, replace it with the shuffled discard deck.

5. The game goes on until one player has 20 points, or for as long as players choose to continue. The winner is the player with the most points.

✐ Before you play the game, try these warm-up problems.

1. Monika turns up a card that says 24_6, and names base 8. What is the answer?

   A 16_8 **B** 20_8 **C** 30_8 **D** 32_8

2. Trenton turns up the number 100_2, and names base 5. Warren gets 4_5. Benton gets 25_5. Who is correct? Explain the other player's mistake.

   Answer: _____ is correct.

   _____

Currency Translations Cards

Starter set of cards. Players can create additional cards. Remember that the largest digit used in a system is always one less than the base. (For example, in base 6, the largest digit you can use is 5.)

01_2	10_2	101_2	111_2	1101_2
4_5	12_5	23_5	34_5	144_5
5_6	15_6	34_6	55_6	342_6
7_8	14_8	57_8	65_8	271_8
2_{10}	24_{10}	73_{10}	96_{10}	319_{10}

Example Cecilia has a ticket for Flight 131. The round-trip ticket costs $379. Usually 3% of the ticketed passengers for flight 131 don't show up. So the airline overbooks seats by 3%. If everyone shows up, the airline offers incentives to people who give up their seats. Cecilia gives up her seat and gets a $200 voucher. She uses the voucher on a later trip of the same price. What percent of the cost of her later trip does she save?

Solve

Step 1: Underline the sentence that tells you the cost of her ticket.

The round-trip ticket costs $379.

Step 2: Next, underline the words that tell you the value of the voucher.

...gets a $200 voucher.

Step 3: Now, calculate the percent of the later trip that she saves.

($200 ÷ $379) × 100% = 52.77%

Answer the Question

Step 4: Cecilia saves 52.77% of the cost of her later trip.

✏️ Now try these problems.

1. Joey has a ticket for flight 57. The round-trip ticket costs $500. The airline overbooks seats by 5%. They offer incentives to people who give up their seats when too many passengers show up. Joey volunteers to give up his seat. He gets a $250 voucher to use in the future. What percent of a repeat trip, costing the same, does he save when he uses the voucher?

   Answer: Joey saves _____% of a repeat trip at the same price.

2. 94% of the time, 3% of the ticketed passengers for flight 245 don't show up. 98% of the time, 2% of the ticketed passengers for flight 245 don't show up. 100% of the time, 1% of the ticketed passengers for flight 245 don't show up. When full, flight 245 carries 300 passengers.

a. Based on these statistics, the probability that all of the ticketed passengers will show up is _____.

b. Make this number line to show approximately 3% of the passengers.

```
|_____|
```
0 passengers   300 passengers

3. Sergio reads an advertisement while waiting for his luggage. It says, *"Carry a suitcase that fits in the overhead compartment or under the seat. Take 50% off your arrival time!"* It usually takes Sergio 45 minutes to get through the baggage claim area and out to his car on a Friday evening. How much time might he save by following the advice in the advertisement?

    A 11.25 minutes   **C** 33.75 minutes

    B 22.5 minutes   **D** 45 minutes

4. Kara goes to a 3-day business conference. Her company gives her $25 per day for meals. Each day she spends $7.50 for breakfast and $4.75 for lunch. The first two evenings she spends $14.50 and $16.80 for dinner. How much money does she has left for dinner on the third evening? Write the number of coins and bills Kara has to show the answer.

☆ Challenge Problem
You may want to talk this one over with a partner.

What is the 2004th positive odd number? Write an expression to explain your reasoning.

_____

_____

_____

Lesson 4 → *Renting What You Need*

Example Bill and his band need a sound system so they can play at a wedding. They can rent the system for one week at the location of the wedding for $185. James says they should take their own system with them. He says that the airline fee for extra baggage will only cost them $50 more each way.

What is the difference in the cost? Suppose *you* have to make the decision to rent or to take the sound system. What factors might contribute to your decision?

Solve

Step 1: Underline the words that tells you the cost of renting the sound system.

They can rent the system for one week... for $185.

Step 2: Next, calculate the extra fee on the airline when they take their system.

$50 × 2 = $100   The fee is $50 more *each* way.

Step 3: Find the difference in the cost of taking their system and renting it for the week.

$185 − $100 = $85

Step 4: Think about factors that might contribute to a decision to take or rent the sound system.

Consider money, quality, ease of travel, possible damage.

Answer the Question

Step 5: The difference in the cost is $85. Factors that might contribute to my decision include these: money I have available; how important it is to have my own system; the quality of the rented system; ease of travel with carrying the system; possible damage to, or loss of, my sound system on the trip.

✎ Now try these problems.

1. Kalani rents ski equipment for her week of skiing in the mountains. The rent is $305. If she takes her own equipment,

the baggage fee will only cost her $40 more each way. What is the difference in the cost? Why might she rent ski equipment?

Answer: The difference in the cost is $_____. She might rent

equipment because _____.

2. At the car rental counter, the assistant offers Riley a collision damage waiver (CDW). This promises that the company will pay for damage to a vehicle in case of an accident. Riley is in a hurry and does not read the fine print. He does not check to see if his own policy covers damage to a car he rents. He pays an extra $10 per day on the rental cost of a car. At this rate, how much does collision coverage cost per year?

    A $10   **B** $120   **C** $520   **D** $3,650

3. Beyonce goes to a regional skateboard championship. She has three options.
   i. If she pays for her hotel room three months ahead, the cost is $315.
   ii. If she pays for her hotel room two months ahead, the cost is $390.
   iii. If she pays for her hotel room at the last minute, the cost is $420.
   Complete the table. The first column tells which rates she compared to find the fraction in the second column. Then calculate the amount of money that Beyonce saves for each choice.

Comparing choices	Fraction that shows the comparison	Amount of money that Beyonce saves
Choosing option i instead of option iii	$\frac{3}{4}$	
	$\frac{21}{26}$	
	$\frac{13}{14}$	

4. Cason goes on a job interview. In the afternoon, he rents an electric cart to tour the town. The rental cost is $25 for the first hour, and $15 for each additional hour or part of an hour. He picks up the electric cart at 2:15 p.m. and returns it at 5:30 p.m.

   a. How much does he pay for his tour?

   b. Suppose he keeps the cart for another 45 minutes. How much *more* will he pay? Draw a line that connects the two correct answers.

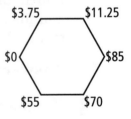

☆ Challenge Problem
You may want to talk this one over with a partner.

A group of students meets in the parking lot after the competition. Twelve girls leave on the first minibus. Twice as many boys as girls are left. Then 15 boys leave. Now, three times as many girls as boys remain. How many boys and girls were in the original group?

Lesson 5

Going Abroad

Example Penelope takes $250 to a bank at London's Heathrow International Airport. She wants to get pounds sterling. Today, the exchange rate for dollars to pounds sterling is $1.6272 to £1. How many pounds sterling can she get for $250?

Solve

Step 1: Use the exchange rate to write the ratio of dollars to pounds sterling.

$$\frac{\$1.6272}{£1}$$

Step 2: Next, write a ratio for $250 to *x* pounds sterling. The variable *x* represents the number of pounds sterling that Penelope can get for $250.

$$\frac{\$250}{£x}$$

Step 3: Now, write a proportion to find the value of *x*.

$$\frac{\$250}{£x} = \frac{\$1.6272}{£1}$$ Set the two ratios equal.

$250(1) = x(1.6272)$ Find the cross products.

$153.64 = x$

Answer the Question

Step 4: Penelope can get £153.64 for her $250.

☞ Now try these problems.

1. Cedric takes £125 to a bank in New York. He wants to exchange pounds sterling for dollars. Today, the exchange rate is $1.5912 to £1. How many dollars can he get for £125 pounds sterling?

   Answer: Cedric can get $_____.

2. Morgan wins a place in the international surfing contest in Australia. Before leaving the country, she goes to the bank to get travelers checks. The fee for travelers checks is 3% of the amount of the purchase. The fine print says that this fee cannot be less than $5, and will not exceed $50. Morgan buys travelers checks

and pays a fee of exactly 3% (not more and not less). Write the range for the value of the checks she could buy.

Answer: From $_____ to $_____

3. Bonita's bank charges a fee of $1.50 each time she uses an Automatic Teller Machine (ATM) owned by another bank. While she is in Europe, she uses an ATM at a foreign bank seven times. She takes out a total of $600 in cash. What can she expect to be the effect on her account?

A a debit of $589.50   C a debit of $610.50

B a credit of $589.50   D a credit of $610.50

4. In one international airport, Raphael reads that bags are valued at $20 per kilogram. He remembers reading somewhere else that bags are valued at $9.07 per pound.

a. How can he check to see if these statements mean the same thing?

Answer: _____

b. If a bag is not weighed in at check-in, the airline assigns it a weight of 70 pounds. Raphael loses his luggage. One bag was weighed in at 145 pounds. The other was not weighed in. Raphael writes an equation for the amount of money that he can claim. Is his equation correct? If not, make any necessary corrections.

$$(145 \times \$9.07) \ + \ (145 - 70)\$20 = \$2,815.15$$

☆ Challenge Problem
You may want to talk this one over with a partner.

The sum of three numbers is 34. The ratio of the first to the second number is $\frac{3}{4}$. The ratio of the second number to the third number is $\frac{2}{5}$. What is the second number? How did you find the answer?

_____

_____

_____

_____

Review

Review What You Learned

In this unit you have used mathematics to solve many problems. You have used mental math and estimation, practiced basic operations, solved equations, and used statistics, ratios, and proportions.

These two pages give you a chance to review the mathematics you used and check your skills.

✔ Check Your Skills

1. Ruma plans a 10-day, 9-night cruise. The cruise costs $635. The round-trip plane ticket to get to the cruise ship costs $152. She allows $500 for other items. Suppose she spreads the cost of the vacation equally over 12 months. Write an expression for the effect on her budget each month. What is that amount?

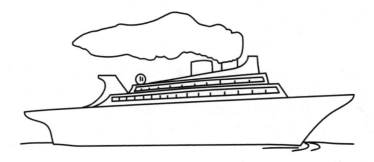

   Answer: _____

   If you need to review, return to lesson 1 (page 80).

2. Arlan has a ticket for flight 67. The round-trip ticket costs $250. The airline has overbooked the seats, and Arlan volunteers to give up his seat. He gets a $200 voucher to use on a future trip. What percent of a future trip that costs the same amount does he save? Draw a diagram to show this percent.

   If you need to review, return to lesson 3 (page 84).

3. Azita rents windsurfing equipment when she goes to the beach. The rent is $106 for a weekend and $18 a day for weekdays. If she takes her own equipment, the extra baggage fees cost her $46.50 more each way. She wants the equipment for Saturday, Sunday, and Monday. Azita takes her own equipment. What fraction of the rental cost does she save? Shade an area of the circle that represents this fraction. Show your calculations.

Answer: _____

If you need to review, return to lesson 4 (page 86).

4. Today, the exchange rate for dollars to English pounds sterling is $1.6272 to £1. How many pounds sterling can you get for $500?

A £32.50   **C** £500

B £307.28   **D** £813.60

If you need to review, return to lesson 5 (page 88).

5. Garrett reads at the airport that bags are valued at $9.07 per pound. If a bag is not weighed in at check-in, the airline assigns it a weight of 70 pounds. Garrett loses his carry-on bag. He thinks it weighs 100 pounds. It was not weighed in at check-in. Write an equation for the amount of money he can claim.

Answer: _____

If you need to review, return to lesson 5 (page 88).

Write Your Own Problem

Choose a problem you liked from this unit. Write a similar problem using a situation and related facts from your own life. With a partner, share and solve these problems together. Discuss the mathematics and compare the steps you used. If you need to, rewrite or correct the problems. Write your edited problem and the answer here.

_____

_____

_____

_____

Keeping the Books

Preview

How You Will Use This Unit

Keeping the books, or financial records, involves many different things. You may track income and expense. You may need to decide what software to use. You may also think about how to keep the books for a club or organization, and even for a large event. As you compare options and make choices, you will often use math. The math skills you use include mental math and estimation, basic operations and equations, statistics, and ratios and proportions.

What You Will Do in This Unit

In this unit, math steps demonstrate how to solve problems. These steps can help you answer questions such as these:

You receive $1,714 in salary. You get paid for an invoice of $300 for this month's tutoring. You pay bills that add to $1,092. You are also paid for new invoices that add to $986. Extra expenses total $623. What are your income and expenses?

Your club decides to go on a bike trip. You estimate the cost of various items for the trip. After the trip, you compare each estimate to the actual cost for each item. What is the variation for each item?

You review the financial results of the summer festival. You make a table of major sources of income and the major categories of expense. After that, can you see if the event made or lost money?

You use a spreadsheet software package to manage your finances. What are some of the advantages that you are looking for?

What You Can Learn from This Unit

When you complete this unit, you will have used mathematics to work problems related to keeping the books. These problems are similar to those that may actually occur in your daily life.

Lesson 1

Keeping Records

Example During January, Mariano receives $1,404 as his salary. He is also paid $543 rent on the upstairs apartment. He pays his mortgage, utility, telephone, and credit card bills for a total of $1,012. He receives payment for this month's invoices for a total of $2,314. Miscellaneous expenses add to $655. Answer these questions for this month.

a. What is his total income?

b. What are his total expenses?

c. What is the difference between his income and expenses?

Solve

Step 1: List all Mariano's income items and find their total.

Income items → $1,404 + $543 + $2,314 = $4,261

Step 2: Now, list Mariano's expenses and find that total.

Expenses → $1,012 + $655 = $1,667

Step 3: Find the difference.

$4,261 − $1,667 = $2,594

Answer the Question

Step 4: a. His total income is $4,261.

b. His total expenses are $1,667.

c. His income is greater than his expenses by $2,594.

✐ Now try these problems.

1. During September, Laurel receives $1,521 in salary. She is paid $400 for her graphic arts project and $310 for an invoice. She pays her rent, utility, telephone, and credit card bills for a total of $1,143. She receives payment for additional invoices totalling $2,877. Miscellaneous expenses add to $474.

a. What is her income?

b. What are her expenses?

c. What is the difference?

Answer: a. Laurel's income is $_____.

b. Laurel's expenses are $_____.

c. The difference is that her _____ is greater than her _____ by $_____.

2. This month Patience receives a credit card bill for $1,906. She pays $25 on this bill. What is the difference between the amount she pays and the amount she owes?

Answer: $_____

3. Elyssa charges one customer $15 per hour for her time. She keeps a record of her hours. Her client offers to pay her a fixed fee of $1,200 for a similar project in the future. Suppose you are Elyssa. Would you accept this offer? Why? Why not?

March	Monday	Tuesday	Wednesday	Thursday	Friday	Saturday
Week 1—hours:	0.0	0.0	8.0	7.5	9.0	9.0
Week 2—hours:	5.0	6.5	8.0	8.0	7.5	7.5
Week 3—hours:	7.5	10.0	9.0	0.0	0.0	0.0

Answer: _____

4. Cody transfers the balances from his three credit cards to a new *Dynamo* credit card. The rate on each card is 18.9%, 12.45% and 14.67%. The new card company offers a rate of 0% interest on all transactions for 12 months. What are some advantages and disadvantages of transferring his balances to this new card?

Advantages: _____

Disadvantages: _____

☆ *Challenge Problem*
You may want to talk this one over with a partner.

You have $7.85 worth of nickels and dimes in the petty cash drawer in your business. You have an odd number of nickels and more dimes than nickels. What is the largest number of nickels that you can have? Explain how you get your answer.

_____

_____

_____

_____

_____

_____

Example *ClubAdventure* decides to go on a field trip to the marine science center. Camille estimates the cost of various items for this trip. The club raises money to pay for the trip. After the trip, Camille compares the estimated cost to the actual cost for each item. What is the difference for each item? Did Camille underestimate or overestimate the total cost of the trip?

Field Trip Finances	Estimated cost	Actual cost	Difference (use a minus sign when actual > estimate)
Hotel	$1,350	$1,390	
Transportation	$255	$250	
Entrance tickets	$240	$240	
Food	$400	$382	

Solve

Step 1: Subtract the actual cost from the estimated cost for the hotel.

$1,350 – $1,390 = –$40

Step 2: Subtract the actual cost from the estimated cost for the other items.

Transportation	$255 – $250 = $5
Entrance tickets	$240 – $240 = $0
Food	$400 – $382 = $18

Step 3: Enter these values in the table.

Step 4: Calculate the total variation.

–$40 + $5 + $18 = –$17

Difference
–$40
$5
$0
$18

Answer the Question

Step 5: Camille underestimated the cost of the trip by $17.

✏ Now try these problems.

1. *ClubSport* decides to go on a ski trip. Michael estimates the cost of various items. The club raises money to pay for the trip. After the trip, Michael compares the estimated cost to the actual cost

for each item. What is the difference per item? Did Michael underestimate or overestimate the cost of the trip?

Ski Trip Finances	Estimated cost	Actual cost	Variation
Hotel	$2,160	$2,135	
Transportation	$2,413	$2,567	
Ski tickets	$2,100	$2,400	
Food	$850	$545	

Answer: Michael _____ (underestimated/overestimated)

by $_____.

2. The lunch special at the *OnTheBeach* cafe costs $4.95. The *Theta4* club has $53.00 in its club account. What is the greatest number of lunch specials that the club can buy with this money?

     A 8   **B** 9   **C** 10   **D** 11

3. The student council budgets $840 for beach cleanup events this year. Last year, the records showed a total of $700 spent on these events. Which sector of this circle graph shows the percent increase from last year to this? Shade and label that sector.

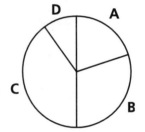

4. The art center's postage cost went from $238.00 in January to $117.60 in February. Complete the equation and find the percent decrease in postage.

Answer: ($_____ – $_____) ÷ $_____ × 100% = _____%

☆ Challenge Problem
You may want to talk this one over with a partner.

Fill in the empty squares with one-digit numbers (choosing from 0 through 9). The numbers in the unshaded squares of each row or column must multiply to give the number in the shaded square that begins the row or column.

	24	15	2
9			
10			
8			

123 A Calculation Game (for Two or More Players)

The goal of this game is to be the first to cover a complete line of answers with your counters. First, someone gives a math problem. Then, you find the answer on your *Bingo Books* sheet.

Materials

Bingo Books sheets (next page); counters; paper and pencils; board for writing the problem

Directions

1. Each player has a *Bingo Books* sheet, a handful of counters, a pencil, and scratch paper. Players sit where they can see the board.

2. Player 1 writes a math problem on the board. The problem must have an answer that is a number from 1 to 60. For example, $9 \times 8 \div 18$. Other players first calculate the answer (for example, 4), and then find the answer on their *Bingo Books* sheets, and place a counter on that square. Player 1 then tags another student to write the next math problem.

3. Players take turns writing math problems as they are tagged. Each one must have a whole number answer from 1 to 60. A player can refer to the answer from the previous problem. For example, "What is the square root of the last answer?" The other players find the answer (for example, 2) and cover that number on their *Bingo Books* sheets.

4. The winner is the first player to get a complete vertical or horizontal line of correct answers. Players check the answers and start again with new *Bingo Books* sheets.

✏ Before you play the game, try these warm-up problems.

1. Anson writes the problem, $4^2 \times 1\frac{1}{2}$. Warren covers the number 8. Lance covers the number 24. Who covers the correct number?

   Answer: _____

2. Anson tags Taylor to write the next problem. Taylor writes this problem: "What number is a factor of the last answer and is also 3 greater than another factor of that answer?"

   A 3   **B** 4   **C** 6   **D** 12

Bingo Books Sheets

Bingo Books sheets can have many different patterns of numbers, but always have 1 through 60. Each sheet must have the same dimensions (columns by rows). Here are two examples.

Players can have identical or different sheets.

1	2	3	4	5	6	7	8	9	10
11	12	13	14	15	16	17	18	19	20
21	22	23	24	25	26	27	28	29	30
31	32	33	34	35	36	37	38	39	40
41	42	43	44	45	46	47	48	49	50
51	52	53	54	55	56	57	58	59	60

16	27	28	39	40	50	51	57	58	60
15	17	26	29	38	41	49	52	56	59
7	14	18	25	30	37	42	48	53	55
6	8	13	19	24	31	36	43	47	54
2	5	9	12	20	23	32	35	44	46
1	3	4	10	11	21	22	33	34	45

Example Vrae reviews the results of the costs and income for the *Summerfest*. He makes a table of major sources of income and major categories of expense. What are the total income and total expenses? Does the event make or lose money?

Income		
Item	**Tickets Sold**	**Total Income**
Participant fee, $25	32	
Vendor fee, $15	50	
Entertainment:		
TGIF band, $5	75	
Saturday, *Brownbaggers* lunch band, $8	150	
Saturday, *NiteWild* band, $12	210	
TOTAL INCOME		

Expenses	Total Expenses
Set up, tear-down, cleanup	$200
TGIF band	$250
Brownbaggers band	$400
NiteWild band	$850
TOTAL EXPENSES	

Solve

Step 1: Find the income for each item. Then, find the total income.

$25 \times 32 = $800   32 participants who pay a $25 fee each.

$15 \times 50 = $750   50 vendors who pay a $15 fee each.

$5 \times 75 + $8 \times 150 + $12 \times 210 = $4,095   Income from bands

TOTAL: $800 + $750 + $4,095 = $5,645

Step 2: Now, compute total expenses.

$200 + $250 + $400 + $850 = $1,700

Answer the Question

Step 3: Total income is $5,645. Total expenses are $1,700. The event makes money.

✏ Now try these problems.

Refer to the information in the example as you work these problems.

1. Vrae reviews his income and expense data from *Summerfest*. He wonders what would happen if the weather were bad. He estimates that only one third of the people would buy tickets to listen to the bands. Suppose all the other data stays the same.

What would the total income and expenses be? Would the event make or lose money?

Answer: Income would be $_____. Expenses would be $_____.

The event would _____ (make/lose) money.

2. Drew manages *Summerfest* the following year. He reduces the participant fee by 10% and increases the vendor fee by 5%. Suppose that the same number of participants and vendors take part.

   a. Write an expression to show the difference in income from the previous year.

   b. How much more or less will the event make than the previous year?

   Answer: a. _____ **b.** $_____

3. Drew retains two bands who charge $350 and $900 to play. He predicts that 80 people will pay $12 to listen to one band, and 150 people will pay $16 to listen to the other band. What would the income and expenses for the entertainment be using his predictions?

   A Income: $3,360; expenses: $1,250

   B Income: $3,360; expenses: $550

   C Income: $1,250; expenses: $3,360

   D Income: $3,080; expenses: $1,250

4. Jayfus advertises early registration for *Summerfest* the following year. He prepares this poster which offers advance tickets to *both* of Drew's concerts at 25% off. 75 people buy these advance tickets. On the day of the event, 60 people buy $12 tickets, and 150 people buy $16 tickets.

   a. What is the price for a set of advance tickets?

   b. How much income does the entertainment part of the event actually make?

   Answer: a. $_____ **b.** $_____

> **Single tickets
> $12 and $16**
>
> **Attend both
> concerts and
> save 25%!!**

☆ *Challenge Problem*
You may want to talk this one over with a partner.

You and some friends organize a big event. You manage the bands. One friend does the tickets. A second friend sees to the participants. A third friend manages vendors. A fourth friend organizes setting up and cleaning, and tracks the income and expenses for the event. What are advantages and disadvantages of each person managing a different part of the event?

_____

_____

_____

Lesson 5

Spreadsheets & Software

Example Jonelle uses a spreadsheet to keep track of finances at her daycare center. Each month she enters the amount of money that she collects for each child. The spreadsheet software gives her the total per month. It also gives the total per child since January. Calculate the total for each child during the quarter (the first three months of the year). What does the TOTAL line of the spreadsheet look like at the end of the first quarter? Does the *1st quarter total* for the five students match the total for the three months in the last row?

Child's name	January	February	March	1st quarter total
Alexandra	$350	$350	$350	
Chase	$275	$300	$225	
Logan	$380	$275	$275	
Michael	$125	$200	$250	
Stacia	$420	$325	$325	
Total				

Solve

Step 1: Columns Use mental math to calculate each monthly totals. Then find the three-month sum. Notice the amounts are grouped for easy adding.

January → $350 + ($275 + $125) + ($380 + $420) = $1,550
February → $350 + ($300 + $200) + ($275 + $325) = $1,450
March → ($350 + $250) + ($225 + $275) + $325 = $1,425
Total for the quarter → $1,550 + $1,450 + $1,425 = $4,425

Step 2: Rows Use mental math to calculate the total collected for each child. Then find the sum for all five children.

Alexandra → $350 × 3 = $1,050
Chase → ($275 + $225) + $300 = $800
Logan → $380 + $275 × 2 = $930
Michael → $125 + $200 + $250 = $575
Stacia → $420 + $325 × 2 = $1,070
Total for the quarter → $1,050 + $800 + $930 + $575 + $1,070 = $4,425

Answer the Question

Step 3:

Total	$1,550	$1,450	$1,425	$4,425

The column total *does* match the row total.

✏️ Now try these problems.

Refer to the information in the example as you work the first problem.

1. During March, Jonelle adds a sixth child and collects a $200 payment.

   a. What does the TOTAL line of the spreadsheet now look like?

   b. What is the new sum for the six totals in the *1st quarter total* column? Does it match the row total for the three months? Why?

   Answer: a.

Total				

   b. The new sum of the *1st quarter total* column is $_____.

   It _____ (does/does not) match the row total because

   _____.

2. Bryant compares the price of several software packages. He calculates the mean price, and buys the package that is priced closest to this number. Which package does he buy?

Fingertip Finances	**Fast Finances**	**Finances First**	**Financial Views**
One package does it all	BEST SELLER	Everything you need	Tailor-made to your needs
Only $209	**$299**	**$599**	**$850**

   A *Fingertip Finances*   **C** *Finances First*

   B *Fast Finances*   **D** *Financial Views*

3. Lucianne conducts a survey to find out what activities are most popular. She uses her software package to present the information in a circle diagram. Out of 425 responses, about how many responses name each activity?

   Answer: ____ choose basketball. ____ choose softball.

   ____ choose robotics. ____ choose chess.

   ____ choose debate. ____ choose band.

   Band 20% — Basketball 29% — Softball 18% — Robotics 15% — Chess 7% — Debate 11%

☆ *Challenge Problem*
You may want to talk this one over with a partner.

You use a software package to help gather, manage, and present data from a community project. The package allows you to look at the data as tables, graphs, and charts. You can calculate percents and relationships among the data with the software. What are some advantages and disadvantages of using software for this sort of project?

_____

_____

_____

Review What You Learned

In this unit you have used mathematics to solve many problems. You have used mental math and estimation, practiced basic operations, solved equations, and used statistics, ratios, and proportions.

These two pages give you a chance to review the mathematics you used and check your skills.

✔ Check Your Skills

1. During November, Jeannianne receives $1,714 in salary and $250 for tutoring after school. She receives payment for an invoice of $165 for tutoring at home. She pays her rent, utility, telephone, and credit card bills for a total of $1,092. She also gets paid for other invoices that total $986. Miscellaneous expenses add to $623.

   a. What is her income?

   b. What are her expenses?

   Answer: Income → _____

   Expenses → _____

   If you need to review, return to lesson 1 (page 93).

2. *ClubArt* decides to go on a photography trip to the botanical gardens. Daran estimates the cost of various items. The club raises money to pay for the trip. After the trip, he makes a table to compare the estimated cost to the actual cost for each item. Complete the table to show the difference for each item. Did Daran underestimate or overestimate?

	Estimated cost	Actual cost	Variance
Hotel	$1,675	$1,654	
Transportation	$125	$134	
Entrance tickets	$160	$140	
Food	$360	$382	

   Answer: Daran _____ (underestimated/overestimated).

   If you need to review, return to lesson 2 (page 95).

3. The heritage club's advertising costs went from $358 in March to $242 in April.

    a. Complete the equation to give the percent decrease in advertising costs.

    Answer: $\$\underline{\hspace{1cm}} \div \$\underline{\hspace{1cm}} \times 100\% = \underline{\hspace{1cm}}\%$

    b. Highlight the portion of the line to show approximately this percent decrease.

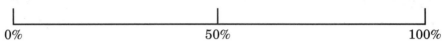

    0%   50%   100%

4. Faith makes a table to review the financial results of the town's *FallBackfest*. Complete the table to show the total income and total expenses. Does the event make money?

Income		
Item	**Tickets Sold**	**Total**
Participant fee, $30	45	
Vendor fee, $15	25	
Entertainment:		
Friday *Bandstand*, $6	60	
Saturday's Child lunch band, $7	90	
Saturday *Freedom* band, $15	180	
TOTAL INCOME		

Expenses	
Set up, teardown, cleanup	$250
Bandstand	$300
Saturday's Child lunch band	$520
Freedom band	$650
TOTAL EXPENSES	

    Answer: The event _____ (does/does not) make money.

    If you need to review, return to lesson 4 (page 99).

5. Keyton uses his software package to track tickets sold for various events. Two different events are scheduled for July through September. So far he has sold tickets that total $1,365 for one event and $785 for the other event. The sum of the totals for the three months should be $\underline{\hspace{1cm}}$.

    If you need to review, return to lesson 5 (page 101).

Write Your Own Problem ✍

Choose a problem you liked from this unit. Write a similar problem using a situation and related facts from your own life. With a partner, share and solve these problems together. Discuss the mathematics and compare the steps you used. If you need to, rewrite or correct the problems. Write your edited problem and the answer here.

_____

_____